D0429913

TOUGH JEWS

RICH COHEN

SIMON & SCHUSTER

SIMON & SCHUSTER
Rockefeller Center
1230 Avenue of the Americas
New York, NY 10020

Designed by Mspace

Manufactured in the United States of America
1 3 5 7 9 10 8 6 4 2
Library of Congress Cataloging-in-Publication Data
Cohen, Rich
Tough Jews/Rich Cohen
p. cm.
Includes bibliographical references.
1. Jewish criminals—New York (State)—New York.
2. Crime—New York (State)—New York.
3. Jews—New York (State)—New York—Social conditions. I Title.
HV6194.J4C64 1998
364.3'492407471—dc21 97-39282
CIP
ISBN 0-684-83115-5

Acknowledgments

Writing this book would not have been possible without the help of many people. First, I want to thank Alec Wilkinson, who is just about the best guy I know. Also, Ian Frazier, from whom I learned that serious people can be funny, funny people can be serious. And Sara Barret, David Lipsky, Jim Albrecht, C. S. Ledbetter III, Helen Thorpe, Melissa Roth, Todd Clark, Ralph and Renee Blumenthal, Debra Eisenstadt, Tad Floridis, Julie Bauer, Bill Brenner, Morris Liebman, Mark Varouxakis, Dennis Cohn, Brendan Lemon, Chris Knutsen, and my grandparents Benjamin and Betty Eisenstadt. I also want to acknowledge *The New Yorker* as it was when I got out of college, where, given a job as a messenger, I began pestering everyone with everything I had ever written. I especially want to thank those editors who gave me my first chance, Bob Gottlieb and Chip McGrath. I also owe a special debt to Jann Wenner, who brought me to *Rolling Stone,* where he has been less employer than friend, a patron who has given me so many opportunities. Also at *Rolling Stone* thanks to Bob Love, Sid Holt, Tobias Perse, Tom Conroy, and Will Dana. At Simon & Schuster I want to thank Dominick Anfuso and Ana DeBevoise. I am also grateful to Jessica Tuchinsky, at Creative Artists, who has become a good friend. And then my agent, Andrew Wylie, who is like Reggie was with the Yanks—the straw that stirs the drink. Also at the Wylie Agency I want to thank Jeff Posternak.

And, of course, Jessica Medoff, the one who is awakened when I have a dumb idea in the middle of the night, without whose support and insight I would not have finished this book.

Mostly I want to thank my parents, the Herb and Ellen of my best stories; my sister, Sharon Levin, and my brother-in-law, Bill Levin; my brother, Steven Cohen, and his wife, Lisa Melmed. And also down in North Miami Beach, the true promised land of the Jews, I want to thank my grandma Esther, thank her and say, "No, Grandma, don't send a brisket. We have plenty of food here in New York."

For my mother and father

Contents

Arnold's Boys

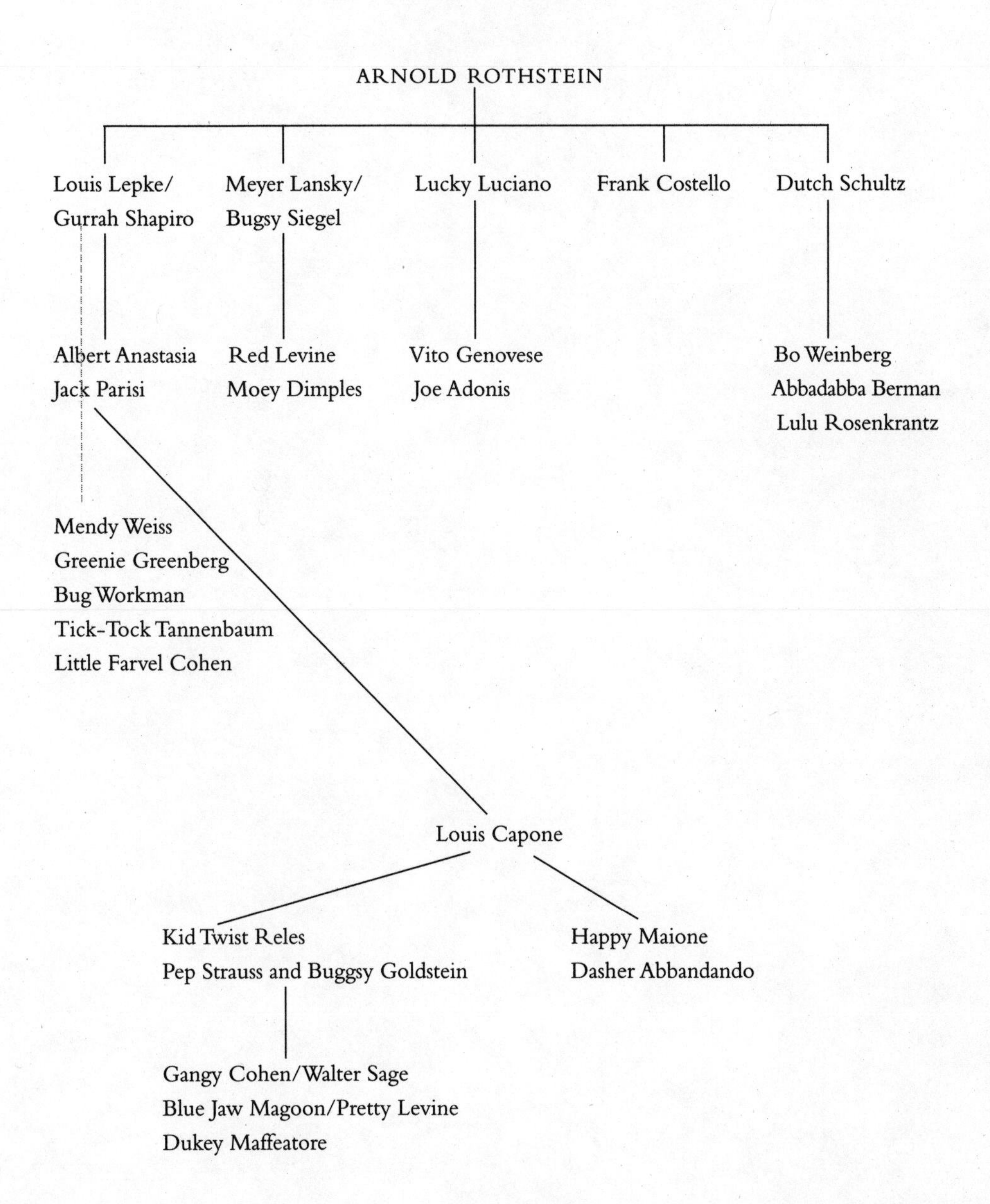

The criminal progeny that grew out of Arnold Rothstein's underworld empire.

Nate 'n' Al's

THEY ARRIVE IN German and Italian sports cars. They double-park and discard the ticket. They come through the door of Nate 'n' Al's, a delicatessen in Beverly Hills, they come in from the glare of Rodeo Drive expecting friendly faces. They are not disappointed. They float in on Italian-made shoes. They jam the aisles, fill the air, talk pseudo-Yiddish. They ask for the pickles, the ketchup, the herring, and they never say please. It's always gimme, gimme, gimme.

"C'mon, you heard Asher," says Herbie, folding his arms. "Give 'em the herring." Asher gets the herring, lays it on his bagel, and never says thank you. It's okay. It's understood. There are lots of things Asher never says.

They sit each morning at the same booth in back of the restaurant. They look over crowded tables and booths, over mingling bigwigs and hustling waiters, over the cigar case, where toothpicks and mints can be had for free. They blink in the half-light known to all true delis, where every morning is the same morning. They sit among Jews who have moved from the East—Baltimore, Chicago, Brooklyn—and are now looking for something that got lost on the way west. They arrive at the hour agreed on the day before. "Nine A.M. tomorrow," Sid had said, tapping his watch. "Last to come, pays. Agreed?" Heads nod. Agreed.

Today, Sid is the last to come. Sid will pay. Sid is a man of his word. He follows the rules. "Especially when they're my rules," he says, sliding into the booth. "A man who breaks his own rules is no man at all."

Sid is a few inches under six feet tall and broad shouldered and burly, but size is not the first thing about him you notice. The first thing you notice are his eyes, which are full of mischief. "Good eyes see the present and the past right at the same time," he says.

Sid has good eyes. Over the last several decades he has moved west with the country, from New York to Los Angeles. He has passed time at real estate conventions in the Midwest, drink in hand, corn and rye ripening all around. He has been to seminars, talked PTA, the future of the Rust Belt, computers, the explosion of the Southwest, the Internet. Still, in all these years, in all the houses with all the women, he never took his eyes off Bensonhurst, the neighborhood in Brooklyn where he came of age fifty years ago. Wherever he goes he surrounds himself with people who remind him in some vague way of those kids who formed his world in Brooklyn, where every son was an immigrant's son, every dream the pipe dream of an immigrant's son. In Los Angeles, where so many of his boyhood friends have also landed, he runs with the old crowd. "Hello, fellas," he says, reaching for a menu. "Happy to see everyone looking so happy."

Sid is a millionaire. He was in real estate. He sold his company. He says being from Brooklyn is a full-time job. When Sid talks, it's in a high singsong that is pleasantly at odds with his frame. "I see I'm the last through the door," he says, motioning for a waitress. "Guess I have to pay. Well, okay. Don't be shy, boys. Eat up. I'm loaded."

They grunt in acknowledgment. They're lost in their food: Asher and his egg-white omelet, runny and covered in ketchup; Herbie and his bagel, light toast, light schmere; Larry picking at Asher's egg-white omelet, runny and covered in ketchup. "I want a bagel and a whitefish," Sid tells the waitress. As he hands her the menu, he says, "Tell the counterman to gouge out the eyes. I don't want breakfast looking at me."

"Hey, Asher, you trying to hide your eggs from me?" asks Larry, looking at Asher's plate. "What's with all the ketchup?"

"Shut up," says Asher. "No one invited you."

A breed of such men thrive in Los Angeles, brokers, lawyers, entertainers, entertaining lawyers, promoters, moguls, former furriers, distributors, importers, exporters, self-promoters, men of leisure. They fled Brooklyn thirty-five, forty years ago and have shed as many outward signs of their heritage as would be shed, yet still retain something of the old world, a final, fleeting glimpse of what their fathers must have been. Their faces are concentrated, their talk full of warnings, premonitions of things to come, of time repeating itself, of good men stripped of all worldly goods and left to fight again with nothing but instinct. Every time he enters a room, Asher notes where each man stands, who poses the biggest threat, and who, if necessary, he'll take out first. "This is the stuff I'm thinking about all the time," he says, wiping his hands. "For me, it's just like a crossword puzzle."

On those mornings when the gang is in high form, when the stories come fast as tracks on a CD, they pull Nate 'n' Al's off into a swamp of time, where old Brooklyn comes face-to-face with modern Los Angeles. On such occasions, the group is an attraction to those who fill the outlying booths, the regular clientele of Nate 'n' Al's, who watch the gang as if they're watching mimes on stage, reading meaning in each gesture, seeing in them everything from how wealth is wasted on the uncouth to the last of a vanishing breed, whose very dialect, a thick Brooklynese, exists nowhere but in such storytelling, backward-looking circles. "They're trying to teach my grandkid Spanish in school," says Asher, yielding his plate to Larry. "What the hell? If he needs to learn anything, it's Yiddish. The language of my people is dying."

And when the men on stage look back across the restaurant, take in the eyes taking them in, what do they see? Many things. People who ruin every sandwich with mayonnaise, who buy high and sell low, who do what they're told, who say things like "It's nice to be important, but it's more important to be nice," who fall for every cheap carnie who comes through the door, and who know nothing of Brooklyn, of days when the old world existed alongside the new, when each roof looked like the scene of a police chase. "I go wherever I want to go and act like me," says Sid, looking around the room. "Everyone else's home is home to me."

Around each other, these men have a kind of ease that makes you want to confide things. The ease of old friends. Late nights. Stories by now more fiction than fact. Stories set on the stoops and corners of Bensonhurst, Flatbush, Brownsville, in a time when Jewish gangsters, that lost romantic breed, still roamed the streets, when Italians had no monopoly on hooliganism, when a Jewish boy could still fashion his future as murderous and daring and wide open, a future shot full of holes. Alleys. Blue smoky rooms. Basements. The ominous echo of footsteps. Leather shoulder holsters.

In his youth, Sid could leave his family's apartment house on Seventy-fourth Street, walk among the row houses to Kings Highway, where he could follow the immortal Sholem Bernstein, who ran "errands" for the Jewish Syndicate, clear out to the waterfront, where the world seemed to open up. If he tried hard, Sid could almost walk like Sholem, duck his shoulder like Sholem, drag his foot. Or like any of the other members of Murder Incorporated, a Jewish gang involved in racketeering, bootlegging, and shylocking. But all this happened so long ago, back when a Jew in jail didn't have to mean white-collar crime.

"Did I tell you guys who I met?" asks Larry, looking up from Asher's plate. "Mike Tyson. I interviewed him in the ring after that farce of a fight with that bum McNeely. We talked a little about the fight, then spent an hour on the old gangsters." Tyson is from Brownsville, the home of Murder Incorporated. And no matter how many middle-class families flee for the suburbs, for the shrubs and hedges of Long Island, heroes never really leave. "When Tyson talks about Lepke," says Larry, "he chokes up like a schoolgirl."

Larry is the television personality Larry King. As Larry Zeiger he grew up in Brownsville and Bensonhurst, tagging after people like Sid and Asher, dreaming of long nights on the radio. "I give Larry a hard time," says Sid, glancing at his friend. "Needle him. An hour goes by and still he can't believe what's happening, that someone's mocking Larry King. Larry Zeiger, maybe, but Larry King?"

Larry, held together by blow-dried hair and suspenders, is hunched over the table, checking his reflection in Asher's plate. Like the others in the booth, his trip to Nate 'n' Al's was an extended ramble over years and landscapes. In 1962 he was seated with a microphone in the window of Pumpernicks, a restaurant in Miami, interviewing any fool who happened through the door. One morning he ate alongside Meyer Lansky, an old man hosting an old friend, triggerman Jimmy Blue Eyes. "Lansky kept saying, 'Jimmy, why do you stay in New York?' " Larry recalls. " 'Do you know the temperature in Brooklyn today? Two. Why do you want to live like that? Move down here. Miami's the promised land.' "

A few years later, Larry picked a bad horse and was himself just about chased from Miami, splashed across the newspapers, and locked in some cracker jail. "I used to be there, but now, thank God, I'm here," says Larry, rapping the table.

Larry is in Los Angeles to cover the trial of O. J. Simpson. He flew in this morning, dropped his bags at the Beverly Wilshire, and walked right over. "Hey, Larry, what's the deal with that Simpson case?" asks Asher, picking up a fork. "What does the jury know? How sequestered is sequestered?"

"They had a conjugal visit last night, so they know everything you know," says Larry.

"Conjugal visit? How often do they have those?" asks Asher.

"Once a week."

"That's enough," says Asher. "I'd have time left over."

Asher is the dashing dark-eyed member of the group. When he smiles, his eyes disappear. His hair is gray, his glasses tinted. He sells real estate from an office around the corner. "When did you get in, Herbie?" he says, looking across the table.

Herbie has dozed off. This means nothing. Herbie dozes off all the time. He is relaxed. He once dozed off while having his teeth drilled. "Hey, Sid, shake Herbie."

"What?" asks Herbie, opening an eye.

"When did you get in?" Asher repeats. "Don't tell me you've been out here hiding from your pals. That'd break my heart."

"No, Asher," says Herbie, closing the eye. "I got in late last night."

Herbie is my father. My whole life, Herbie has been happy to see me. When he sees me, he acts in a way entirely unlike the way he acts before he sees me, something I know from overhearing him and from the way he is described by friends. When he does not see me, his language is filled with obscenity, with cocksuckers and motherfuckers and fuckin' pricks. One thing that frequents his stories—before he sees me—are dead men. "That motherfuckin' cocksucker and those fuckin' pricks he calls a crew are dead men." After he sees me, the talk is about the future, the way one should act, God, the mysteries of life, the neighbors, what Hank Greenberg would hit in this park, funny road signs, Jewish sports legends.

Before he sees me, his talk revolves around Louis Lepke and Gurrah Shapiro. After he sees me, it's Sandy Koufax and Sid Luckman. Of course, the same thing that drives his conversation (without me) to Louis Lepke drives his conversation (with me) to Sandy Koufax. It's all about Jews acting in ways other than Jews are supposed to act, Jews leaving the world of their heads to thrive in a physical world, a world of sense, of smell, of grit, of strength, of courage, of pain. "The day Koufax refused to pitch in the World Series on Yom Kippur was a great day for our people," says Herbie.

In the house where I grew up, we had no fewer than three books on the exploits of Jewish sports legends. My father used to point out the entry in *The Baseball Encyclopedia* that encapsulates the entire experience of the Jews in America: "Mo Solomon. 'The Rabbi of Swat.' At Bats 8. Hits 3. Born New York, N.Y., 1900. Died Miami, Florida, 1966." In my house we did not have a single book on Jewish gangsters. And though I enjoy the conversations I have with my father (home runs, no-hitters), I sometimes wish I could talk to him before he sees me, a conversation about Lepke and Shapiro, a conversation riddled with obscenity, a bloodbath of a conversation where every other sentence hides a dead man.

My father has a highly expressive face, where every emotion registers like a shade of light. The lines in his face run north to south, like furrows in a mountain. He talks in a slow, drawn-out manner that pulls people in and holds them longer than they intended to stay. Friends call looking for me and spend hours on the phone with him, at last agreeing he is right, they are on the wrong career track, heading nowhere fast.

My father grew up with Sid and Asher and Larry in Bensonhurst. They formed a gang called the Warriors but never really had the opportunity or inclination to emulate Murder Incorporated in any way other than language and dress. And nicknames. They gave themselves the sorts of loopy nicknames gangsters are supposed to have: the Mouth Piece, Who-Ha, Inky, Bucko, Lefty, Gutter Rat, Moppo. My father named himself Handsomo, a name that to me sounds ridiculous. Still, some of the old gang insist my father really was good-looking. "Your old man deserved to be called Handsomo," Larry told me. "He had dark black hair and green eyes, a rare combination in our neighborhood." Larry has written at least two books that chronicle Herbie's childhood exploits. My father moves through such texts the way the youthful hero, the hero destined to fall, moves through all coming-of-age novels: "There was a stage in my life when I wanted to be Herbie," wrote Larry. "Herbie was a provocateur. He was a schemer and a troublemaker, but he was in it for the sport, and he got just as much satisfaction getting into trouble as getting out. . . ."

After serving in the army and graduating from NYU law school, my father was hired by Allstate Insurance Company, where he announced his daily arrival saying, "Company Jew passing through." Several transfers later (New Jersey, Long Island, Illinois) he quit Allstate and set out on his own. He would consult, lecture, negotiate. "Just who will you consult?" his father asked at the time.

"General Motors," said Herbie.

"How long has this General Motors been in business?"

"For decades, Dad," said Herbie.

"And have they done okay without you so far?"

So my father found himself starting over in the wilds of Illinois, where the "s" is silent. And as I grew up, I found that I was becoming in some ways very different from him. I came to see myself as a midwestern character, as open and friendly as the plains, while he only wrapped himself more tightly in Brooklyn. By age fifty he had developed a great man theory of history, whereby all men of significance are from Brooklyn. "You like that guy?" he would ask, looking at the TV. "Well, that's another one from Brooklyn."

About ten years after he quit Allstate, my father wrote a book that went on to become a best-seller. The book was called *You Can Negotiate Anything,* a title for which I was punished in high school. "You can't negotiate everything in this class, Mr. Cohen."

Oh, yeah? Fuck you.

To me, that title, *You Can Negotiate Anything,* sums up the ethos of his old block, an ethos that means as much to Sid and Asher and Larry as it does to my father. It's about being savvy, about never letting anyone know if you're real or fake, crazy or sane, righteous or fallen, good or bad. It's about risks. On family trips, my father would steer the station wagon as he read the paper (stretched wide across the wheel) and ate a hamburger (left hand). "Any damn fool can drive a car," he would say, turning a page. "Reading the paper, eating a meal, *and* driving a car, now that's something!"

During the Korean War, my father, like Elvis—who, incidentally, was not from Brooklyn—was stationed in West Germany. He was stationed in Bad Kissingen on the East German border a decade after the Second World War. One day, looking over some grainy photos of him in fatigues, I asked if this scared him, being surrounded by men who may have been Nazis so soon before. "Scared?" he repeated, as if I were a fool. "Hey, baby. I had a thirty-eight on my hip. That means when I talk, you listen. Army of occupation, baby. I wasn't the one who had anything to be scared about. The Kraut, the Jerry, the Hun, that's who was shaking."

And this is a lesson many Jews of my father's generation took from the war. Shooting is bad. Shooting is to be deplored. But if shooting should break out, make sure you're on the right side of the gun. *Army of occupation, baby!* Which is one reason my father's friends cling to the romantic image of the Jewish gangster. In their formative years, those following the Holocaust, as they were faced with the image of dead, degraded Jews being bulldozed into mass graves, here was another image, closer to home—Jews with guns, tough, fearless Jews. Don't let the yarmulke fool ya. These Jews will kill you before you get around to killing them. Bugsy Siegel, Abe Reles, Louis Lepke, antiheroes whose very swagger seemed to provide another option. If Jewish gangsters still thrived today, if they hadn't gone legit, if Jews of my generation didn't regard them as figments, creatures to be classed with Big Foot and the Loch Ness monster, I think the Jewish community might be better off. After all, everyone needs someone who gives them the illusion of strength. How else to explain the sacred position in which American Jews hold the Israeli army? *Army of occupation, baby!*

The Jewish gangster stories told each morning by my father and his friends are really the remnants of old neighborhood stories, legends that have been passed from clubrooms and street corners to boardrooms and delis and on to suburban towns, like the one where I grew up. Over the years, in tellings that have worn them smooth, these stories have certainly been worked up and embellished, fitted less to the need of the subject than the teller. The story I am left with is therefore not so much one of facts as the noise those facts make passing through time. It is a story of shifting perspective, the way a group of Brooklyn thugs, each with his own rise and fall, fills a need in the lives of my father and his friends, and also in my life. So what follows is less a straight history than the story of a Brooklyn gang as seen through the eyes of my father and his friends, and then that story (my father looking at gangsters) seen through my eyes, like laying colored glass over colored glass.

And though this story sprawls across decades and time zones, from the stoops and candy stores of Brooklyn to the driveways of suburban Chicago, where fathers let their sons win at basketball, it is really just the story of three generations: the gangster generation, that handful of early century Jews who tried to bust into the palace with a crowbar; my father's generation, diligent sons who carried us over the threshold with hard work; my generation, cool-thinking suburbanites who wonder what it was like back on the outside. For people like me, who grew up hearing only of the good Jews, fund-raisers and activists, the gangsters offer a glimpse of a less stable time, like the Ice Age, when a greater variety of species thrived on earth.

The Jewish gangster has been forgotten because no one wants to remember him, because my grandmother won't talk about him, because he is something to be ashamed of. Well, to me, remembering Jewish gangsters is a good way to deal with being born after 1945, with being someone who has always had the Holocaust at his back, the distant tom-tom: *six million, six million, six million*. The gangsters, with their own wisecracking machine-gun beat, push that other noise clear from my head. And they drowned out other things, too, like the stereotype that fits the entire Jewish community into the middle class, comfortable easy-chair Jews with nothing but morality for dessert. Where I grew up, it was understood: Even the most reckless Jew winds up in medical school. Well, the gangsters helped me clear this trap, showing me that since the worst is possible, so is everything else. If a Jew can die in the electric chair, anything can happen.

After living in Chicago for twenty-seven years, my parents repatriated east, settling in Washington, D.C. Every now and then, however, when my father is in Los Angeles on business, he spends his mornings at Nate 'n' Al's. Once there, he picks up the narrative of the Jewish gangsters like something he left off only a moment before. "One day, I'm coming home from school and this guy comes running onto Eighty-fifth Street," says Herbie, coming out of his doze. "A car lurches after him and two guys come out. They're wearing hats. They throw the guy against a wall. They get him by the neck, punch him in the stomach. He doubles over and they kick him in the head. The guy slumps against the wall. As the thugs walk back to the car, they see me and one says, 'What the fuck are you lookin' at?' That was the first time I saw real violence—cruel, unprovoked violence. This wasn't two guys fighting. This was something else."

In a real way, people like my father, Sid, Asher, and Larry are the offspring of those old gangsters. They grew up on the same blocks, were part of the same world, were being pulled toward the same future. They were children on streets where Lepke and Reles were parents, grandparents. In some way, Sid, Asher, Herbie, and Larry are the dream the gangsters had of the future. Jews who are indistinguishable from Americans. Jews who are Americans. Jews who go to temple with all the nonchalance of a President Clinton going to church. Jews washed clean of Odessa, the shtetl, the camps, the tenements, millionaire Jews who drive German cars, who make legit deals before breakfast that pay off just after lunch.

And still, these Jews, are they happy? Can they ever be happy? Is any real Jew ever happy? Happy, is that a word you would use to describe Moses? Jesus? Freud? Einstein? Groucho? Hell, no, they're not happy. They crave the physical power of gangsters. They've seen *The Godfather* dozens of times. They talk tough in the produce line. Mess with them, you'll get hit with something heavy—maybe. No. They're not happy. They long for the past, for a time when all the old assumptions about Jews were like the German mark after the Great War—worthless.

Each day, after the eggs but before the coffee, after the box scores but before the futures, conversation turns back to those old criminals. And in the gang's deliberate way of speaking, you hear again the voices of killers under the bridge, the Gowanus Canal at dawn, sharpies and sharks, washlined streets and early morning walk-ups where young hoods make their last nocturnal rounds as sucker big brothers are just rousing for another chicken-shit payday at work.

Abe and Buggsy

ABRAHAM RELES AND Martin Goldstein were just coming home. The light was already on the eastern horizon, so it had to be something like four-thirty, five A.M. They were coming back from East New York, a nighttime world of young Italians in sheeny suits and old Italians in ribbed T-shirts, foreign accents, and fire escapes. They drove down Van Sicklen Avenue to Livonia, left the car at a garage, and made their way on foot. Walking through downtown Brownsville in 1931, the height of the Depression, they would have seen an occasional ice wagon and only those men who worked the first shift at the mills and packing houses. In the early morning, such men must have seemed like apparitions, the ghosts of lives Abraham and Martin would have led had they followed the rules and done as they were told.

Reles was known on the block as "Kid Twist," a name he gave himself, partly in tribute to an East Side gangster of an ancient era, partly in acknowledgment of his style, which was to get his enemy around the neck and twist the life out of him. To friends he was simply "the Kid," a short man with long arms and huge hands and fingers a cop once described as "spatulate." Reles had just turned twenty-five but looked half that age, with the soft, unlined features of a prize pupil or, worse still, a mama's boy. He looked young the way the most vicious criminals look young—like something in his development had been arrested or thwarted or turned into something else. Goldstein, who was known to everyone as Buggsy, must have found it comforting to have a friend like Abe.

As Reles and Goldstein walked along the steel-shuttered, early morning street, their words must have been end-of-the-day weary. They probably talked about the last few months, the bad things that had happened, the bad things that were to happen still, and how they would make up their losses.

In those days, the power in Brownsville was the Shapiro brothers. The oldest brother, Meyer, was born in the neighborhood, a fat kid who had grown into a fat man. Everything about him was fat: fat eyes, fat nose, fat ears, fat mouth. His kid brothers (Irving, William) were like cheap knockoffs of the original; not quite as fat, not quite as dangerous, not quite as smart, they mostly helped Meyer with his loansharking, bullying, pimping. The brothers ran fifteen bordellos in the slum. They were like the nineteenth-century Jewish bosses of Odessa, Russia, terrorizing shopkeepers and merchants who, like them, were confined to the Pale.

The big money, their future, was in slot and vending machines. Any store or restaurant owner who wanted to buy or rent a slot machine in Brooklyn in the early thirties had to go to the Shapiros, who, in addition to taking a percentage of the earnings, got five dollars for each machine. And if the Shapiros don't get paid? If you get your jukebox or cigarette machine or pinball machine somewhere else? Well, then something unfortunate might happen—your store might burn down or get robbed or who knows what else? These things happen.

If you were a young neighborhood tough wanting to steal, intimidate, raise hell, then you too went to the Shapiros. In Brownsville the brothers were the only way into crime, the only ramp onto that particular expressway.

Abraham Reles and Martin Goldstein—neither made it past the seventh grade—went to work for the Shapiros in the late twenties. By the time the boys were fifteen, Meyer had them stink-bombing restaurants, beating up strikers, collecting loans. And does Meyer show any appreciation? Does he give the boys a sign of thanks? Promote them? Pay them? Of course not. Mostly he just taunts and teases Abe, who really was funny looking. The Kid was near the end of his patience the night the cops caught him at Meyer's dirty work. And do the Shapiros come through with a lawyer or bail? No. Not even a visit. This is probably all the Kid thought of as the cops handed him to the lawyers who handed him to the judge who handed him to the guards who put him on a bus that ran north to the Elmira Reformatory. Reles got two years upstate. He must have sworn that if ever he made it back to Brownsville, he'd pay back the Shapiros.

On April 1, 1930, the New York Department of Corrections played a prank on Brooklyn—they let Abe Reles out of prison. While the Kid was away, Buggsy bought a pool hall, a run-down joint beneath the Sutter Avenue elevated. Reles spent much of his time at the pool hall, hustling whoever happened through the door. One night in comes this handsome kid looking for a game. The kid takes almost a hundred dollars off Reles. After that, Reles and the kid were friends.

It did not take Abe long to figure out just who this kid was—George Defeo, kid brother of William Defeo, who was tight with Meyer Lansky and Ben Siegel. Even out in Brownsville, the edge of the map, the names "Lansky" and "Siegel" were magic: they conjured up the whole story, the rise of two Jewish kids from the Lower East Side slums to the heights of the underworld. "So your brother's William Defeo," Reles must have said. "Not a bad brother to have."

A few weeks later, in the middle of a casual afternoon pool game, Reles said something like "Hey, George, your brother's gang, they do some work with slot machines, right?"

"Sure," said Defeo. "What about it?"

"Tell him, if he can supply us with machines, we can put them in Brownsville and East New York."

"You can't do that," said Goldstein. "That's still the Shapiros' territory."

"To hell with the Shapiros," Reles said. "If we're backed by Lansky and Siegel, what can they do about it?"

Defeo said he would look into it.

A few weeks later Reles and Goldstein were in business with Defeo. They had a supply of slot machines, which they leased to bars and restaurants. Though they kept a percentage of each machine's earnings, there was no five-dollar per-machine charge. What's more, since Lansky and Siegel saw this as a way into Brownsville, virgin territory, they gave the Reles gang the machines on credit. When the Shapiros threatened bar and restaurant owners, the Kid laughed it off. "Don't worry," he told customers. "We've got real power behind us."

Reles soon moved in on other Shapiro strongholds: bookmaking, shylocking. Less than six months out of prison, the Kid had gotten

Meyer Shapiro's attention. After deals and threats failed to deter Reles, Shapiro took the next step: around Brownsville, people who knew, knew that Abe Reles, Martin Goldstein, and George Defeo did not have long to live.

Jews of my father's generation and mind-set have a favorite gangster the way Catholics have a patron saint: a mythic figure who has left them a life lived, a style, a way of doing things. There was a kid on my father's block who would not fight on the Sabbath, who would rather let himself be whipped by a man half his size than fight on Friday night, because that's how Red Levine did it. For my dad, who tried and rejected several gangsters as either too brutal or not brutal enough, the greatest of all the old hoods was Abe Reles. "I once saw the Kid come out of hiding to buy a newspaper," my father told me. "The paper cost a nickel, but he gave the lady a fifty. That's how you get to be a hero. Lay green on everyone you meet. When you overtip, you're not throwing money away. You're investing in your legend."

The Reles legend was handed down from my father to me. I have learned each detail, each step, each misstep, each act of bravery. I have also learned to generalize, to see beyond the details to the poetry inherent in the timeline of every man's life.

Reles grew up on Pitkin Avenue and Watkins Street in Brownsville. He grew up in the years just before the First World War, before America plunged headlong into the twentieth century. At night the streets were full of faces, dark scowls and sly smiles, babies crying. There were people on the street at night in Brownsville, and they were all trying to get out, move on, get going, keep on, get settled, get rich, get home.

Like most adults in the neighborhood, Abe's father, Sol Reles, came from Europe, Galicia, a desolate part of eastern Austria. Fleeing pogroms, Sol left his village. By the time he reached Ellis Island in the first year of this century, he had nothing. A few years later he met a woman who had also come from Austria, and she too had nothing. They were married and had nothing together. In 1905 they had a child and for the first time did not have nothing. They had a son, and someday that son would have everything. But even as Abraham made his way in the underworld, Sol continued to struggle. "My Abie was always a good boy," Mrs. Reles told a reporter when the Kid was arrested for the forty-third time. "If he is such a big man, would his papa have to sell neckties and suspenders from a pushcart?"

Abraham Reles was raised a Jew. He was told of Abraham and Isaac; he was told of the binding of Isaac and must have pictured the blade Abraham held to Isaac's throat. He was told of the Flood, the plagues, the Exodus, the Commandments. But the life around him, the hum of the streets, must have been infinitely more vivid than those old stories. The time of Abe's youth was an in-between time for Jews in America. Like many others, Kid Twist was born in the course of a long voyage, knowing neither from where he came nor to where he was going; he was expected to finish a journey his parents began the day they fled the villages and shtetls of Eastern Europe, a trip that would eventually lead to Nate 'n' Al's in Beverly Hills.

As they became adults, men like Abraham Reles set out to conquer the new world. They took the dream of America and turned it into their own personal dream. They made fortunes. They rode in fancy cars. They walked in the street without fear. In the end, however, it was they who would be conquered, hunted and hounded and sent to jail. Some of them, the most murderous, the most daring, would die in the electric chair. Later, all that was left were bits of stories and colorful names, amusing anecdotes used to adorn the conversation of men like my father. Later still, their great-grandchildren would intermarry and lose their way. Their traditions and their past would evaporate like water on a hot plate. But this was far in the future, and by then there was no longer an old world to dream of returning to.

As a boy in Brownsville, Abe surely heard stories of the old country. Of the flat horizon and the high, white sky. Of horses and mules and chickens. And about land and how it's the only thing worth a damn. And about America, a beautiful nation of beautiful people. The way the kids of immigrants heard about America, you would think it was not down the stairs and out the door but still across the ocean, a distant place where everything is promised and, for hard work, everything is given. From the day he left his parents' house, Abe had to know his father was right, that America promises everything, but he also had to know his father was wrong—America gives nothing. Those things that are promised, they cannot be worked for but must be taken, conned away with good looks, obsequiousness, mimicry; or traded for with bits of your soul or the morals of the stories your parents told; or tricked away with lies; or wrested away with brute force. In Brooklyn, home was the old country, the land of the shul and shtetl, but the street, that was where the deals went down, where Rockefeller struck oil, where all roads led to Tammany Hall, where Jimmy Walker was king. In Brooklyn, the street was the new world.

Back then the borough was in a state of flux. Every day more immigrants poured into the narrow streets. Things broke down. Strife was the order of the season. Strikes and threats of strikes. In the middle of a crowded market, a young man would be attacked, beaten, and left bleeding. It was all over in a minute, the assailants disappearing down alleyways. And each day, all over the borough, brothers and sisters woke to another day of school, a useless exercise conducted in alien tongues. The wildest among them ran off, passing the hours however they could—hustling bums, playing cards, picking fights, unloading crates, pitching coins.

On blocks just like the one where Abraham grew up there was already a generation of accomplished Jewish gangsters. Veterans. They ran all kinds of penny-ante scams, and they too had dreams. They would be stronger than their fathers, stronger than the cops. They would be their own nation, with their own laws, loyalties, and justice. The most notorious of these kids were named Buchalter (Louis Lepke), Flegenheimer (Dutch Schultz), and, of course, Lansky and Siegel. Some of them were rumored to have done killings. Reles tried to emulate these older men. They showed what was possible. So even in the early days, before Meyer Shapiro was even a cloud on the horizon, the Kid was on the lookout for other kids, Jewish kids mostly, who took the lessons of their parents seriously, but not too seriously. Mostly he was looking for kids who weren't afraid—of the Italians, the Irish, the cops, the consequences. From the beginning, Reles knew that where you end up is the thing, not how you get there. How you get there, that's just something to be debated by the suckers who never make it out.

Over time, Reles emerged as a leader. Though he was just over five feet tall, something in him demanded respect. The smallest provocation, something only he knew the meaning of, could throw him into a rage. One day in the early twenties, he felt a group of older kids were giving him the high hat and so jumped a curb with his motorbike and rode them into a wall. This side of him, this wild, cowboy side, was usually hidden by an easy, laid-back, just-off-the-boat demeanor. He spoke in a slow, guttural lisp. He had a funny way of walking; going down the street, he looked like a man trying to kick off his shoes. Whenever booked for a crime, he listed his occupation as soda jerk.

When Reles was growing up, Brownsville was a hothouse of criminal talent. Just across the way, on Alabama and Dumont Avenues, Harry Strauss was coming of age. The Kid knew Strauss from school. He was one of those kids you admired but stayed away from, who ate alone in a corner of the playground. They called him Big Harry—he really was very big. Or Pep—he could be the kind of friendly that demanded a cute diminutive. Or Pittsburgh Phil—it sounded tougher and more interesting than Big Harry or Pep. As he grew into a man, Pep was often enlisted by the desperate to even the odds. He was big, strong, reckless. He had a sense of fair play, of right and wrong, of justice. Still, he was a head case. Violence was something he liked too much. Violence is something you can't fear, but you can't love it, either. One vice is as bad as the other. Excess is the beginning of the end of any ambitious youngster. Big Harry was good to have in reserve, like mustard gas, but he wasn't the first person you went to.

The first person the Kid went to was Martin Goldstein, who lived a few doors from the Releses. Marty was timid, but the Kid saw something in him. If his timidity was challenged, he could be thrown into a psychotic fit. That's why he was called Buggsy—because he was a little buggsy, a little crazy, a quality that's always recognized in some gangsters and is always called Buggsy.

Everyone familiar with the Brooklyn boys was convinced Edward G. Robinson based his film persona on Buggsy Goldstein, who had the same side-talking, duck-walking, tough-guy attitude as the movie star. And this, too: Buggsy had a real sense of style, a wise-guy sharpness. If you were in the underworld in the thirties and your first name was Buggsy but your last name wasn't Siegel, you'd better have a sense of style. A cop once asked Goldstein what name he went by.

"Buggsy," he said.

"Known by any other name?"

"Not that I know of," said Buggsy. Of course, this was a kind of joke. He was known by lots of other names: jerk, Jew, asshole, schmuck.

Over the years, Buggsy and the Kid pushed each other into crime the way friends always push each other from one dare to the next. He was there at the beginning, and Abe would make sure he was there at the end.

When they were twelve, Reles and Goldstein stopped going to school. What could it teach them? They instead took part-time jobs, Abe working for an engraver, Marty for a plumber. And they robbed: stores, cars, apartments. They were arrested. They were released. Their stock rose. On the block their friendship was admired as a partnership.

There were other guys around, too. Hundreds of them. You would see them on the corner, say hello, good-bye, that's it. Some were named for old gangsters, or for daring acts, or for no intelligible reason at all. Others were named for their physical deformities: Fatty, Big Head, Little Ears. Some would be your best friend for a day, a week, a month, then again fall into the background. Others you tried to help, like Joey Silver, a neighborhood kid who was always tagging after Reles and Goldstein. When Abe spoke about the future, the things he would do, Joey hung on every word. Joey was a cheering section, and the Kid liked having him around.

Just before he was sent up to Elmira, Reles got Joey a job with the Shapiro brothers. Three years later, when Abe started his own gang, Joey stayed with the Shapiros. But that was okay. It was expected. A job is a job. Besides, Joey was only running nickel-and-dime errands for the Shapiros. And if things ever got really bad, the Kid knew he could always turn to his old protégé for help. And things were bad now. A death sentence had been passed. So Abe asked Joey for a favor. "Tell me when Meyer and the other Shapiros go out together," he said. This way, the Kid would know when the hit was coming; he would also know when the Shapiro headquarters was unguarded, when he could stage his own guerrilla raids.

One night, as Reles, Goldstein, and George Defeo were hanging around the pool hall, the phone rang. Maybe Buggsy took it in the back room. As Defeo racked the balls, the Kid could hear Marty talking in low tones. He heard Marty say thank you, hang up. "That was Joey Silver," said Buggsy, reaching for his coat. "The Shapiros just went out."

Abe, Buggsy, and George parked a distance from the Shapiros' clubhouse. They walked to the Shapiros' parking lot. Beyond the trucks and sedans, the clubhouse, a squat building, sat in the dark, not a light anywhere. A car went by in the distance. Abe crept alongside one of the sedans. After taking a knife from his pocket, he drove the blade into a tire, releasing a sharp hiss of air, like the disapproving sigh of a parent, the Kid's mother, say, wearing a housedress, holding a brisket, shaking her head. "Why, Abie? Why?"

Across the lot, as Defeo watched the street, Buggsy tossed a rock at a truck. In the windshield, shattering into a thousand tiny images, Buggsy might have seen the men spilling from the clubhouse behind him. He must have heard the gunshots and seen the sparks dancing off the pavement where the bullets hit. Buggsy made it to the corner, his face bloody, the tip of his nose shot off. Defeo was shaken but untouched. Reles was the last to get away. He had been shot in the back, a bullet he would carry until the day he died.

As he ran, the Kid must have been thinking, Shit. Joey. Joey Silver. Cocksucker. Kike. Fucking bastard. Set us up. Chose the wrong gang. Better hope we don't live.

In the distance, Abe could hear an engine turning over, followed by the crunch of tires on broken glass as the Shapiros drove off. Meyer Shapiro went around Brownsville that night, looking for the Kid's girl. At last, spotting her, he called her to the car. He flashed a gun. "Get in," he said. The men in back slid over. Meyer drove to a deserted street. He dragged the girl from the car, beat her, raped her, beat her again. He left her in a field.

It was a bad night for the Kid—his own personal Night of Broken Glass. Still, the Shapiros had made a mistake. They had hurt Reles in every way possible, and still he was alive. The Kid spent the next several weeks, first in the hospital, then at Buggsy's, fighting to recover. When he again stepped into the street, he was thin, pale. If he was not a killer before, the Shapiros had made him into one. He went to see his old friend, Big Harry Strauss.

Harry lived in a brick house fronted by a narrow wood porch. "Come in," he said to Abe.

Abe told the story, his problems with the Shapiros, how he wanted to pay them back. "We'll run Brownsville and you can be a part of it," he said.

Though Pep normally stayed out of this kind of thing, what Meyer Shapiro had done to the girl—what had she ever done to him?—offended his sensibility. "Sure, I'll help," said Pep. "Just tell me what we do."

Reles and Buggsy then drove to East New York, where the sky opened and the air filled with garlic. After parking on Pacific Street, just off Eastern Parkway, they went into a *pasticceria,* a tiny shop where men drank cups of thick black coffee and studied race results in Italian-language papers. From behind the counter came a man, forty-five, maybe fifty, gray-haired, heavyset, a blue shirt with bone white buttons. He took the Kid's hand.

Louis Capone broke his nose years before, so now, when he looked at you, his nose seemed to be looking elsewhere. He had watery blue eyes. Very sympathetic. And the way he stood—back on his heels, stomach out—he looked like some old advice-giving chef. Capone's shop, over the years, had become a hangout for local thugs. They first came when they were kids. Louis fed them and they came back. Now, when Capone needed a favor, he called one of his tamed thugs. If he saw an especially promising kid, he would pass word to one of the more established gangsters in his circle—Albert Anastasia, Louis Lepke.

After feeding Reles and Goldstein—food is always of some comfort—Capone sent them to Sally's Bar and Grill. "Frank Abbandando and Happy Maione are down there," he said. "They're good kids. They have no love for the Shapiros. See them."

Of course, the Kid knew all about Maione and Abbandando—they ran the Ocean Hill Hooligans, the toughest gang in East New York. Yet even here, on their own streets, they were second to the Shapiros. The Kid had actually met Abbandando once before, up at Elmira, where Frank was doing time for robbery. The Kid used to watch Frank play baseball in the prison yard—shortstop. People said Frank was a very good ball player, that with a little dedication, he could probably make the Yankees or Giants. Some even said he got his nickname—the Dasher—on the base paths at Elmira. Others said he got the name early one morning in Brooklyn, when he was trying to shoot an enemy. When Frank's gun jammed, he was chased by his victim. Having lost him, Frank ran around the block, caught the man from behind, and shot him in back of the head. Hence: the Dasher. These men were different than the Brownsville Boys. They were the real thing. Gangsters. Killers. But what choice did the Kid have?

Sally's was a jukeboxy little bar on Euclid Avenue. Coming through the door, the Kid spotted the Dasher in back. He had small eyes, a high forehead, dark hair with a part as sharp as the spine of a book. He was thick necked. When he raised his head, a roll of skin gathered above his collar in back. Even in mug shots, his head is held high. And always that same smug, go-fuck-yourself smile. His biggest smile was saved for the worst times. When things got especially bad, when the cops came around asking questions, he would appear on the street with a suitcase, shake hands, look in windows, then gone, one week, two weeks, a month; then, when the heat was off, he would reappear—"The Dasher is back!" That night he would again be at Sally's, buying drinks, blowing money. "Hey, Frank," someone would say. "Where've you been?"

"On adventures," he might say, raising a glass.

"Hey, Frank," someone else would say. "Where'd ya get all the cash?"

"More adventures," he might add, looking at Happy.

Frank was always looking at Happy, seeing when he should and should not talk. Happy could give such instruction with his eyes alone. He was a little guy—five feet four—but charismatic as hell. He wore a size five shoe, the size of Chinese feet *after* binding. He was well dressed, wearing custom-made suits on even the most trivial errands. His black hair was slicked back—a dramatic backdrop for his dark, melancholy face. He was arrested thirty-one times before he was thirty-one. He knew everyone in the neighborhood and helped everyone he did not have to hurt. He loved to be out among them, spending, talking, boasting, laughing. People came to him with stories. He was the best audience in Ocean Hill.

Happy listened carefully as the Kid told him about the Shapiros, what they had done to his girl, how they shot him and Buggsy, and also about his plans: shylocking, slot machines. "If we teamed up, we can run the Shapiros out for good," he said. Several drinks later, Buggsy and the Kid stumbled off, with a promise from Happy and the Dasher to meet the following night at a diner in Brownsville.

As Kid Twist and Buggsy made their way home in the early morning, they must have been satisfied with their progress; from the edge of defeat they had rallied, cobbling together a kind of army. As they turned to say good night, it's hard not to imagine Buggsy grabbing Abe's sleeve and saying, "Hey, Kid, nine P.M. at the diner tomorrow. Last one through the door pays. Agreed?"

One of the diners frequented by the Reles gang was on Livonia just off Pitkin. The restaurant occupied the ground floor of a four-story brick building. There was a long lunch counter, fronted by stools. The counter was polished to a shine. Behind the counter was a grill, which the cook scraped clean with a spatula. Beyond the counter were booths and tables. It always looked as though a rush had just ended in the diner, or else as if something were about to happen. The place was never more than half-full. For years it was owned by a family of Irish immigrants. Then, around 1927, this family, deciding to move on, put the place up for sale. My mother's grandfather pulled together some cash and bought the restaurant. Why he did this, I don't know. Owning a diner doesn't seem like the most obvious way to the American dream. Still, it did a decent business and still occupies a mythic place in our story, recalling a more jaunty, experimental period in family history. At one time the place must have had a name, but everyone, even my great-grandfather, just called it "the diner."

Soon after my mother's grandparents bought the place, they discovered it was a hangout for Jewish gangsters. In the future, these gangsters would come to be known as Murder Incorporated, and the diner would become a sort of shrine to their bravado. The gangsters had a regular booth in back. Often there were many people in this group, and another table had to be added. Louis Lepke himself once sat in the corner of the booth, his back to the wall.

When he was old enough, my mother's uncle Abraham went to work in the diner. One night, before closing, Pittsburgh Phil came up behind my great-uncle, who was stacking dishes. "A big husky kid like you?" said Strauss. "Why you wasting your time doing ladies' work? You could make a nice penny running errands for me and the boys."

My uncle did not answer and instead went on stacking dishes. This upset my grandmother, who thought this might be taken by Strauss as a sign of disrespect. "That man would kill you as soon as look at you," she told me recently. "I was positive Abraham was going to wind up dead."

She was right. Several years later Abraham was killed in combat in the Second World War, the same result in a larger cause. The men in Murder Incorporated, they too were willing to die for a cause. They were just selfish enough to know what their cause was—themselves. They were not fool-sucker enough to die for something as vague and abstract as freedom or liberty. Of course, after V-E Day, when the particulars of Hitler's war became clear, these feelings would change.

Around this time, my mother's mother married Benjamin Eisenstadt, my grandfather. Though he had passed the bar exam, work did not come easily for lawyers, especially Jewish lawyers, during the Depression. After trying just about everything else, Ben took a job as a counterman at the diner. If you go to the house in Flatbush where my grandmother still lives, you will see on the wall a newspaper clip from that time: the photo, Ben in apron with coffeepot, is accompanied by text that reads, "If you want a cup of joe *and* a legal brief, come see Benjamin Eisenstadt." After several years in the diner, my grandfather, tired of countertop sugar dispensers and how they crusted over (he found this unsanitary), invented the sugar packet, which finally freed him from the service industry. Much later he came up with Sweet'n Low, but that was far in the future, when my grandfather had already become a very different kind of man.

My mother's recollections of the diner are vague, but my grandmother still dreams about the place. When I told her of my interest in writing about the restaurant and also about the gangsters and their table in back, her face clouded over. "They'll kill you," she said. "These men, they're not like you. They'll kill a boy like you."

When I pointed out that these men—Reles, Strauss, Goldstein, Maione, Abbandando—were long dead, she shook her head and said, "They'll kill you." That's when I realized that to my grandmother, and to a lot of other people, too, the Jewish gangsters who came to power in the twenties and thirties were less like men than weather systems, wild and unpredictable and unstoppable by a small thing like death. "I beg you not to ask any questions about these men," she went on. "They hear everything and will enjoy killing you."

One night in 1931, at nine P.M. all the men whom Abe had called were seated at a booth in back of the diner, all but George Defeo and the Dasher. There was Pittsburgh Phil, who would soon be known as the most efficient killer in Brooklyn; Happy Maione, who sneered long before Elvis; Buggsy Goldstein, whose mother called him Mot'l; Walter Sage, who said he stole to support his study of the Talmud; and Gangy Cohen, a huge tank of a man who talked fast and clear, as though his words were connected by hyphens. Now, when I think of these men and their nicknames, each carefully chosen and solemnly given, I imagine them as colorful, gun-toting action figures.

"Would-somebody-please-tell-me-please-where-is-this-fellow-they-call-the-Dasher?" asked Gangy Cohen. "Where-the-hell-is-this-fellow?"

A window near the table was open, and through the window came the sound of the street: cars, kids on stoops, mothers calling sons home. "Look, I've been thinking about this and decided we need to kill everyone associated with the Shapiros," said the Kid. "If we don't kill them all, they kill us. And listen: Meyer and Joey Silver. Those are special. I want to be there for those."

Pep, who was seated next to the Kid, nodded. Strauss was tall and well built, with wide-set eyes, dark hair, high cheekbones, a long nose, thin lips, and small teeth. When the waitress came over, he ordered first. He always ordered first, and always sturgeon, the most expensive item on the menu. "Gimme a plate of sturgeon," he would say proudly. Though Strauss was not yet rich, sturgeon was something he had to have, something his parents could never afford. The meat of the sturgeon was white and soft and came apart on his fork. For Strauss, one bite of sturgeon took the place of all his father's morality. The other men ordered coffee, hamburgers, brisket sandwiches, doughnuts.

"Hey, fellas," said the Dasher, coming through the door. "Did you get the news?" When the men looked up, Dasher could probably tell they had not heard and must have felt the thrill of delivering bad news. "I heard it coming over," he said, stripping off his coat. "George Defeo caught it."

And that was all. Abe and Marty had spent much of the last few months with George, but in the end it must have been like hearing about a stranger. All they got was the one cold fact: George is dead. But they did not see him fall. They did not see him backed against a wall on Atlantic Avenue. They did not see the pattern the exit wounds made on the bricks. The cops would be all over this one, so they would not even attend the funeral. "We'll have to look for someone to take his place," said the Kid.

A long time later, Reles and Goldstein probably went to see the tombstone at Mount Zion Cemetery. George Defeo. Born 1910; Died 1930. And that was it. Nowhere in there was there any hint of the real George, how well he played pool, how he wore his hat.

The men sat in the back booth until closing. They talked in hushed tones. Sometimes there was a long silence, somebody mumbling, followed by an explosion of laughter. At such moments the back of the diner seemed to fill with teeth. Those moments made my great-grandmother nervous, but the men in the back tipped well, and they made the idea of the diner ever being robbed a kind of joke.

At the end of the meal, the Kid went over assignments, sending men like soldiers across the neighborhood. He was preparing for war; he wanted to fight the Shapiros in the street, so everyone could see the corpses. George Defeo was the first casualty of that war, but the real fighting would not come until the summer, and it would be the first test of Kid Twist and his gang.

The Moderns

WHEN ABE RELES and his gang went to war with the Shapiros, it was a rite of passage—for the Italians, it was making your bones; for the Jews, it was a kind of underworld bar mitzvah, like becoming a man. And it was yet another installment in the long history of gang warfare in New York City, which stretches clear back to the eighteenth century, when a bad night out meant drinking knockout drops, getting blackjacked and rolled, then waking, hours later, on a broken-down ship bound for China, the captain saying, "Work or swim."

Each kid who makes his way in the city's underworld, whatever his background, inherits this tradition as even the lowliest bush league baseball player inherits the mantle of Gehrig and Ruth. It's why Reles named himself after Kid Twist Zweibach, a gangster who was killed one night in 1908 by Louis the Lump in Coney Island; why, in the 1920s, Arthur Flegenheimer, a Jewish kid from the Bronx, called himself Dutch Schultz after a German gangster from a century before.

For living gangsters, the stories of dead gangsters, their exploits and failures, the way they died, is the only history that really amounts to much. It's a story that most ambitious gangsters are trying to make themselves a part of, a story that begins over two hundred years ago in the Five Points and the Bowery, the toughest, most storied slums in New York, and follows the great gangs that dwelled there: the Bowery Boys, who fought just north of Grand Street, on Bunker Hill; the Dead

Rabbits, who were sometimes joined by Hell-Cat Maggie, a ferocious female gangster who filed her teeth to points; the True Blue Americans, who wore stovepipe hats and ankle-length frock coats; the Daybreak Boys, who worked the docks, killing vagrants and night-watchmen, pillaging ships and warehouses; the Plug Uglies, who wore oversize plug hats, which, before fighting, they filled with wool and leather, fashioning an early version of the sports helmet; the Buckoos; the Hookers; the Swamp Angels; the American Guards; the Slaughter Housers; the Short Tails; the Shirt Tails; the Patsy Conroys; the Border Gang; the O'Connel Guards; the Atlantic Guards; the Forty Thieves; the Roach Guards.

And later: the White Hands, a Brooklyn gang that stole across the Brooklyn Bridge each night, terrorizing downtown neighborhoods; the Whyos; the Hudson Dusters; the Gophers; the Potashes; the Chichesters; and the Stable Gang, who hung out in a barn on Washington Street in Greenwich Village, just a few blocks from where I now live.

Going back through police files, or the pages of old books, you can find pictures of many of the early century gangsters. They have names like Red Rocks Farrell, Slops Connolly, Big Josh Hines, and Googy Corcoran. Their faces are dark and tight, their features pressed like fingers in a fist. They probably did not have what we would today call a balanced diet. They were surprisingly small: a hundred years ago the average New York gangster was not more than five feet three or heavier than 135 pounds.

If you go back further, to the time of President Ulysses S. Grant and the Tweed ring, the pictures give way to police drawings. Looking at these hastily made sketches—a line here, a shadow there—it's hard to believe in the actual, day-to-day life of such men. They look like characters in a fairy tale.

And going back before that, to the decades preceding the Civil War, you are left with only a few legends—the creation myths of New York's underworld, stories as mysterious and full of portent as those in Genesis. The characters in such stories stand forever behind reputation-minded criminals like Reles and Goldstein, a backdrop against which their most daring crimes are cast.

In his 1927 book, *The Gangs of New York,* which is really the Old Testament of the New York underworld, Herbert Asbury wrote about one of these early gangsters:

> The greatest of the Bowery Boys, the most imposing figure in all the history of the New York gangs, was a leader who flourished in the 40s, and captained the gangsters in the most important of their punitive and marauding expeditions into the Five Points. His identity remains unknown, and there is excellent reason to believe that he may be a myth, but vasty tales of his prowess and of his valor in the fights against the Dead Rabbits and the Plug Uglies have come down through the years, gaining incident and momentum as they came. Under the simple sobrique of Mose he has become a legendary figure of truly heroic proportions, at once the Samson, the Achilles and the Paul Bunyon of the Bowery. And beside him, in the lore of the street, marches the diminutive figure of his faithful friend and counselor, by the name Syksey, who is said to have coined the phrase, "hold the butt," an impressive plea for the remains of a dead cigar.

When Jews began arriving in New York in numbers in the middle of last century, they at once found themselves among the gangs. On the Lower East Side, in rickety tenements, on narrow streets, in brick alleys and crowded warrens, they came face-to-face with Irish thugs. Late at night, when the only light came from the moon or a flickering gas lamp, the streets would fill with toughs who moved among the newcomers. Some preyed on immigrants, Italians and Jews, who could often be tricked out of what little they had; those who could not be tricked could be bullied; those who could not be bullied or tricked could be killed. In those days, before the spread of handguns, an old immigrant would often be found in some dark alley, his skull smashed, his pockets turned out, a timesaving message to scavengers: Nothing more here.

To some Jews still trying to find their way through the streets, this was just a continuation of the past, more of the same harassment they had known in Europe. There was a real anti-Semitism in the air, a hatred often dressed as civic pride. Frank Moss, who worked with the preacher William Pankhurst, claimed he was trying to clean up the city when he wrote of his visit to the Jewish slums:

> Ignorance, prejudice, stubborn refusal to yield to American ideas, religious habits and requirements, clannishness and hatred and distrust of Christians; these combine to hinder any device for raising the condition

> of the poor of the great Jewish district . . . there is no part of the world in which human parasites can be found in more overpowering numbers. . . . The criminal instincts that are so often found naturally in the Russian and Polish Jews come to the surface in such ways as to warrant the opinion that these people are the worst element in the entire make-up of New York City.

The strongest of the immigrants took such words as a challenge. Jews were bullied in America, but in America Jews could fight back. They were not confined, in a legal sense anyway, to any particular place or profession—they were free to be criminals. And they had an advantage that Irish gangsters, many of whom were born in the United States, did not quite understand: the Jews had little to lose. Nearly two million of them left Eastern Europe in the last two decades of the nineteenth century, washing up here like driftwood, with nothing but a few names, a few riddles. How the hell do we get out of the Lower East Side?

And the pogroms of Europe had taught them something. Some it taught how to die; others it taught how not to die. When he was an old man, Meyer Lansky, who came to the Lower East Side in 1911, talked to Uri Dan, an Israeli reporter, about the pogroms that swept through his hometown of Grodno, Poland. Lansky talked about those who threw up their hands, who saw the situation as hopeless, a punishment from God; but he talked about others, too, a new generation determined to fight back.

"One man—I don't remember his name, but I wish I did—held a meeting in my grandfather's house," said Lansky. " 'Jews,' he shouted. 'Why do you just stand around like stupid sheep and let them come and kill you, steal your money, kill your sons, and rape your daughters? Aren't you ashamed? You must stand up and fight. You are men like other men. A Jew can fight. We have no arms, but it doesn't matter. We can use sticks and stones. Fight back! Don't be frightened. Hit them and they'll run. If you're going to die, then die fighting.'

"This speech is burned in my memory," Lansky went on. "I carried the words with me when I finally traveled with my mother to America and the Lower East Side. I remembered those words when I fought back at the Irish as a boy on the East Side. They were like flaming arrows in my head."

By the time many Jewish immigrants reached New York, they too were ready to fight back. Some because they had to—for their wives and children. Others because they had to, but also because they wanted to. And still others, who came from middle-class families and did not have to, because they would rather fight than go to school or work. They fought for sport. The most skillful of them became gangsters, mastering things like stealing and killing, which Jews are not supposed to master.

Unlike the gangsters who came later—gangsters truly of the twentieth century, men like Crazy Joe Gallo and John Gotti—these early figures, who often went straight from the boat to the street, were not going into a family business, not following a blazed path. Their fathers were peddlers or tailors, butchers or merchants, and here were their sons, good Jewish boys, going into crime, which to their fathers must have seemed as strange and exotic as investment banking or advertising might seem to the Gallos or Gottis today. Like many Americans of the first generation, these gangsters were taking on the hard task of reinventing themselves, of creating a new identity for a new country.

"They were tough because they had to be tough," said John Cusack, formerly an agent for the Federal Bureau of Narcotics, now the head of drug enforcement in the Bahamas. In the fifties, Cusack testified on organized crime before the McClellan Rackets Committee. "If these men had grown up in another place, in another time, who knows? But they were playing what was dealt. They were just trying to survive on the streets where the wind had brought them."

Though there were many accomplished Jewish gangsters in the years before 1900, the first truly famous one was Monk Eastman. His real name was Edward Osterman. He was born in Williamsburg, Brooklyn, around 1873. His father was solidly middle-class, a restaurant owner. Before Monk was twenty his old man gave him a store to run, a pet shop on Broome Street in Manhattan. Monk sold the store and went instead to work as a bouncer at New Irving Hall, a nightclub on East Eleventh Street, where he became renowned and feared for the easy manner in which he dispatched drunkards, defeating men twice his size with a few sharp blows. Like the hero of a calypso song, he whipped every man and loved every woman.

Monk was ugly in a way you don't see anymore—nineteenth-century ugly. His face, the aftermath of smallpox and brawls, looked like a stretch of Carolina landscape after a hurricane has blown over, with boats in the middle of town, cars overturned, cows hooked on flagpoles. You know what his face looked like? Like an art class sculpture by an eight-year-old: his ears cauliflowered, his nose really just the suggestion of a nose, his mouth a dark gash. His hair was parted neatly—an odd, dandified touch, like a hat on a horse. He was around five feet five and weighed 150 pounds. Coming down a dark downtown street, he must have looked like death itself.

By the time Monk was in his early twenties, he had gathered around him most of the East Side Jewish thugs. The Eastmans, as he called the gang, hung out in a clubroom on Chrystie Street near the Bowery. Monk could call out over a thousand soldiers. These men mostly fought an Italian gang headed by Paolo Vaccarelli, a former prizefighter who called himself Paul Kelly. One night the gang leaders fought, one on one, for supremacy. Eastman and Kelly brawled under klieg lights for two hours, until each man, bruised and battered, had to be carried off by his troops.

The Eastmans were not tightly organized. There was no schedule of events, no newsletter. They were either fighting or not fighting. When soldiers were needed for a fight, the call was shouted in the streets, whispered in the dives—in Gluckow's Odessa Tea House on Broome Street, in Sam Boeske's Hop Joint on Stanton Street, in Dora Gold's candy store on First Street. The Eastmans fought wars inconceivable today: all-day gunfights with hostile gangs, passersby falling here and there; pitched battles with entire police divisions. Barricades were erected, stones hurled. Though they sometimes had guns, most of these battles were fought with clubs or blackjacks or pipes. Raiding the Eastmans' clubhouse, the police came away with two cartloads of slungshots.

When not fighting, the gangsters were left to make their living—robbing, looting, stealing. Mostly they dressed like river rats, in tattered shirts and mothy jackets, fingerless gloves and broken-brimmed hats. At night they drank blue ruin, the cheapest rotgut whiskey, chased girls, started fights. The victims were found in the East River the next morning. This was New York's Wild West era, when the most important gangsters were really just street thugs. The underworld had not yet made the transition to the twentieth century. Parts of lower Manhattan made Tombstone, Arizona, look like a sleepy border town.

In 1904 Monk bungled a holdup, shooting at a Pinkerton detective in the process. He was sent to Sing Sing. In his absence, a succession of Jewish gang leaders rose and fell, passing like picture cards in a fast shuffled deck: Kid Twist Zweibach, who died in a fight over a girl; Big Jack Zelig, a broad-shouldered, arrogant young man whom enemies called the Big Yid ("Where's that Big Yid?" an Italian assassin asked one night. "I gotta cook me that Big Yid"); Dopey Benny Fein, the sleepy-eyed trailblazer who led the way to labor racketeering; Kid Dropper, who was shot while in police custody in front of the Essex Street courthouse by a mysterious figure who said his name was Louis Cohen; Little Augie Fein, who was killed in 1927 by Louis Lepke and Gurrah Shapiro at Norfolk and Delancey Streets as his bodyguard, Legs Diamond, looked on.

Monk Eastman was released from prison in 1916. All of a sudden the word was out: Monk is back! But things had changed. The old gangsters had died or gone straight; the young gangsters were different. No longer did people fight for the sheer joy of it. Monk could not raise an army. Not yet thirty, he was an old man, a relic. He worked as a sneak thief, a pickpocket, a dope peddler. After a half dozen small-time arrests and short stints in prison, he decided to go where there was sure to be fighting. In the spring of 1917, Monk Eastman joined the U.S. Army. At the enlistment, when he was stripped and examined, the doctors, noting the dozen or so knife wounds on his torso, asked, "What wars have you served in?"

"Just a lot of little wars around New York," said Monk.

He was sent to France. I like to think of him arriving in Paris not too many years after the Dreyfus affair—this big, ugly, broken-nosed, backbreaking Jew. How could the French, with their ideas about Jews—what they looked like, what they did—deal with a man like Monk Eastman?

On the battlefields of France Monk was a hero. He led charges, gave orders. He did things, courageous things, in the face of enemy fire. It probably reminded him of the old days on Chrystie Street. In New York a year later, he was rewarded for the same behavior that once sent him to Sing Sing. On May 3, 1919, Governor Al Smith signed an executive order restoring Monk to full citizenship.

The police helped him find a job, but how could they help him settle down? When most people see extravagant window displays, they think: Wait until I get my paycheck! When Monk saw extravagant window displays, he probably thought: Where's a rock? At night he went for long walks by the river—the hero back from the war, realizing he is still not home. Monk was soon mixing with criminals. On December 26, 1920, he was found dead in front of the Bluebird Cafe on Fourteenth Street. He had been shot five times. He was buried with military honors.

The death of Monk Eastman marked the end of the old-time gangster, whose world had been one of brute force and blunt instrument, whose money had come in dribs and drabs. Already, in the first years of the century, there were hints of the future, when gangsterism would at last become Americanism—as much about remaking yourself as about striking it rich. Monk actually spotted this future years before, in a seedy gambling house downtown. Here was this skinny kid (thin hands, thin wrists) leaning over the crap table, throwing dice. "Who the hell is that?" asked Monk.

"That's Rothstein," someone said.

Though Arnold Rothstein was just a boy—fifteen, sixteen years old—there was already something great about him, something just coming into focus. Monk sensed it right away. Not only was Rothstein the future of Jewish crime in New York, he was the future of all crime everywhere. In the coming decades, this skinny kid, who was probably losing that night at craps, would find that perfect mix of grace and violence, bluff and bravado, sophistication and brutality, that would become the modern American gangster. "Look out for number one," Rothstein told a reporter years later. "If you don't, no one else will. If a man is dumb, someone is going to get the best of him, so why not you? If you don't, you're as dumb as he is."

Arnold Rothstein was a rich man's son. He grew up in a town house on the Upper East Side. His father, Abraham Rothstein, owned a dry goods store and a cotton processing plant. Abraham had one of those dark, haunted Jewish faces that seemed to disappear with the last century, or else survived just long enough to die in Treblinka or Auschwitz. He had a beard, a nose, eyes. By certain friends he was called Abe the Just. A dinner given in his honor in 1919 was attended by Governor Al Smith and Judge Louis Brandeis. Whenever a Protestant politician had trouble with the poor, downtown Jews, they sought the advice of Abe the Just. From an early age, Arnold must have known he would disappoint his father, that he was not very much interested in his father's sense of justice.

When he was around fifteen Arnold began slipping away from his father's house and heading downtown. Though just a few minutes by train, it was like crossing into another country. He walked along flaring streets, jostled by drunken men and mysterious women, surrounded by accents, shouts, the clang of buoys, the cry of gulls. Running together, these sounds built to a roar—the song of the slum. Arnold sought ghetto life the way white teenagers later sought black music—jazz, rock 'n' roll, rap. Here was a world beyond the humorless conventions of middle-class society. Arnold went to the Lower East Side the way Teddy Roosevelt went to Africa—in search of big game.

What he loved most were the card and dice games being played on every corner. When Rothstein first threw a pair of dice, something magical must have happened, a flash illuminating the next twenty years: smoky rooms, late nights, laughter, bluffs, tells, codes, straights, guns, bootleggers, casinos, horses, showgirls, Saratoga, Miami, bets won, bets lost, more bets lost. Though Rothstein would eventually tire of most things—friends, cities, states, styles, girls—he never lost his interest in gambling. It built him in the beginning and destroyed him in the end. From the day he first went below Fourteenth Street, his life was an endless succession of bets.

Gambling put a distance between Arnold and his father. If you could come away from a card game rich and fulfilled, if a seamless bluff brought respect and money, what did that say about the old morality? Was hard work really the way to the good life, or was it just a path for suckers? But despite that first rush, Arnold intended to come home. He would quit slumming, go into the family business, attend shul. He always wanted to be the good son. So what happened? The same thing that always happens. Arnold Rothstein met a girl.

When Arnold brought his girl home to meet his father, when Abe the Just hobbled downstairs, tugged his beard, straightened his yarmulke, when he heard his boy out, the plans to get married, when the girl told the old man no, she was not Jewish, and no, she would not convert, the old man shook his head and said, "Well, I hope you'll be happy." And after the wedding, when the old man pronounced his boy dead, when he covered the mirrors and read the Kaddish, it was a great development in American crime. It set Arnold free.

For Rothstein this was the decisive break, an excuse to turn his back on the old laws, subjecting himself instead to the rule of the street—a father/son split that was mirrored throughout Jewish America. "We saw it everywhere," wrote reporter Lincoln Steffens. "Responding to a reported suicide, we would pass a synagogue where a score or more of boys were sitting hatless in their old clothes, smoking cigarettes on the stoops outside, and their fathers, all dressed in black, with their high hats, uncut beards and temple curls, were going into the synagogue, tearing their hair and rending their garments. . . . Their sons were rebels against the law of Moses; they were lost souls; lost to God, to the family and to the Israel of old."

Rothstein was darkly handsome, with a high forehead, sloping nose, downturned eyes, thin lips, and a mole on his left cheek. Every line in his face, every crevice, seemed as carefully placed as war paint on a Sioux, each mark declaring his dread intent: to win every bet, whip every foe, meet every challenge, take every sucker. In rooms where other men wore cloth jackets or shabby suits, he wore tuxedos and top hats. "I had no idea he was a gambler," said Carolyn Greene, his showgirl girlfriend. "He looked like a successful young businessman or lawyer."

In the early 1900s Rothstein was making his way in the small gaming houses and pool halls of the Bowery. He changed this world as he passed through it, showing the young hoods how a gentleman carries himself. In the way that every great stylistic invention seems a convergence of high and low, a cultural cross-pollination, Rothstein was taking his uptown sophistication to the Jews downtown. He had more influence on the look of American criminals than Jackie O had on middle-class American housewives. Jackie brought hats, gloves, big sunglasses. Arnold brought wing-tip shoes, silk suits, expensive hats. He kept his money, his bankroll, in his front pocket. Whenever a friend needed a loan, he whipped out the entire roll, which, thanks to winning hands and gutsy bets, was getting fatter all the time. "No problem," he would say, tearing off a few bills. "How much do you need?"

Like most great men, Rothstein can be judged as much by his enemies as by his friends. In 1911 some of these enemies—sour old gamblers—decided to teach him a lesson. Arnold thinks he's great at pool? Well, let's get a real shark in here and show him he's wrong. So they got Jack Conway up from Philadelphia, a pool prodigy. They took Conway to Jack's, a popular bar with the Broadway crowd, where he struck up a conversation with Rothstein. "I hear you play pool," Conway said. "Maybe you think you can beat me. What do you say? Do you want to play some pool?"

Before Rothstein sensed all those gamblers smirking in the dark, he had accepted the bet. And then it was too late. Once you're in, you're in. Okay, said Rothstein. First man to one hundred points wins.

Since Conway was the challenger, Arnold got to choose the pool hall. Easy. John McGraw's Billiard Parlor, next to the Herald Building. McGraw was then the manager of the New York Giants. One of the great baseball men of all time, he was one of the great sports of his time. He followed the races, the fights. On off days he could be seen at the track, leaning on the rail. He was friendly with all the big New York gamblers. For Rothstein, McGraw's was home court.

Arnold took the first break early Thursday evening, the sky already more black than blue. The only light in the room came from lamps that hung over the tables. The light showed only the felt of the tables and the lay of the balls. When Rothstein leaned to shoot, you would see his face and veined hands. Standing around the table, or watching from the bleachers along the wall, the other men in the room were just shadows or the glow of cigarettes.

When the balls crashed, the shadows shifted, the voices murmured. The room was full of voices. Every important New York gambler and gangster was in the room that night. The men who brought Conway up from Philly were there, betting anyone fool enough to believe in Arnold—who, by the way, was betting on himself, which he would do up to the very end.

Conway reached a hundred points first. "Nice game," said Arnold. "What do you say, do you want to play some more pool?"

"All right," said Conway. "Let's play."

Arnold won the second game, and the third. Over time, he wore Conway down. By sunrise Rothstein was up three thousand dollars. "That's fine pool," said Conway. "Let's play some more."

So they kept at it, the big hand circling the clock like a device in an old movie. The sun came and went. The shadows lengthened and shortened. The noise in the street changed. Daytime noises: kids, dogs, crowds. Nighttime noises: rain, laughter, footsteps. A hat was filled with money for the kids racking the balls and keeping score. Black coffee was served on silver trays. When the sky paled Saturday morning, the gamblers backing Conway were down more than ten grand. Conway, who had yet to win a single best-of-three series, shook Arnold's hand. "Nice shooting," he said. "What do you say, do you want to play some pool?"

Before Arnold could answer, John McGraw stepped in. "That's it," he said. "If I let you go on, I'll have you dead on my hands."

Rothstein put his hand on Conway's arm. He thanked him. They must have been in that region of exhaustion where every word is a joke and every joke is unnecessary. As the spectators—some happy, some not—went off into the morning, Rothstein took Conway downtown to the Turkish baths.

By evening the news had made the rounds: Arnold Rothstein had pulled off a great feat in an era of great feats—he had prevailed in an epic encounter, an underworld spectacle. It was a triumph of will. Even in hour forty, when every eye in the room was itchy and crying for sleep, when the balls moved in trails across the table, when the outside world was just a blur beyond the glass, Rothstein stayed cool. He did not rattle or break.

The underworld was now open to Rothstein. Each night he wandered as far north as Harlem, as far south as Delancey Street. If you went out to a Manhattan nightclub in those years, a dark place at the bottom of some stone stairs or maybe a casino hidden in back of a tall office building, you would have seen gangsters in parrot-colored shirts and hats, backs and shoulders, faces. If, in a corner of one of these rooms, you saw a well-tailored young man with a curled lip and downturned eyes, surrounded by other men fighting for his attention, this was Arnold Rothstein making the rounds. Athletes, starlets, tycoons—they sought him out. They wanted to shake his hand, collect the encounter.

It was around this time that Rothstein was befriended by Big Tim Sullivan, the great Irish political boss of the Lower East Side. Throwing an arm around Arnold, Sullivan would say, "This is one of my smart young Jew boys."

Wondering about Sullivan's new protégé, a ward leader once asked, "How can you tell what a Jew's thinking? They're different from us."

"Rothstein's a good boy," said Sullivan. "You stick with him and you'll make a lot of money."

With Sullivan's protection—from gangsters, from cops—Rothstein took the next step, opening an opulent midtown casino. In addition to money, the casino, which brought in about ten grand a week, gave Rothstein stature. He was now the house, the establishment, the meeter and greeter who accepts or does not accept markers, who sees people in their true nature, how they act in the wee hours when the table is just a sea of chips. His regular customers included Charles Gates, the son of John W. "Bet-a-Million" Gates; Julius Fleischmann, the yeast king, whose family would later found *The New Yorker* magazine; Joseph Seagram, the Canadian whiskey baron whose heirs now run MCA; Harry Sinclair, the oil magnate. For lots of wealthy New Yorkers, Arnold Rothstein was a door to the kind of fun that could not be had legally.

One night, Percival H. Hill, the president of the American Tobacco Company, lost $250,000 in Rothstein's casino. Hill left Arnold a marker, which he said could be redeemed from a Mr. Sylvester the next day at the American Tobacco Company.

When Rothstein showed up with the IOU, Mr. Sylvester shook his head and said, "A gambling debt, I presume?"

Rothstein was not only getting rich—he now had more money than his father—he was climbing the underworld ladder from brash young gambler to elder statesman. Coming out of his own casino, he was less the smart young Jew boy than the Brain, the Bankroll—names he answered to on Broadway. To those who never met him he was A.R. the way James Pierpont Morgan was J.P. Biographer Gene Fowler compared him to "a mouse standing in a doorway, waiting for his cheese."

When Arnold had enough money, he went still further, becoming the financier of the underworld, backing any shady project that caught his fancy. He was involved in the drug trade, raised horses, fixed fights. To downtown Jews he was the Jew with money, "the Man Uptown." They called him Ph.G.: Pappa has gelt—the old man has cash. He could be found each night at Lindy's, a diner on Broadway and Forty-fourth Street, hearing get-rich-quick schemes. It was here that he was first approached about fixing the 1919 World Series. Though Rothstein turned down the members of the Chicago White Sox who approached him—"You'd get lynched if it ever came out," he told them—popular imagination has fastened this piece of corruption to his legend.

In his 1925 book *The Great Gatsby,* F. Scott Fitzgerald based the character Meyer Wolfshiem on Rothstein:

"He's quite a character around New York—a denizen of Broadway," Gatsby tells narrator Nick Carraway.

"Who is he anyhow—an actor?" asks Nick.

"No."

"A dentist?"

"Meyer Wolfshiem? No, he's a gambler." Gatsby hesitated, then added coolly: "He's the man who fixed the World's Series back in 1919."

Fitzgerald had already described Wolfshiem: "A small flat-nosed Jew raised his large head and regarded me with two fine growths of hair which luxuriated in either nostril. After a moment I discovered his tiny eyes in the half darkness."

Of course, in the real world, Arnold Rothstein was just as smart and well put together as F. Scott Fitzgerald. (If they had nose-hair clippers in the twenties, you can bet Rothstein owned a pair.) And that was the point. There was no easy way (reptilian eyes, Jew nose) to tell Rothstein from the other successful businessmen skulking around Manhattan. He was a businessman just like so many of those fathers who, returning each day from the city, disappear into neat suburban homes—whose wives, when all is said and done, have no idea what their husbands do. He had broken through the traditional confines of the underworld and come out in a place where the line between the criminal and the commendable is vague and unreal. He worked the underworld the way a great aristocrat works the upper world: moving gracefully through rooms and thresholds.

In the fall of 1920 Arnold Rothstein was approached by Irving Wexler, a small-time dope peddler and sneak thief whom everyone called Waxey Gordon. Waxey and his partner, Big Maxie Greenberg, who had just arrived from Detroit, had come up with a way around the Volstead Act, which enforced the Eighteenth Amendment, which made the sale or transport of alcoholic beverages illegal. Waxey and Maxie would speedboat cases of whiskey across Lake Michigan from Canada to Detroit. The whiskey would then be smuggled and sold across the country. Simple. Only thing: Waxey and Maxie needed $175,000 to get it going. A.R. was the only gangster anyone knew with that kind of money. After meeting with Maxie the next day on a bench in Central Park, Rothstein said he would think it over.

The best gangsters act like the best businessmen: it's not their job to come up with the great discovery, the flash of inspiration. Their task is instead to recognize the great idea in others. See it, back it. Sometime in the next few days, as Rothstein considered Waxey's plan, he must have realized that here was a key to the future: that by banning alcohol, the U.S. government was turning a legitimate, multimillion-dollar business over to criminals, like walking into an abandoned factory and everything clean and shiny and ready to go; that young thugs who would have once gone straight would now stay in crime, at last having an illegal business to grow up in; that this new business would demand a new type of criminal, men with enough polish to move in the upper world, enough muscle to move in the lower, who could kill but could also intimidate, corrupt; that, if things went well, organized crime would soon change from an urban menace to a great moneymaking American industry, like steel or oil; and that he, Rothstein, was perhaps the only gangster in New York with the connections, money, sophistication, and smarts to turn East Side street punks into an army of business thugs.

The thing in Rothstein that recognized this, that saw beyond the patterns organized crime had followed until then (street brawls, gambling) to a glimmering world of gangster statesmen, is what separates old-timers like Monk Eastman from moderns like A. R. Rothstein was to the back alley what the money baron was to the boardroom: he pushed the barriers, bent the rules. He understood the truths of early century capitalism (hypocrisy, exclusion, greed) and came to dominate them. When a friend was in trouble, Rothstein offered the use of his lawyer. The lawyer told A.R.'s pal to refuse to answer questions, saying he might incriminate himself—that is, stand on the Fifth Amendment of the U.S. Constitution. This had never before been tried, and the lawyer went clear to the Supreme Court to make it law. So, in a way, A.R. created even this—taking the Fifth, a tactic that would come to define the American gangster. If the world of organized crime were a university, this alone would assure Arnold Rothstein tenure.

When A.R. again met Waxey and Big Maxie, he told them yes, he would back their plan—only he wanted some changes. Instead of A.R. financing Gordon and Greenberg, he would hire them. He would become the first big-time American bootlegger and they his employees. Another thing: Instead of bringing cases of alcohol on boats from Canada, which struck A.R. as small-minded, they would bring in a shipload of whiskey from England. After crossing the Atlantic—a hard, dangerous crossing—the ship would sit just outside American waters, about three miles off the coast of Montauk, Long Island, where it would be met by cutters fast enough to outrun Coast Guard boats. Rothstein bought six speedboats, each to carry ashore between seven hundred and one thousand cases of whiskey. The alcohol would then be trucked to a warehouse in Manhattan, from where it would be sold and shipped to speakeasies and clubs throughout the city.

In 1920 Montauk was just a sandy, unprotected, windblown point. Lighthouse. Shacks. Rock. I like to think of A.R.'s boys meeting the cutters on the beach out there, city men in black city suits, lugging heavy cases of whiskey across the dark sand in black city shoes; starting the truck and heading east down an empty ocean road, leaving in their wake a trail of sand and dust, the road a black ribbon beneath a black sky. They drove through a darkness composed of farms and fields, towns, houses, church spires, railroad platforms. City crime making its first groping contacts with a world beyond the last city light, the sticks, where everyone is assumed to be a sucker.

Rothstein had paid off cops all along the way. When the truck went barreling through some lonely crossroads, the patrolman just looked the other way. Or maybe he pulled the truck over, made small talk, then asked for a bottle. "Just something to keep me going," the cop might say. No, the problem wasn't the cops or the locals. It was the other gangsters. Coming out of nowhere, in dark sedans and coupes, bandannas below their dark eyes, guns flashing, these hijackers would stop the truck, hold up the drivers, and make off with a few dozen cases. And who could protect A.R.'s product? When a smuggler is robbed, can he go to the cops? No, not really. What Rothstein needed were his own criminals, men tougher and smarter than those robbing him. In the future, each of his trucks would head out with a driver up front and two soldiers in back, riding shotgun, like heroes of the Old West protecting the mail from bandits or Apaches.

These recruits came from the Lower East Side. They were Jewish and Italian—but mostly Jewish. If A.R. didn't find them, then they found A.R. (Meyer Lansky met Rothstein at a bar mitzvah.) This was a generation miles removed from gangs like the Eastmans. Many of these men came here as boys from Italy or Poland or Russia, but already they were Americans. Already they had the pragmatism of the new world—Jews and Italians who saw that they were more alike than different, that old rivalries meant less than new money. When Irish gangs came down to beat up immigrants, young Italians and Jews fought them off together. It was the beginning of an alliance that, for many Jews, was a great part of the American experience. "When Lucky Luciano was deported from America and was living in Italy, you know what he talked about missing?" John Cusack asked me. "Jewish corned beef, pastrami, rye bread. He said just thinking about it made his mouth water."

And these men, growing up on the same streets, learned the same lessons: that in America it isn't enough to be strong, you also have to be smart; that in America it isn't enough to be strong and smart, you also have to play a role, making others feel that you are really just like them, only younger or older or from a different place; that in America people help you only when they are convinced they are really helping themselves, either through a mutual interest or through identification, a belief that by helping you, they are actually helping themselves in some other incarnation.

Rothstein picked out the best of these young thugs, those he could train, who shared his views, who got it. In the first years of Prohibition, riding shotgun for A.R. was like fighting for the Mujahdeen—it taught you, hardened you, marked you for life. The men Rothstein hired included Lansky, Siegel, Luciano, Frank Costello, Legs Diamond, Waxey Gordon, Dutch Schultz, Louis Lepke, Gurrah Shapiro—men who would eventually turn A.R.'s lessons into a national obsession and would themselves become the most notorious criminals of the twentieth century. "Meyer Lansky went on to become the king of illegal casino gambling," a retired New York detective named Ralph Salerno told me. "I think the first time he ever saw the green felt of a crap table was in Rothstein's place. Arnold taught Lansky about style. He was maybe the first guy to take craps off the street and put it indoors, up on a table."

As far as I'm concerned, Arnold Rothstein was the Moses of the underworld: he led the next generation to the promised land but himself could not enter. He was shot in the stomach on November 4, 1928. A Sunday night. Earlier that evening he had received a phone call at Lindy's. He was asked to come to the Park Central Hotel on Fifty-sixth Street to discuss a debt. Having lost at cards some weeks before (fifty grand in a single hand), he now owed a California gambler a few hundred thousand dollars. Small change. But A.R. refused to pay, saying he had been cheated. "I don't pay off on fixed poker," he told a waitress. The same thing that gave Rothstein the strength to play pool for forty-five hours would not let him pay off that chicken-shit marker. Leaving Lindy's, he gave his gun to a friend. Weapons were not allowed at such meetings. Rothstein was found an hour later, slumped over a banister in the lobby of the hotel. "Call me a taxi," he told the doorman. "I've been shot." Later, at the Polyclinic Hospital, when the cops asked Arnold who shot him, he waved them off, saying, "I'll take care of it."

Though Rothstein had seen dozens of underworld figures fall—Louie the Lump, Monk Eastman, Kid Twist Zweibach, Dopey Benny, Little Augie—he could not believe in his own death. He spent the next few days promising to recover as he dissolved into delirium. Slipping away, his hospital window showing nothing but river and sky, he must have felt less like an underworld genius than a lost son, a boy who has disappointed his father.

A few years before, Arnold heard his father was in trouble. The cotton market had collapsed. Abraham Rothstein's cotton processing plant was worthless, creditors were after him, he couldn't get a loan. Arnold learned of this from his kid brother, Jack. "He needs a lot of money," said Jack. "More than two hundred thousand."

"Why doesn't he just ask me?" asked Arnold.

"You know he wouldn't do that."

"Okay," said Arnold. "Tell him to go to the main office of the Bank of the United States tomorrow and ask for a loan."

"He's been there," said Jack. "They refused him."

"I'll see to it that they change their minds," said Arnold, who then went to the bank and gave the president $300,000 in Liberty bonds—enough to secure the loan. "When my father comes in, give him his loan," said Rothstein. "My father is not to know that I was here."

Rothstein was no longer an observing Jew, but here he was living the Jewish experience—giving anonymously. No one but Arnold and God would know of this gift. No matter the bad things Rothstein did, I like to think this act carried weight with God. Rothstein was looking after his father long after his father stopped looking after him.

One afternoon Rothstein's estranged wife came to see him in the hospital. "I want to go home," he told her. "All I do is sleep here. I can sleep home." He died a few hours later. The funeral was overrun by sharks and gamblers, superstitious men hoping to take away some part of A.R.'s magic. In front of the crowd stood Abraham Rothstein, old man in prayer shawl, saying Kaddish a second time for his son.

For the most part, Rothstein's legacy would be carried on by the young criminals he had influenced. "He taught me how to dress," Lucky Luciano recalled years later. "He taught me how to not wear loud things, how to have good taste. If Arnold had lived longer, he could have made me pretty elegant; he was the best etiquette teacher a guy could have—real smooth."

A.R.'s legacy was powerful, finding its way even to those who never met him, who would not make their names until much later. The connection between Rothstein and the Jewish hoods of later generations like Abe Reles and Buggsy Goldstein was tenuous but real—like the relation of a photograph to a copy made from a copy made from that photograph. Though years had passed and the image had blurred, some of the original features—a hint of style, a dash of color—could still be made out. To this day, every gangster in America, in ways they probably don't even understand, is imitating Arnold Rothstein.

The time of Rothstein's death was an in-between time for organized crime in America. Rothstein had left disciples behind, a cadre of young criminals determined to carry the word forward: Money is money, everything else is bullshit. But the streets were still in the grip of the last generation, traditional Italian gangsters whom A.R.'s boys disdainfully called "Mustache Petes." These were old world criminals with thick mustaches, dark eyes, creased brows, heavy hands, strong loyalties, ancient hatreds, deep suspicions. The Petes traced their roots to the Black Hand of Sicily, secret societies, vendettas, stylish symbolic killings: shoot out the eyes, stealing the last sight accorded even the dead; cut out the tongue, telling the world, "Here lies a squealer."

These men were bothered by what they saw as the corruption of the new world, where promising young thugs like Charles Luciano consorted with Jews like Meyer Lansky. When Frank Costello introduced Vito Genovese to Bugsy Siegel and Meyer Lansky, Genovese said, "What are you trying to do? Load us with a bunch of Hebes?"

"Take it easy, Don Vitone," said Costello. "You're nothin' but a fuckin' foreigner yourself."

The Mustache Petes were small-minded, parochial men who really belonged to the past. And soon the past would come looking for them. The resulting fight—the Castellammarese war—would be perhaps the most important battle in underworld history. It was to organized crime what the Civil War was to the United States: a battle of ideas, economies, vision: Do we go forward, do we go back? It was a war in which Jewish gangsters would play a decisive role.

By 1930 everything seemed settled, with the underworld, the Italian part of it, at least, run by those men—Costello, Luciano, Anastasia, Gambino—loyal to Joe Masseria.

Masseria had come to the Lower East Side from Sicily—where he was wanted for murder—in 1903. He was a short, roly-poly guy a shade above five feet, but something in his eyes, some steadiness, froze people. As a young man he had a reputation for athleticism, an agility that defied his physical appearance. Once, when an enemy came after him on Second Avenue, he literally dodged the bullets. After killing Masseria's bodyguards, the assassin fired several shots at Masseria, who bobbed and weaved, the bullets lodging in the wall behind.

In the coming years, Masseria rose to power. Behind this rise, as behind the rise of all powerful men, stood a troop of shattered friends and rivals: Lupo the Wolf, Peter Morello, Ciro Terranova. By the late twenties, Masseria, having defeated his enemies and tricked his friends, declared himself *capo di tutti capi,* boss of bosses. To those working for him, he was simply Joe the Boss.

Masseria was not a popular leader. He was disliked even by his own lieutenants, especially those who had worked for Rothstein. Costello and Luciano distrusted the boss, his love of ritual, his prejudice. "When I started hanging around with Jewish guys like Meyer and Bugsy and Dutch, Masseria used to beef me about it," Luciano later wrote. "He said someday the Jews were going to make me join a synagogue."

But what could Luciano do? Masseria was the power on the street. What he lacked in foresight he made up in guns. A well-armed past can, for a time, hold off even the most prosperous future. Joe the Boss would be Joe the Boss until someone took that title away. And it wasn't going to be Luciano or Costello or Lansky or Siegel. Not yet, anyway. In the meantime, Luciano would just have to wait, all the while playing the role of top man behind the boss.

All things in the world are connected. Throw a switch here, a light goes on over there; break a promise here, make an enemy over there. In 1926, when Benito Mussolini began cracking down on the Mafia in Sicily, he probably did not think it would affect life over there, in New York, but it did. Soon after the dictator pushed the crime bosses out of Italy, they began turning up in Manhattan. They came mostly from the area around the Bay of Castellammare, a rugged country of squat white houses running over scrubby hills to the sea. Some of these men—Joseph Bonanno, Joseph Profaci—would later become powerful gangsters. Arriving on the East Side, though, they were just hungry exiles. And they were a threat to Joe the Boss. The newcomers did not respect the current order. Why should they? They ran things in Sicily. Why not run them here, too?

These men were led by Salvatore Maranzano, who in 1927 settled in America with his old world ways. A thug who met Maranzano later wrote: "When we arrived, it was very dark. We were brought before Maranzano, who seemed absolutely majestic, with his two pistols stuck in his waist and about ninety boys who were also armed to the teeth surrounding him. I thought I was in the presence of Pancho Villa."

Setting up headquarters in an office tower near Grand Central Station, surrounding himself with lieutenants, Maranzano went to war with Joe the Boss. All over Manhattan, in blue smoky rooms and underground clubs, in pool halls and all-night diners, gangsters took sides. They fired from moving cars, rooftops, doorways. Pistol shots punctuated the night. In the morning the cops came for the bodies. Between 1927 and 1930 at least fifty men fell. Luciano spoke to young soldiers on both sides, telling them the war was a waste, how nothing would come of it, how it was costing everyone money, how here was another example of old generals fighting with young lives.

Charlie Luciano had come to New York from Sicily in 1906. He had a dark fleshy face, curly hair, and a quality smile. On a fall night in 1929, four thugs dragged him from the West Side docks, where he was unloading a shipment of heroin, and into a car. As the sedan ghosted through Brooklyn, Charlie was beaten, blackjacked, pistol-whipped, ice picked, cut across the throat and face, then left for dead on Huguenot Beach in Staten Island. At dawn he was found by a cop and rushed to the hospital. Later, when he was asked who attacked him, he shook his head, saying, "I'm pals with everybody. Nobody's after me. Everybody likes me."

Gangsters suffer the same setbacks as everyone else, only their losses can be more easily seen. Luciano's defeat could be seen in the scars that ran across his face. The muscles below his cheek had been severed. As a result, his left eye drooped, giving him a sinister aspect. Women in his world found this attractive. "I never liked a pretty man," an old gangster doll I met in Miami told me. "I like a man that's been marked up." On the street, Luciano was now called Charlie Lucky—the only man lucky enough to be taken for a ride and survive. The very term "going for a ride" was really just code, another way of talking about death, the way American soldiers in Vietnam would later talk about "buying the farm." Charlie was a religious man. He must have believed God had saved him for a reason, that there was still work to be done.

Whenever he could get away, Luciano went down to Delancey Street, a crowded little delicatessen—silverware ringing, voices chattering—for breakfast with Meyer Lansky. Luciano first met Lansky years before, on a January afternoon at the beginning of the century. Meyer, a scrawny immigrant kid with huge features, was walking alone through the snow on Hester Street. Looking up, he saw he was surrounded by young Italians. "If you wanna keep alive, Jew boy, you gotta pay us five cents a week protection money," said the leader, Charlie Luciano.

Meyer looked up. Two sharp eyes met two sharp eyes. They saw something in each other, something familiar. "Go fuck yourself," said Lansky.

It was one of those moments—Mick Jagger meeting Keith Richards; Otto von Bismarck meeting Kaiser Wilhelm—that would have consequences. "He stood there, this little punk," Luciano later recalled. "I was five years or so older than him and could have smashed him to pieces. But he just stood there staring me straight in the face, telling me to stick my protection up my ass. He was ready to fight. His fists were clenched."

Luciano respected the kid's nerve. He hit him with some small, face-saving insult, then walked away. Later he came back alone, looking for an ally—someone who would fight with everything he had. In the coming years the boys looked after each other, protected each other. Crossing one was crossing both. Gangster arithmetic. They forged one of the great friendships in criminal history. "We had a kind of instant understanding," Luciano later said. "It was something that never left us. We didn't have to explain things to each other. It may sound crazy, but if anybody wants to use the expression 'blood brothers,' then surely Meyer and I were like that, even though we had come from totally different backgrounds."

Here was an example of gangsters living ahead of their time. In an era when much of the country was hyper-aware of background and religion, Lansky and Luciano got beyond that. They believed that in America your brother can be born to any parents, in any house. "Gangsters who never made it out of high school broke social barriers thirty years before anyone else got near them," Ralph Salerno told me. "Much more than people in other parts of society, gangsters are pragmatic and realistic. Why the affinity between Italians and Jews?" he went on. "It was a marriage of convenience. They were in the slums at the same time; they went against Prohibition at the same time. It was a marriage of the three M's: moxie, muscle, money. The Jews put up the moxie, the Italians supplied the muscle, and together they split the money."

Whenever Luciano talked about the war between the Mustache Petes, Lansky urged caution. *Wait this thing out. Let the bosses kill each other off.* But by 1931 both men had tired of waiting. Too many people had died; too much money had been lost. Something had to be done.

That spring Luciano went to see Maranzano in his headquarters, a real estate office in the Eagle Building at 230 Park Avenue. Lucky spent an hour in the office, nodded at the bodyguards in the outer room, took the elevator down, and disappeared into midtown. At that point, only one person other than Lucky knew what would happen next—Meyer Lansky. Whatever happened, some of Meyer's boys would be involved. After all, the future Lucky and Meyer were planning was Italian and Jewish—so Jews and Italians should ring it in together.

On April 15, 1931, Luciano asked Masseria to lunch. "We'll go over to Scarpato's," Lucky told the boss. "Scarpato fixes sauce like in the old country, with the clams and good olive oil."

They took Masseria's steel-plated, bulletproof limousine. From the East Side it was a short drive through lazy red brick Brooklyn, alleys and stoops tumbling past the window. Now and then a kid stood watching the car go by, dark windows, mystery.

They drove along the harbor, schooners and sloops stretching to the horizon, masts making lines against the sky. The restaurant was on West Fifteenth Street in Coney Island—one of those run-down Italian joints by the boardwalk. You can still go there today. The restaurant is gone, but the building is there. It's now the General Iron Corporation, but it looks pretty much the same: narrow facade, slender columns, arched windows. The street runs under stunted city trees down to the ocean. Standing out front, clouds moving fast on the horizon, you think: This is how it must have felt in 1931, only less carefree, less picturesque, less sinister; romantic now only in the way of a ruin, a place where something important happened long ago.

That afternoon, Luciano and Masseria took a table in back. They had the kind of long, leisurely lunch known only to the very rich and the very poor. Masseria probably talked about the war, how it was going, how he still hoped to win. Maybe he talked about the Jews, again telling Charlie how a man can only trust his own. They drank Chianti. Plates were cleared. A waiter brought a deck of cards. They played poker. At around three P.M. Luciano excused himself, saying he had to go to the toilet.

A moment later the restaurant's front door flew open. In came a ragtag collection of killers: Ben Siegel, Albert Anastasia, Joe Adonis, Red Levine. They walked to the back room and began shooting. Twenty shots. When the killers returned to their car, Adonis got behind the wheel. He was shaking so, he couldn't turn the key. Siegel pushed him aside, started the engine, and drove off.

When Luciano returned from the bathroom, he saw panicky waiters, Masseria slumped on the table, holes in the wall, holes in the boss, an end (to some) of his problems. In newspaper photos the only thing visible is Masseria's bloody hand, palm up, holding the ace of diamonds. Among gangsters, that card was ever after cursed. Receiving an ace of diamonds by messenger was another way of learning of your own death.

When cops later asked Luciano where he had been during the shooting, he said, "In the can taking a leak." He thought a minute, then added, "I always take a long leak."

That night, when Maranzano heard about the killing, he declared himself the victor of the Castellammarese war. He got a message to Luciano: Thank you. Lucky was named Maranzano's first lieutenant, perhaps the second most powerful job in the underworld.

A few weeks later Maranzano called a meeting. Just about every Italian gangster in New York was there, a huge warehouse in the Bronx, a few blocks from the Harlem River. The doors were patrolled by armed guards, the roof by sharpshooters. Like at the Congress of Vienna, which followed the defeat of Napoleon, or the Yalta Conference, which followed the defeat of Hitler, the survivors were meeting to redraw the maps. Standing before the boisterous crowd, with his guns and bodyguards, Maranzano laid out a blueprint for the next generation. The Italian underworld would now be divided into five criminal families. Each family, which was really just an affiliation of like-minded thugs, would operate like a trade union. Low-level members of a family, soldiers, would pay the boss a percentage of their earnings, a tribute. In return, the soldier is protected—from other criminals, from cops. If a soldier from one family is wronged by a soldier from another family, he has someone to go to—his capo, a neighborhood leader, who may then bring the matter to a lieutenant, who may then bring it to the boss, who may then bring it to the boss of the rival family, quietly settling what might once have led to a bloody war. And if a soldier is arrested on family business, the family posts bail, hires a lawyer, fixes a judge. If a judge cannot be fixed, the soldier's wife and kids are taken care of while the soldier does his time. It was a good system.

Maranzano named bosses to run each family. The selections were not random. Maranzano was not betting hunches. These were already powerful underworld leaders. Each man gave his family his name: the Lucky Luciano family; the Albert Anastasia family; the Tommy Luchese family; the Joseph Profaci family; the Joseph Bonanno family. For the most part, these families still exist today, operating on the same basic principles Maranzano set up in the warehouse in the Bronx, running restaurants, stores, guns, bakeries, trucking companies, hotels, resorts, drugs, whatever. When most successful, their operation is as fluid and invisible as the wind.

Over the years, as bosses have been killed or jailed or deported, new bosses have risen to take their place, giving the families new names. When Albert Anastasia was shot dead in midtown, his family became the Carlo Gambino family and was still called that when it was being run by John Gotti. When Lucky Luciano was deported to Italy, his family became the Frank Costello family, then the Vito Genovese family, then, when Genovese was wanted for murder and was hiding in Sicily, it again became the Frank Costello family. When Genovese came back to New York and realized Costello would not relinquish power, he organized a coup. As Costello passed through the lobby of his Upper West Side apartment building, a hulking youth stepped from the shadows and shot him. Though Costello survived, he surrendered power. When Genovese died, family leadership went to the kid who allegedly shot Costello—Vincent "the Chin" Gigante, who is said to still run the family, even though he was convicted in 1997 of racketeering and conspiring to kill John Gotti. Since Maranzano first set up the families, underworld politics have supplied more intrigue, color, and drama than even the most backward state in the Balkans.

As far as the younger generation saw it, Maranzano made only one mistake. He placed himself above the family bosses, making himself the boss of the bosses. So, after all that, after the gunfights and stabbings, here was yet another would-be dictator, another *cappo di tutti capi*. Maranzano must have known his decision was not popular, that downtown clubrooms were filled with young men who would not bow to absolute rule, who were determined to make the underworld a republic, who in every important way were more American than Sicilian. Maranzano could call himself whatever he wanted—boss of bosses, boss of the universe—but it wouldn't mean a thing until he dealt with these young men, who were led by Luciano and his friends. That's why Maranzano made Charlie his chief lieutenant—keeping Lucky close was a way of controlling him. And when it was time to kill Lucky, he wouldn't have to go far looking for him.

Luciano knew the truth—that he was an obstacle, something in the way. And if he didn't know it, he had only to ask the Jewish gangsters, who were sufficiently removed from the Sicilian underworld to see the pattern. Luciano was being warned, not only by Lansky, but also by Louis Lepke, who was the first gangster to come into real conflict with Maranzano after the war.

In the summer of 1931, during a season of strikes, one of the most important garment workers' unions, the Amalgamated Clothing Workers, splintered into factions. One faction, run by Phillip Orlofsky, was allied with Lepke, who supplied protection. The other was led by the union president, Sidney Hillman, who would later serve on Franklin Roosevelt's kitchen cabinet. When relations between the factions turned ugly, Hillman went with money to Luciano, asking for help. Though Lucky said he would like to help (money is money), he couldn't. Lepke was his pal. How can you go against your pal? So Hillman instead went to Maranzano, who took the job. Maranzano told Luciano not to worry. He knew he and Lepke were pals. There would be no fighting. This was just about the money. A few weeks later, though, Maranzano's men opened fire, killing a few of Lepke's soldiers. "Don't you see?" Lepke told Luciano. "He's not just shooting my men. By going after me, he's going after you."

September 10, 1931. Sometime that morning, the phone rang in Luciano's clubhouse. It was Maranzano. He wanted to talk business. Could Lucky come up to the office? And could he bring along his friends Frank Costello and Vito Genovese?

To Luciano, Maranzano's call was a warning bell—it said, "You're about to be killed." Just a few weeks before, Lucky had learned of the plan, probably from Tommy Luchese, a Maranzano confidant who was secretly working with Luciano. Maranzano had drawn up a list of men to be killed: Luciano, Costello, Genovese, Willie Morretti, Joe Adonis, Dutch Schultz (the only Jew to make the list), and, in Chicago, Al Capone. The killings would start that afternoon with the murder of Luciano, Costello, and Genovese. They were to be shot dead by the Irish gangster Vincent "Mad Dog" Coll, whom Maranzano hired special for the job.

Coll was a gawky Irish kid, twenty-two years old, with a big toothy grin, blue eyes, freckles. He looked less like a killer than someone you see leaning on a wall at a country club social, hoping to God no one asks him to dance. In the twenties he worked for Dutch Schultz. The men later had a falling-out, which turned violent. While trying to shoot the Dutchman, Coll accidentally killed a five-year-old boy. Though never convicted, Coll was ever after reviled. By hiring him, Maranzano was hiring the most hated gunman in town.

When he got off the phone with Maranzano, Luciano called Lansky. It was time to set in motion a plan they had arranged weeks before. The killers could not be Italian—Maranzano would recognize them. And they could not be Jewish gangsters of too much prominence. He would recognize them, too. No, the killers had to be strangers to Maranzano, men who could walk by all his guns and bodyguards the way a jet can fly under radar. So Lansky went to work, assembling a team of Jewish gunmen from across the country. This group included Red

Levine, from Toledo, Ohio, an Orthodox Jew who would not kill on the Sabbath; and Bo Weinberg, a top Dutch Schultz lieutenant.

To me, these killers seem about as skillful as the Israeli commandos who slipped into Entebbe, freeing Jews held hostage at the airport in Uganda. These were men hand-picked by Lansky for their cool. Posing as federal alcohol agents, they went into Maranzano's headquarters, said something about a raid, flashed badges, and lined the bodyguards against the wall. As two men covered the guards, the others went with Maranzano into his office. As he pleaded his case—"There is no liquor here!"—Red Levine stabbed him. He stabbed him six times. When Maranzano, wild-eyed and dying, lunged at the killers, they shot him four times. The killers then ran through the office and into the hall. I like to think of them out there, the sound their shoes made on the floor, sliding around corners, wheels spinning.

Years later, Dixie Davis, Bo Weinberg's lawyer, talked about Weinberg's involvement in the killing, which he said Weinberg had confessed to him. Davis talked about Weinberg's escape, how the killers made a wrong turn and wound up in a ladies' room; how they saw Mad Dog Coll waiting for the elevator in the lobby. "Beat it," one of the killers said. "The cops are on their way." How they ran into the street, flushed, heart pounding, crowds, traffic, horns, colors, sirens; how they scattered, some down side streets, some into getaway cars; how Weinberg, finding himself in the rush-hour crush of Grand Central Station, smoothly slipped his pistol into the pocket of an unsuspecting commuter.

Some historians talk of a purge that followed the killing: the slaughter of the Sicilian vespers, in which forty Mustache Petes were executed across the country. Many scholars say this never happened, that it's an underworld myth. But even if it didn't happen, the fact that gangsters tell the story—Joseph Valachi, who was one of Maranzano's bodyguards, told it to prosecutors when he turned state's evidence—is itself of interest. The slaughter of the Sicilian vespers is a kind of underworld Bible story, like the story of Noah and the Flood, that marks the destruction of one world, the birth of another. The world of the Petes was gone—what survived was a generation raised by Rothstein, Prohibition, the twenties, the slums. For them violence was not the end—it was a way of getting there; it filled the void between wanting and having. They were Americans.

Over the next few months, these leaders created new rules. The five families would still exist, only now they could work closely with Jewish gangsters, as the Luciano family did. "The Italian gangs with Jewish friends did better than the others," Ralph Salerno told me. "The Genovese family, the Gambino family, they had Jewish friends and prospered. What did they care about a guy's religion? Do you like him? Do you trust him? Can you make money with him? That's all that matters."

And there would be no boss of bosses. The system would instead run like a corporation, with a board of directors voting in policy. The members of the board included Lansky, Luciano, Lepke, Anastasia, Siegel, Costello. Together these men and the troops they commanded were called the Mob or the Syndicate or the Combination; it was the birth of modern organized crime; it was the disciples of Rothstein putting the teachings into practice. Before anyone could be killed anywhere, the Syndicate had to okay it. In hotel rooms across the country, these men held court, questioned witnesses, passed judgment. If some family member had to die, the board hired the killers. Since having killers from one family kill wrongdoers from another family could lead to a war, Lansky and Luciano decided to create an enforcement wing, a group of gunmen who would kill just for the Syndicate. They looked for these gunmen mostly in Brooklyn. Since the Williamsburg Bridge went up in 1903 and the Manhattan Bridge in 1909, the slums had moved with the subway to the end of the line. The Lower East Side was melting away. Brooklyn was the place for young criminal talent.

Then somebody (Anastasia? Lepke?) remembered the kids making their way in Brownsville, the young toughs Louis Capone was always talking about. Maybe their names were mentioned: Abe Reles, Buggsy Goldstein, Happy Maione, Frank Abbandando, Harry Strauss. Lansky must have remembered them, too. Maybe, turning to Ben Siegel, he said, "Didn't we supply them with slot machines?" And someone probably mentioned the feud between Reles and the Shapiro brothers. What was going on out there? There had already been shooting. Who was coming out ahead? If anyone could test the Reles gang, it was Meyer Shapiro. If the Brownsville Boys could handle the Shapiros, they were probably the gunmen the Syndicate was looking for.

So, as the new era began, all eyes were trained on a few ragged streets in Brownsville, where Kid Twist, Buggsy, Pittsburgh Phil, Happy, and the Dasher were set for the fight of their lives.

War in Brownsville

IN THE SPRING of 1931, the war came to Brownsville. It was one of the first springs of the Depression, and the corners were full of young jobless men. Vendors huddled pushcarts along curbstones, warming their hands over red charcoal fires. The butcher shops were full of meat no one could afford to buy, and the wind carried the sweet smell from bakery ovens into the sky, where old women in windows sat stitching seams for the great middle class. At night Brownsville was like Manhattan in negative: empty alleys, tumbledown facades, dark windows. No glamour. And then the intriguing, too close sound of gunfire, where killers were doing business.

Abraham Reles and Buggsy Goldstein were busy each night with the Shapiros, hunting the brothers like game. Kid Twist didn't like fair fights; they were something he worked to avoid. He preferred taking enemies by surprise. If surprise was impossible, he overwhelmed them with numbers. If he had neither numbers nor surprise, he used all kinds of sly tricks. Reles thought he was the smartest man around and was forever trying to figure it from the other guy's point of view. When he thought he knew what the other guy was likely to do, no matter how low-down or cheap, he would do it first himself. And though he tricked the Shapiros many times that spring, his luck was bad, and his dream of killing Meyer must have sometimes seemed as impossible as the American dreams of all those poor out-of-work men on the corners.

Reles and Goldstein shot at Meyer maybe ten times that spring—in alleys, streets, garages, hallways—and not a single bullet found its target. The bullets instead lodged in walls or skipped off concrete floors or sailed harmlessly into the dark. And the screech of tires taking Meyer away. It must have become a neighborhood joke: Reles can't hit the side of a barn; Meyer has the power of the hex. Who knows? Maybe the Shapiros had access to some old Sioux war cry that turns bullets to water in midair?

In April Reles paid some neighborhood punk a few bucks to lead the brothers out of their clubhouse and into a trap. While the punk was in there, saying whatever, Reles was crouched in an alley around the corner. When the punk, followed by Meyer Shapiro, came into the alley, he looked at Reles, nodded, ran. The scene was probably still arranging itself in Meyer's head as Reles stepped forward and fired. Meyer felt his arm—warm with blood. He had been hit at last, only it was a nothing flesh wound. Meyer fled to his clubhouse.

Reles and Buggsy ran to the candy store on Livonia and Pitkin, where they had their headquarters. They called the Italians in Ocean Hill; someone from the Italian gang could always be found drinking in Sally's Bar. Sitting in the back room of the candy store, Reles explained the situation, how Meyer had been wounded and would now be even more dangerous. The war was entering a phase of dark images running across a small screen. Cars driving up out of gloomy garages, rumbling down blue streets, spent weapons being tossed into turbid rivers. Sometimes there were two or three sets of killers on the street, trailing Meyer. What the Shapiros were doing just then is hard to know. It's a clear case of history being written by the winners. In the coming years, Meyer would not be around to tell his story to police or reporters or friends. The Shapiros were on their way out, so their significance comes only in moments of conflict with Reles and his gang. When the Shapiros appear in the Kid's world, they are on our map. Otherwise they are off screen, somewhere in the wings, conducting affairs in those parts of the past that contribute nothing to the present.

Meyer came back on screen one afternoon in May, when Reles and some friends were hanging out at Buggsy Goldstein's pool hall. It was one of those middle-of-the-day middle-of-the-week nothing doing afternoons that, in small towns and on the outskirts of big cities, comes to even the most important men. And then it was gone. Maybe someone heard the car, or maybe the first thing they heard was glass shattering and gunshot peppering the walls. Maybe a stray bullet struck the eight ball, rolling it across the table and into the corner pocket. Probably not. The Kid crawled to the window. He could see Meyer shooting from the rumble seat of a dark sedan. His brothers fired from the back. The man at the wheel was a stranger: a handsome, sad-faced rich boy looking straight ahead, like a hack unconcerned with the behavior of his fare. The shooting stopped and the car drove on.

No one was hurt. Not a scratch. And the attack was over. It had to come, and now it was over. And it was a good thing. The attack was Meyer's way of acknowledging the corner he was in. Reles must have known that by joining the battle, Meyer was accepting his vulnerability. He was just another soldier now, and soldiers die all the time.

In June Reles and the boys cornered the Shapiros on Sheffield Avenue, outside the City Democratic Club. Caught by surprise, the brothers made a break for it, each running a different direction. Pep, Happy, and Dasher gave chase, leaping fences and running through backyards, a kind of youthful suburban race from danger. Reles and Buggsy instead went to one of the apartments the Shapiros kept. Like great athletes, they were playing the ball where it would be, not where it was. They walked to the fifth floor, where the Shapiros had a two-bedroom place. After wrapping a handkerchief around his hand, Reles unscrewed the hall light bulb. He and Goldstein then crouched in the dark. They waited ten minutes, twenty minutes, an hour. They heard someone on the stairs. When the man stepped to the door, Reles got him from behind. It was Irving Shapiro. Reles dragged Irving outside, pushed him against a wall, and shot him eighteen times, twice in the face.

It was like the domino theory. After the first brother fell, the others went just like that. Reles caught up with Meyer on a deserted street a few days later. Pep and Dasher were there, too, but they let the Kid take care of it. Reles shot Meyer only once. Maybe he wanted to show the neighborhood that Meyer was not Rasputin, that the life in him could be snuffed out as it could be snuffed out of any living thing. He shot Meyer through the ear. When they found Meyer he looked just fine, except for the blood coming from his ear.

A few days later Reles and Happy trapped Joey Silver. Joey was the kid who betrayed Reles and Goldstein, leading them into an ambush. Backing him against a tree, Reles blew Silver's head off.

After each killing, a squad car would answer the call, coasting down some deserted Brownsville streets (Pitkin, Van Sicklen, Livonia), a dashboard searchlight sweeping the pavement for evidence, illuminating a piece of ground: concrete, cobblestone, glassy puddles. After a killing, the gangsters would often leave their weapons at the scene. The guns they used were wiped clean of serial numbers and fingerprints. The only way a weapon would ever be tied to the criminal was if it was found on him. So the best way to dispose of a gun was to leave it at the scene. This was also a way to tell the cops to give it up, that they were dealing with professionals.

Sol Bernstein worked for the Shapiros. Against him there were no grudges. No one wanted him dead. He was just an order taker, a piece that could fit into any machine. But really, it was up to Bernstein. Could he accept the death of his boss? Would he seek revenge? About a week after Meyer was killed, Bernstein came to the corner by the candy store, asking after his boss. "You mean Meyer Shapiro?" said Pep, scratching his head. Pep had one of those faces you see all the time on the subway. A city face—sly, concealing, waiting for something even he knows will never come. "I don't know what happened to Meyer," he said. "Come to think of it, I haven't seen him around."

Bernstein then went to a bar at 161 Rockaway Avenue where the Shapiros hung out. Meyer wasn't there, either. As he walked out, Bernstein was surrounded by maybe fifteen men. Happy and Dasher were in the crowd. "What do you want?" asked Bernstein.

"We want you to drink," someone said.

They stayed at the bar through the afternoon and into the night, making Bernstein drink whiskey until he could barely stand. The Dasher then led Bernstein to the candy store, where he was seated at a table with Reles, Goldstein, and Pittsburgh Phil. As neighborhood kids milled around up front, Reles spoke softly in back, telling Bernstein, detail by detail, how he killed Irving, Meyer, and Joey Silver, how he would kill still more.

Telling the story this way—when Bernstein was drunk enough to spin the walls—Reles was making sure Bernstein's guard was down, that his feelings could not be easily hidden. Alcohol as truth serum, something that brings out honest emotions. Telling Bernstein this way might also soften the blow, making it all blurry and unreal—as if the Kid had entered Bernstein's dream and were telling him there. The faces at the table turned to Bernstein, seeing how he would take the news. "Listen," said Pep. "We know you, and we just took care of your friend. Go home and don't worry about nothing."

The Dasher followed Bernstein home.

The next day a kid came up to Bernstein on the street. "Pep wants to see you," he said.

"Who is Pep?" asked Bernstein.

"Harry Strauss."

Bernstein went to the candy store, where Pep was waiting. "What is going on?" said Pep. "Anything important happen lately?"

"Nothing," said Bernstein. "Nothing at all."

And that was it. Bernstein was a civilian.

Willie Shapiro wore silk gloves and cashmere scarves. When his brothers died, he must have felt alone. Probably he never felt so alone in his life. The fight in him, whatever it was that made him a threat to the Kid, was gone—a light that went out with the bulb Reles unscrewed before killing Irving. And though there was no rush to kill Willie, it had to be done. A sentence passed must be carried out.

Willie was killed a few years later in a bar in East New York. Reles killed him with a garrote, strangling Willie until his time ran out on the floor. Then, just in case some part of Willie was still alive, Pep tied him up, put him in a laundry bag, dumped him in a car, and buried him inCanarsie. A few years later, when he was dug up and autopsied, a coroner found dirt where Willie's lungs had been. He had been buried alive.

Something about Reles's nature is mysterious; it runs away from me like mercury. The reason is, until he fought the Shapiros, he gave no indication of just how deep within him the violence ran. Before he got mixed up with Meyer, I don't even think he was that violent. He probably could have gone on and lived a life like other people—got a job, raised a family, *not* killed handfuls of men. But the way he was treated by the Shapiros—abused, humiliated, threatened, shot, girlfriend raped—turned him into a killer. I'm not saying he was just like everyone else. He surely had a tendency to violence. Something in his makeup or upbringing made killing something he could deal with, a direction in which he could go. But the Shapiros, together with his neighborhood and the nature of his times—the twenties, the Depression—revealed in Reles what might otherwise have remained hidden.

In the course of the war, Reles and Harry Strauss emerged as partners. Their personalities, taken together, were bittersweet and could at once repel and attract. While Reles moved on impulse, Strauss lived in a deeply moral world. His views—on punishment, responsibility, covenant—were, in many ways, Jewish views. For Strauss, God was present in every move, gesture, act. If you were associated with him, you would, sooner or later, cross a line, defy his code. And when you did, he was there, beyond hearing but within view. He sometimes couldn't tell where his authority ended and that of the world began. He was like the God of the Old Testament, seeing, judging, punishing. Punishing was more fun than forgiving. Forgiving meant a sit-down, coffee, a handshake. Punishing meant a rope, an ice pick, a fire. His world was like one of those early Puritan communities where suspicion is guilt, where being seen coming from the wrong building—the Shapiros' clubhouse, say—is enough to be declared a witch, hunted, hounded, burned. It was a world where, though killing might not be a sin, talking behind the back of a friend usually is; where murder is better than cowardice; where the rules of loyalty are fluid and complicated; where the word "rat" is as indelible and damning as a concentration camp tattoo. You never knew just how things would look through his eyes and what he would declare a sin.

The war had also remade the other members of the troop—from mercenaries to nationalists. The gang members were now less in it for themselves than for honor, fame, each other. You can see it in pictures taken at the time. In mug shots the gangsters look as different from each other as you would expect men with different parents to look. They are tall or short, fat or thin, dark or fair, with sharp or wide noses, blond or brown or black or red hair, curly or straight, or else no hair at all. What they have in common is in their eyes. Not the color of their eyes, which are brown or black or gray or green or blue, but something beneath the color, a kind of icy calm, like something seen at the bottom of a river. After my grandmother met Strauss in her family's diner, what she talked about were his eyes, which she said were disturbing and beautiful. On their own, these men were dangerous. Together they were something new in Brownsville—a crew of killers at once predictable and mysterious: *You will die, but where? When?*

And slowly, word of the gang—their success, how they handled the Shapiros—made it back to Manhattan, to ballrooms and suites where Charlie Luciano and Meyer Lansky were planning the future of crime. *The Brownsville gang passed the test!* It would be hard to find a more effective, artistic, single-minded band of killers anywhere in the underworld. "We were good before all this happened," Reles later said. "But when we added Pep, it was like putting on a whole new troop."

The winter and spring slipped by in a haze, a blur of late nights in tumbledown local bars or seedy nightclubs and dance halls or else the smoky back room of the candy store, playing cards, making plans, wondering who will next come through the door. When Meyer Shapiro was killed, the candy store became a capital of crime. Like London after the Spanish Armada was sunk, it was a new seat of power, where dreamy locals went with their best ideas. Sometimes, if a gangster wanted to leave a gun or bullets or an ice pick or rope for another gangster, he would stash it under the toilet in the back of the store. A few hours later the other killer would say, "Jeez, I gotta take a leak," go back, and retrieve the package. Young toughs stood on the corner in front of the store all day, the way longshoremen stand on docks, hoping someone will call them to work.

The store was run by Rose Gold, a cantankerous, tough-talking sixty-something immigrant who could neither read nor write English. To gang members she was Midnight Rose, partly because her store stayed open all night, partly because she reached her true magnificence only in the small hours, when her light was the only thing going in Brownsville. Over time, Rose became godmother of the troop. When one of the boys was arrested, she bailed him out. In the late thirties hundreds of thousands of dollars went from her account to the state and back again. Later, when she was arrested, she chose jail over telling on her boys. When at last she came to trial and a lawyer asked, "Why do you let so many criminals frequent your store?" she said, "Why don't the police keep them out?"

The store was on Saratoga Avenue directly under the elevated tracks of the number two train. On summer afternoons the sun came through the rails, leaving shadows on the brick facade. On winter evenings the store's yellow light could be seen for blocks. It sometimes seemed the whole neighborhood was in there, the slosh of galoshes across warped wood floors: old men in shirtsleeves with cigars and stories; young machinists and dockworkers getting a free read of the *World Telegram* or the *Brooklyn Eagle* or the *Forward;* long-skirted lady garment workers stopping in for a soda or a date; kids wide-eyed before cases gleaming with licorice, ring-dings, sourballs, lemon drops. A few times each hour, when the pay phone rang, Rose sent one of these kids out to find the man or woman being called. Few people could afford a phone in those days, so they took calls at the local candy store. After completing the call, this man or woman would give Rose some money—a nickel, usually—that the kid could redeem in candy. A nickel could buy a lot of ring-dings. And always, from the back room, the low, mysterious murmur of gangsters being gangsters. For many kids, the first image of adulthood—other than their parents, who never count much anyway—was that secret laughter in back of the candy store.

As summer approached, Reles and the boys must have heard the distant rumblings of armies over larger landscapes, as Lansky and Luciano remade the underworld. Maybe they could even hear the echo of other wars in other cities—Detroit, where the Purple Mob was fighting the Little Jewish Navy; Cleveland, where Moe Dalitz and the Cleveland Four were cementing control; Chicago, where Al Capone was fighting the remnants of the Bugs Moran gang. But mostly the Reles troop was too busy being bosses of Brownsville to worry about much else. Like politics, all crime is local. The troop hosted crap games, loaned slot machines, muscled merchants, hounded rivals, shylocked.

Why live this way? Well, as far as Reles was concerned, it was the only way to live. It was the other guys—who went to work, came home, went to work, came home, went to work—who were hard to figure. The nine-to-fivers were fools. The men in back of the candy store were wiseguys. Wiseguy, a term that appeared around this time, refers to any crook hooked up with the rackets. By nature a wiseguy should be realistic, worldly, not a kvetcher, not sentimental about women, family, or cars, not eager, naive, or romantic. "There was nothing special about what we did," Reles said later. "We just did what we could to turn a dollar."

Late that year, when the snow covered Brownsville in drifts, things began to change. The first call probably came to the candy store, where Rose would have sent a boy to the back room. "Mr. Reles," the boy would say, "there's a man for you on the phone."

"Uh-huh," Reles would say, setting down his cards.

It was Louis Capone. He had a piece of work for the boys. A few weeks later there was another call, another piece of work. Then another. After each killing, Capone got word back to the boys: *You boys done a real good job. Real good!* Maybe he even let slip a few names: Luciano, Lansky, Lepke. Reles would have known how important these names were. He was not a dumb man. At this time, though, similar pieces of work were being farmed out to other wiseguys in other neighborhoods. It was like an open call—the Syndicate casting heavies. And it was not until a few years later, when the Brownsville troop had clearly emerged as the best killers, that Reles went to Manhattan to meet Louis Lepke.

Louis Buchalter was born in Williamsburg, Brooklyn, in 1897. He was one of fourteen children. His parents were Russian-born Jews. His mother called him Lepkeleh, a Yiddish way of saying Little Louis, which friends shortened to Lepke. His father, Burton, owned a hardware store on the Lower East Side, one of those dreary little shops with a bell above the door. Burton sometimes took his son to work. They would walk across the Williamsburg Bridge, over the East River and the rooftops of Chinatown. Whenever he had the chance, Louis would slip from his father's sight into the narrow immigrant streets.

Louis was one of those reckless kids who spring from large middle-class families, the youngest brother, out of reach, who for parents come as a last piece of busywork at the end of a long semester; a wild kid who everyone says can go either good or bad, but almost always goes bad; a kid on Ritalin; a kid you either want to like but don't, or want to hate but can't; a kid who makes some teachers believe in God: *If something is this bad, there must be something somewhere just as good.*

Lepke was abandoned when he was thirteen: first by his father, who died of a heart attack; then by his mother, who, after the death of her husband, moved to Colorado, leaving her son in the charge of an older sister. Father dead, mother gone—the law had run out of his life in an instant. And he must have been angry: at his sister, who thought she was his mother; at his mother, who was off with the Buttes and Indians while he was left to find his way here. Skipping school, he would cross the bridge, losing himself in the streets. Walking from the Bowery to the mansions along Fifth Avenue, taking it all in, a thoughtful, narrow-shouldered adolescent.

He had a dimple, which did not make him cute; it just highlighted his toughness, like a blue sky above a graffiti-covered wall.

He fell in with a group of older men—gangsters who had worked for Big Jack Zelig and Dopey Benny Fein—who taught him the old tricks: how to pick a pocket, roll a drunk, wield a slungshot, spot a nose (a spy working for the cops). This was a primitive society of deals in dark cellars, a world far removed from the one being staked out by Arnold Rothstein. And though Lepke would grow into the epitome of the modern gangster, he would always carry this world with him. Whenever he was in a jam, instinct would tell him to revert, to take care of it the old way, as his first heroes would, with a gun and a shovel.

On those streets, Lepke met other young Jews—Lansky and Siegel, but also Joseph "Doc" Stacher, who smoked huge cigars behind which his face was a planet in eclipse; Louis "Shadows" Kravits; Hyman "Curly" Holtz; Phil "Little Farvel" Kovolick. These young men made up an elite youth group: Jews not afraid of parents or cops, who would keep on until they were knocked down. For such kids, life would unfold as an unending effort to get up more times than they were knocked down.

Lepke was first knocked down in the winter of 1915. Caught robbing a store, he was sent to live with an uncle in Bridgeport, Connecticut, where he was knocked down again, this time for stealing a salesman's sample case. Sent to a reformatory in Cheshire, he must have again felt abandoned, lost to a world that had pushed him to the margins. He was not yet sixteen. In future years, as childhood trauma hardened to middle-age neuroses, Lepke's fear of abandonment would prove deadly to those he was convinced would betray him. But that was much later, when all that remained of the kid in the reformatory was the dimple and the fear.

When he got back to the Lower East Side, Lepke made his way stealing from pushcarts. One day he robbed a pushcart that was just then being robbed by someone else. When the thieves ran off in the same direction, they began talking and Lepke soon realized who this other thug was: Jacob Shapiro, already a notorious downtown figure.

Shapiro was known to most people as Gurrah. He was always walking around with hunched shoulders, telling people, "Get outta here!" And somehow, when he said it, because of his gruff voice and thick accent, it came out as one word—Gurrah. "Hey, what are you doing here? I thought I told you to beat it! For the last time, Gurrah!" I have tried to say "Get outta here" again and again, with all kinds of fake accents, yet it never sounds anything like "Gurrah." I guess that's just another thing lost in the translation of the years, the way, no matter how hard I try, I cannot make Yiddish words sound as sensible or elegant as my grandmother can.

Shapiro and Lepke formed a great partnership. Where Lepke was reserved, Shapiro was out front, every emotion crossing his face like a weather system. Two years older than Lepke, Shapiro had a sidewise way of talking that made people think, Gangster! On the street he could be seen coming from a long way off, tacking toward you, like a yacht. With thick, gangly arms and a powerful circus strongman torso, he was the exclamation point at the end of Lepke's every sentence. He had come to New York as a boy from Odessa, Russia, home of the brutal, farcical Jewish gangsters immortalized in *Odessa Stories* by Isaac Babel, whose descriptions could apply as well to the Jewish hoods of New York as to those of Russia. "Tartakovsky has the soul of a murderer, but he is one of us," Babel wrote in "How It Was Done in Odessa." "He has come from us. He is our blood. He is our flesh, as though born of the same mother. Half Odessa works in his shops."

Lepke and Gurrah were soon accepting tributes from vendors all over the East Side. But they were really still small-timers, running big risks for nothing prizes. In 1918 Louis was caught robbing a loft downtown. He was sent first to the Tombs, a jail his old gangster friends called City College. He was then sent for postgraduate study to the state university at Sing Sing.

On the road between the East Side and Sing Sing he left behind the person he had once been, the reckless energy, the small-time glee that drove his first felonies. When he got back to the city in 1923, he already had the face he would carry with him to the death house: spaniel eyes, sad mouth. He was famous for his reserve, a man who never lost his temper. Yet his exterior hinted at some desperation within; his eyes could cloud over in an instant. And all around him, like an overcast sky, hung a threat of violence. He was twenty-five years old.

Soon after prison, when he got some money, he took himself for clothes, changing his outside to reflect the changes within. He now wore dark suits, conservative ties, loafers, cuff links, wing-tips, fedoras. He tried to dress like a businessman, just another trader on his way home from work, but never got it quite right. If he was standing in a crowd of white-collar boys, something in him, some pride or defiance, would jump out at you.

Lepke and Gurrah, back together, climbed from pushcart vendors to merchants, theft to extortion. People called them the Gorilla Boys. They told strangers they were in the bakery business. While others supplied flour, pots, pans, they supplied protection. "Please get your boss," Lepke might say, showing up at some bakery. "Please tell him Mr. Buchalter and Mr. Shapiro are here on business."

As Shapiro walked the kitchen, smelling this, touching that, Lepke wound through a speech, a lecture on the city, the sorry state of things, immigrants and how they had brought along bad habits, a lack of respect, a disregard for property; he would talk about business and how, no matter how meticulously you build, someone always comes along to destroy; about man, how he is driven by dark forces, vanity, greed, ambition, and how these flaws lead him to do wildly brutal things. Maybe he would let his eyes move around the room, then say, "Why this should be, who knows?"

If a baker asked if there was a point to all this, Lepke might shake his head and say something like "No, not really. Most of the important things in life, they have no point. They're just like a crossroads, and you go one way or the other. I'm here to protect you from going the wrong way, which can lead to problems. With my help, that won't happen. Crazy immigrants won't come burn your store."

Such protection went for a monthly rate, a fee Lepke based on the requirements of a particular job. If the head man said yes, he could use such protection, the details were worked out there and then. If the head man said no, then a few days later crazy immigrants really would burn the store.

Though Lepke and Gurrah would go into many fields, travel the country, make millions, bakeries would always hold a special place. Over the years they extorted money from the biggest bakeries in New York: Gottfried's, Levy's, Fink's, California Pies, Rockwell's, Dugans. By the mid-thirties Lepke and Gurrah were receiving about a million a year in tribute from the industry.

Arnold Rothstein was always on the lookout for smart young Jew boys. And who was smarter, younger, more of a Jew boy, than Louis

Lepke? So sometime in the mid-twenties Rothstein gave Lepke the call; getting the call from A.R. was like getting called to the majors. Lepke started riding shotgun on liquor runs; he also did odd jobs, like baptizing the whiskey—watering it down. Later, when all hell broke loose in the garment industry, Lepke and Gurrah went to work in the labor wars.

Jewish gangsters first went into the garment industry for the same reason wealthy Jews later went to Miami Beach—because that's where the other Jews were. The men who owned clothing factories and sweatshops were mostly uptown German Jews; their employees were mostly downtown Jews from Eastern Europe. Among these men were the future leaders of the American labor movement, ideologues every bit as tough as the thugs leading gangs on the Bowery. One of the first unions in New York was the United Hebrew Trade Union.

In 1897, when garment workers first went on strike, the bosses took their problems to the Jewish gang leaders. Jews seeking help from Jews. One employer hired Monk Eastman to drive the strikers back to work. Monk and his boys attacked the strike leaders on Allen Street. While breaking strikes, gangsters often beat workers with a length of metal pipe wrapped in newspaper. They called this schlamming. In the coming years, as the nation was rocked by strikes, even the most down-on-his-luck hood could get work as a schlammer, the way even a blacklisted actor could later get work at one of the resorts in the Catskills.

Over the years, as factory owners complained about labor, how hoodlums lurked on the edge of every strike, it was good to remember this: It was the bosses who first brought in the gangsters. Union leaders then followed their employers to the clubhouses; how else could they protect themselves? It was Arnold Rothstein who eventually agreed to help the unions, assembling (for a fee) a counterforce, schlammers to schlamm the schlammers. These men were paid $7.50 a day; their leaders were put on the union payroll, at about fifty bucks a week. One of these leaders was Little Augie Orgen, an experienced gangster who had worked for Dopey Benny Fein, one of the first schlammers.

The thugs went to work for the unions, protecting strikers and also taking it to the bosses: setting fires, lobbing rocks, throwing bombs. Gangsters had learned lessons labor leaders were just beginning to grasp: that a bad deed unpunished is another way of asking for it; that noble sentiments, without muscle, are about as useful as get-well cards; that an enemy will make peace only when he has felt the sting of battle.

It was only natural that some gangsters identified with the workers—they came from the same streets as the workers, the same neighborhoods. They too descended from the Jews of Eastern Europe; they too resented the bosses, German Jews who looked down on Eastern Europeans, acting as if they were members of an inferior race, as if this were something more than a dice game, what happens when a distant ancestor, on the long road from Zion, takes a right instead of a left. Now, because they had been in America longer, because they had more money, were better educated and more assimilated, the Germans had lost the very otherness that makes a Jew a Jew. As bad as the gangsters were, as far outside the law as they lived, they thought they were, in some way, more in touch with Jewish experience than uptown Jews like the Schiffs. The gangsters were out where the Jews had always been, living by their wits, where the difference between living and dying is a single bad decision. The gangsters only wondered why the workers weren't *more* like them. Why did they suffer? Why did they take it?

"You say labor unions hire dynamiters and sluggers," a racketeer told a reporter. "Well, I may be a low-down criminal pervert, but I don't think there's anything the matter with that. How do the capitalists treat labor? Is it worse to dynamite a building than to turn out of work, in the middle of the winter, thousands of men whose families live hand to mouth? Why isn't there more dynamiting? If there were, I'd get a little more respect for the working class. Now, to hell with them. These goddamn stiffs, with their docile suffering, make me sick."

The real problems began when the strikes ended, when the union leaders came to the gangsters and said, "Thank you very much. Your services are no longer needed." The gangsters didn't want the war to be over. Yes, they liked the steady paycheck, but it was more than that. Working in the labor movement gave the thugs a cause. It also gave them something to tell people at parties. "Me? I work in garments. I'm a furrier!" And at some point, as Little Augie was figuring what to do next, the question fell on him like a light: Why not run the union? Collect the dues? Call the strikes? Be the boss?

This question came to Augie in that moment where all corrupt generals realize that they don't have to take orders, that they can head the parades, declare the wars, be the president. When Augie went with this alternative to the union leaders, there was not much they could do.

Behind the leaders stood experience, philosophy, dreams. Behind Augie stood a few hundred armed thugs. Over the years, the few labor leaders who did resist racketeers turned up dead in lots or were buried beneath grain elevators or crushed in freak accidents on the docks or else disappeared only to wash up weeks later on some weedy Staten Island beach.

For some gangsters, labor racketeering offered one way out of the twenties, out of the speakeasies and into the factories. A steady income, a title, an office. With labor racketeering began the long run of euphemistic job titles, wiseguys describing themselves as organizers, overseers, fixers. As the power behind a union, a gangster would not only have access to dues—that went without saying. He could also take kickbacks from workers—cash in exchange for jobs or promotions. But the real money would come from the factory owners. Just like a holdup: Give us what we want or your employees walk. And it was good work, like a real job, with an office and a secretary. All they needed was a telephone and the threat of violence, which danced between their words, as abstract and real as sunlight on water.

A few years later, when federal officers tapped phones in a racketeer's office, they captured how this part of the job was done:

(Phone rings.)

Moe: Hello. Moe speaking.

Racketeer: I have something to tell you. You won't like to hear it. I am sending you an extra man.

Moe: No good. I have enough men now. I know Sam is the best man in the flour business, but I can't use him.

Racketeer: Listen, Moe. Don't be tough over the phone, then come down here and you're like a kitten. Talk to your delegate. Listen to reason.

Moe: Listen. I am going to run my own business.

Racketeer: No, Moe. I'll run your business for you. If that man don't go to work, somebody will suffer.

The bosses and union leaders had invited in the gangsters, and now they couldn't get rid of them. It would take the federal government years to do that. Meanwhile the factory owners passed their additional costs on to consumers. During the Depression, for every two hundred dollars spent in New York, an additional twenty-three went to mobsters; it was a gangster tax.

Within a few years, battles between labor and management no

longer mattered much. In many cases the boundaries of those relationships had been drawn. What mattered now were struggles within the unions, as racketeers fought for control with honest labor leaders or else with other racketeers. Soon after they joined the struggle, Lepke and Gurrah were called in by their new boss. Little Augie, who was about ten years older than Lepke, had big doe eyes and a soft mouth.

Augie wanted the Gorilla Boys to take care of Dopey Benny Fein, who was clawing his way back into the union game. Lepke and Gurrah cornered Dopey Benny in a bar on the Bowery. The old gangster got off several rounds before slipping into the night. Looking around, Lepke saw Gurrah was down, blood spreading beneath him. Shapiro had been shot in the back and spent several weeks in the hospital. A few months later, the bullets Lepke had fired that night finally found Dopey Benny. He was killed in front of the Essex Street courthouse by Louis Cohen, a mysterious figure who slipped out of a crowd and shot the gangster where he sat, in the back of a squad car between two cops.

The underworld has no peaceful way of bringing the next generation to power, no way, other than killing, to ring in the future. So, in 1927, when Lepke and Gurrah seized on some petty issue to split with their boss, everyone knew it was really about succession. Who could know this better than Little Augie himself, who for so long had been the next generation, the kid feared by old-timers? It was only a year before that he had tried to have Dopey Benny killed. Now he was the old man. (Things happen so fast in the underworld, time there should be gauged in dog years.) And even if Augie wanted to step down, even if he said, "Fuck it; I retire," Lepke wouldn't let him. Lepke had to kill Augie for the same reason Lenin had to kill all the Romanovs: because even a retired Augie was a challenge. Besides, killing Augie was the only sure way Lepke could secure power. Power flows from a dead gangster to his killer as through an IV. The only thing Augie could do was play the part of the incumbent: wait and see where the attack will come.

He hired himself a new bodyguard: Jack "Legs" Diamond, a free-wheeling gunman who scared even the scariest men in town. Legs once guarded Arnold Rothstein. Though still in his early twenties, Legs was already a glamorous nighttime figure whose very name conjured images of hotel rooms with ice buckets and champagne, limousines, starlets, showgirls, all-night cabarets where the singer is interrupted by gunfire and shattering glass, or a small hotel upstate, his wife in one room, his mistress in another down the hall. Legs was a great dancer. He had slender shoulders and a thin, tapered bullfighter's waist. He was handsome, but his head was weirdly small, with sunken, emaciated cheeks, like something you imagine at the end of a cannibal's stick. Having Legs Diamond on his side must have made Augie feel better, but it was a desperate act, like piling sandbags before a flood; a defensive, already defeated maneuver that any dedicated foe would easily find a way around.

On October 15, 1927, Little Augie was standing in front of his clubhouse on the corner of Norfolk Street near Delancey—a narrow street running between wooden facades, doorways along the street low and uneven, something built for a smaller race of men. From above, the neighborhood was just roofs and chimneys. Augie was talking to Legs on the sidewalk. Everyone on the street (men working, kids playing) must have been aware of the gangsters (where they stood, how they held themselves), so they probably saw what happened next.

A sedan came very fast around the corner. Before it stopped, two men jumped out: Lepke and Gurrah. "Get back," Gurrah yelled at Legs. He yelled the way parents yell at kids standing too close to the train tracks. Lepke then walked up to his old boss, close enough to read the time off his watch, shot him four times, got back in the car with Gurrah, sped off. Legs fired at the car, probably for appearance' sake. Gurrah returned fire, grazing Legs. In the future, when people talked about the legend of Legs Diamond, his amazing power of survival, they usually cited his escape from harm on Norfolk Street.

The next morning, Lepke and Gurrah went to the police station and surrendered. They knew the cops were looking for them. They also knew the cops would have no reason to keep them. Suspicions, yes. Evidence, no. They presented themselves like a pair of overdue books: Buchalter and Shapiro for questioning. A few hours later, when the police were through interrogating the suspects, they hesitated. They didn't want to just let these men go. As soon as Lepke and Gurrah walked out the door, they figured some trigger-happy Little Augie loyalist would shoot them dead. The last thing the police wanted was a repeat of the Dopey Benny thing—a killer killed leaving the police station.

The police decided to make sure Lepke and Gurrah stayed safe, seeing them home under guard. The Gorilla Boys came out of the station behind an army of cops. They walked through the streets. It was like a parade. Two East Side Jews behind a blue wall of Irish cops. Merchants watched from doorways, kids from stoops. A man, darting between parked cars, snapped a picture. The next day, when the photo appeared in the newspaper, it looked as though the cops worked for Lepke and Gurrah. The police, without realizing it, had crowned the Gorilla Boys. They killed Augie and got a police escort home. Besides, no one wanted to avenge Augie anyway. Gangsters are realists. Augie was dead. No use feeling bad about it. It was part of history. The thing now was to figure out who the next power would be, and the picture in the paper answered that. Lepke was the new king of the labor rackets—Gurrah his lieutenant.

What Augie built, that was just a starting point for Louis. He raised an army: 250 men. He was soon moving factory to factory, picking up unions like properties on a Monopoly board. He went after entire industries. In each field he targeted the key union, the piece on which all else hung. In the garment industry, for example, he went after the cutters, a small, easily controlled union. The cutters cut the fabric that made every garment in New York. If the cutters went on strike, the entire garment industry would be crippled. Following the old formula, Lepke presented himself to the union as a savior, someone with the muscle to take on the bosses. To arenas of cutthroat competition and undependable paychecks, he quickly brought a prized stability. You were paid on time; you were promoted as promised; if injured, you were compensated; scabs did not cross your picket lines; the boss kept his promises because now the boss had something to fear. Even enemies said Lepke succeeded where government regulators had failed.

And all the while, as he was raising salaries and securing benefits, he was taking over. Though he never made himself president of a union—he was, after all, a notorious criminal—he put people loyal to him in power. When he took control of the cutters, for example, he put Philip Orlofsky in charge. It was Orlofsky who later fought for union control with Sidney Hillman, the fight that led to a shooting war with Salvatore Maranzano, then to Maranzano's death.

Lepke and Gurrah had joined Little Augie in the winter of 1925. In those first years they were small-time hoods, out there with the workingman, on picket lines in nights so cold they must have cracked apart in their fingers. By the early thirties, when Lepke asked Abe Reles to his office, he controlled thousands of workers through unions of truckers, motion picture operators, and painters. He and Gurrah were adding about $1.5 million of yearly costs to the flour end of the trucking business. They also acquired interests in legitimate businesses: Raleigh Manufacturing, the Pioneer Coat Factory, Greenberg & Shapiro. Each took home about a million dollars a year. No one called them the Gorilla Boys anymore; they were now the Gold Dust Twins. In 1933 the U.S. Subcommittee on Racketeering suggested officials fighting racketeers consider "martial law or renewal of the public whipping post."

Different gangsters bought different things with their money. Some bought apartments or cars or girls. Many bought their way out of the old neighborhoods, into the best rooms of the best hotels. In the twenties Lucky Luciano lived in the Waldorf-Astoria, and so did Ben Siegel and Frank Costello. It was a kind of gangster dorm, a stop on the way from the East Side to Vegas or Cuba or the suburbs. While Gurrah stayed in Brooklyn, moving to Flatbush, Lepke bought a place on the Upper West Side: lobby, doorman, park view. He lived with his new wife, Betty Wasserman, the daughter of a London barber. Lepke was not one of the glamorous gangsters. He did not go to bars or date showgirls. He did not dance in clubs. He was in it not for the girls, but for the money, the power. He was also in it for the long haul and knew publicity, especially good publicity, is just the worst thing for a gangster. A gangster's name in the paper is an advertisement telling cops and DAs: "Make your name here!"

To people in his building, Lepke was just another businessman. I see him riding the elevator up to his apartment, nodding to other riders, cringing at the sight of his name in a stranger's *Herald-Tribune.* When his home phone rang, he would answer only to the name Murphy. Code. A way of avoiding enemies. And the phone rang all the time. Lepke was now sought after in the underworld, his advice prized. To fellow gangsters he was Judge Louis. When people talked about backroom deals, about men powerful men fear, they were talking about Lepke. J. Edgar Hoover said he was "the most dangerous criminal in America."

By the early thirties Lepke was actually living the life of a businessman. Each morning, after breakfast and a nod to the doorman, a private car took him to his Fifth Avenue office. There were phone calls, accountants, negotiations. There were several meetings before lunch and several more after. So the meeting he had one morning in 1933 probably just seemed like something on a schedule. How could Lepke know it would turn out to be one of the most important of his career, that it would bring someone new into his life, someone who would help him realize his worst fears.

Delegates at Large

ABE RELES FIRST met Louis Lepke on March 3, 1933. Reles's features already hinted at the sneering condescension that would mark his middle years, the kind of face people hate at first sight. "If a total stranger walked up to Kid Twist and, without a word, bashed him in the face, I could understand it," Assistant District Attorney Burton Turkus later wrote. "That was the reaction you got from one look at him."

Reles must have been nervous. Who in the underworld was more important than Lepke? Sure, there was Lansky and Luciano, but those guys lived in a different world, the stratosphere, where violence and street fights were just nostalgia. Reles, Goldstein, Strauss, Maione, Abbandando—these were working-class thugs. How could they identify with the elegance of Luciano, the temperament of Lansky? But Lepke, he was different. In Lepke, Reles must have seen a mirror of his own story, his own brutality raised to the highest power.

When they met, Reles and Lepke were separated by a desk, and by other things, too: age, reputation, motivation. Reles was looking to impress an older man, take the next step, move up; Lepke was looking to fill an order placed by Lansky and Luciano, who had asked him to recruit an execution squad for the Syndicate. As far as Lepke could tell, no killers were better suited for the task than Reles's gang. Since they weren't affiliated with any of the crime families, they were untouched by the old rivalries; since they were ethnically mixed, their victims could not gripe about Jews killing Italians or Italians killing Jews. And by so thoroughly dispatching the Meyer Shapiro gang and so easily handling the jobs Lepke had already given them, the gang proved themselves first-rate killers. By the time he met Judge Louis, Reles already had the job.

For Lepke, meeting Reles was something of a risk. For a man like Lepke, meeting anyone is a risk. Talking in person is not the same as sending word through a middleman like Louis Capone. It's the difference between a man coming to court saying, "I heard . . ." and a man coming to court saying, "I saw . . ." So Lepke was probably careful that day, steering clear of specifics. He probably just wanted to get a good look at Reles, an impression. Could he work with this man? Could he trust him? What he saw was a hungry young thug, someone desperate to climb. And desperation was something Lepke could work with.

Over the next several months, as Reles and the boys tended their own business, the specifics of the Syndicate's murder operation were worked out. From now on, the troop would kill only for the Combination. In return they were given a free hand in Brownsville and East New York. That was their territory. No questions asked. They could use any muscle necessary to protect this territory. They were also given the concession to crap games throughout Brooklyn. And, of course, they were paid. For Syndicate killing, the boys were kept on a retainer at $250 a week, or twelve grand a year. For an especially spectacular killing, they might receive a bonus or a gift, some small sign of appreciation.

What's more, they now had something like underworld guidance counselors, older, powerful men to look after their interests. While Lepke took on the Jewish members of the gang, the Italians answered to Albert Anastasia, an important Brooklyn thug. Though Reles, Strauss, and other Jewish gangsters spent lots of time with Albert A., there was always a sense that Jews should tend to Jews, Italians to Italians. Though Jews and Italians worked together, they never confused the other with themselves. Jewish and Italian gangsters somehow sensed they were each following their own plotlines. In the future, as these lines diverged, the gangsters and their offspring would remember each other fondly, as you remember someone you spent a summer with as a boy.

At work, the troop followed a line of command as obscure and tricky as the Russian criminal code. The whole thing would start with a grievance. One gangster is mad at another gangster, some humiliation or double cross or breach of etiquette. Tempers flair. Threats are made. Someone decides to go to a boss with the matter, and soon a court date is set. A few days later high-ranking mobsters gather in a hotel room or clubhouse. The judges at the trial, depending on the severity of the matter, might include Meyer Lansky, Ben Siegel, Frank Costello, Joey Adonis, Louis Lepke, Vito Genovese. Each gangster is represented by counsel, usually another gangster who thinks himself especially eloquent.

The judges hear it all out, nodding, frowning. And then the room is cleared, the door closed, and voices can be heard murmuring on the far side. Sometimes there is shouting or pleading. The gangster lawyers are called back into the room and told the verdict. Sometimes the whole thing is dismissed. Other times a gangster apologizes or agrees to pay the injured party.

Still other times, when there has been a double cross or a ratting out, the judges bring back a death sentence. A few days later Lepke talks with Albert A., who talks with Louis Capone, and then the phone rings in the candy store. The troop spends whole days in there, playing cards, overcoats thrown over chair backs. They wear pinky rings, their cuffs turned back on dark hair curling around gold watchbands. They enforce not only Syndicate law, but their own law, rules they have drawn up for Brownsville. If they hear some young crook is defying their law, they might give him a scare, forcing him into a car, driving him out to a weedy, end-of-the-world beach on the south shore of Canarsie or Plumb Beach, walking him to the edge of the white-capped waters of the harbor. On the other side, beyond the docks and sheds of Neponsit, they can see hills. "Like the scenery?" one of the troop might ask. And before the kid can answer, they say, "How would you like to be part of it—permanent? You want to make money in Brownsville, you do it through us. Got it?"

When such warnings are ignored, a member of the troop might rush out of the candy store and into the street, find the punk, push him against a wall, shoot him. Or else take him on a drive to talk things over, and no one hears from him again.

But when it was a killing for the Syndicate, everything was meticulously planned. Nothing left to chance. The killers were chosen as carefully as the starting lineup for a World Series team. The hit men then went all over town, looking for the best place to finish the mark. Then murder weapons. A couple of local kids were then pulled from the corner and sent out to steal a car: a kill car that would carry the mark and later the corpse. Then a getaway route was chosen—every turn, every stop the car would take after the murder was planned. A second car, a crash car, would ride behind the kill car. If cops or rivals gave chase, the crash car would block the way or supply backup.

Sometimes the members of the troop were forced to improvise; that's how it was with Puggy Feinstein. Albert A. had put word out that Puggy had to die. Maybe he had done something he wasn't supposed to. Maybe he had pissed off the wrong guy. Or maybe he owed something he could never repay. Who knows? He had to die, that was the important thing. But no one, not even Albert A., knew what Puggy looked like. Buggsy Goldstein had met Puggy a few years before but could not picture him. And the others—Reles, Pittsburgh Phil, Dukey Maffeatore, a kid who ran errands for the gang—they didn't even have that. They had nothing but the name. So there they were, looking for a finger man, someone who could point out the mark, when who should walk in on their nightly card game but Puggy Feinstein.

Puggy made his name years before as a small-time prizefighter. He was one of those boxers who takes nothing from the ring but a nickname. Some fighter had flattened his nose, and he was ever after known as Puggy. After leaving the ring, Feinstein rented an apartment in Borough Park and each month made his rent gambling on cards and horses. He bet and lost; he bet and won. Because of a woman he once tried to go straight; because of a woman he could not go straight. One day, when things were especially tight, he borrowed fifty-five dollars from a small-time Brownsville shylock named Tiny Benson.

A few months later he got a couple of his Borough Park friends together and drove to Brownsville. Puggy wanted to pay back Tiny. At around ten P.M. Puggy and his friends walked into the back of the candy store. Goldstein, Reles, Strauss, and Dukey Maffeatore were playing cards. It was like one of those westerns where the strangers come in and no one even raises their eyes. "Hey, Buggsy," Feinstein said. "Remember me? We met a long time ago. My name is Puggy Feinstein."

"Puggy, huh?" said Goldstein, looking up. "Sure, I remember you. Hey, guys, this is Puggy Feinstein. Remember, I mentioned him. What's up, Puggy? What brings you to Brownsville?"

"I'm looking for Tiny Benson. I owe him some money. I thought he might be here."

"No, Puggy, he's not here," said Buggsy.

Strauss nudged Reles. "That's Puggy," he whispered. "You can tell by his kisser."

"Tiny's not here," said Strauss. "But we can take you to him. Hey, Buggsy, take Puggy in your car and drive him over to see Tiny Benson. You know where Tiny is, right?"

"Sure," said Buggsy. "Let's go."

Never go with strangers, especially if those strangers have names like Kid Twist, Buggsy, Dukey, Pittsburgh Phil; not names you hear and say, "Here are fellows I can trust." Still, this was just what Puggy did; he followed Buggsy Goldstein and Dukey Maffeatore from the store into a maroon Pontiac. Before leaving, Puggy told his friends to wait, that he would be back shortly.

As Puggy talked to his friends, Reles said, "Now that we got him, what are we going to do with him?"

"Well, you're moving anyway," said Pep. "Let's take him to your house."

"Are you crazy?" said Reles. "My house!"

"What's the difference?" said Pep. "I won't make no noise. Once I mug him, you know, he stays mugged."

Buggsy broke in: "My wife told me she's going over to meet Rose [Reles's wife] and go to the movies with her."

Pep told Buggsy and Dukey to drive Puggy around for at least an hour before bringing him to Reles's. Pep and Reles then went to Albert A.'s clubroom in Ocean Hill to make sure it was okay to take Puggy off the corner. "What are you doing?" asked Reles at one point. "You want to burn up our own corner?"

"What the hell," said Albert A. "Take him however you can take him. Just take him."

So they went back to the Kid's house, which was supposed to be empty. Buggsy's wife and Rose Reles were supposed to be at the movies, but here they were. "I thought you were going to the pictures," said the Kid, throwing his coat over a chair. Pep went to the kitchen to pour himself a glass of milk.

"We missed the picture," said Rose. "Besides, there's nothing to see."

The Kid gave each lady a fifty. "*Find* something to see," he said.

The Kid's mother-in-law was asleep in a bedroom in the back of the house, but it was okay. This was a railroad flat; between the old lady and the living room were three rooms, six doors.

"All right," said Pep, setting down his milk. "Let's get ready."

Pep told Reles to get rope and an ice pick. Reles rummaged through the kitchen, garage, and bedroom and found nothing. At last he made his way through those six doors and woke the old lady. "Hey, Ma," he said, kneeling by the bed. "Ma, where is the rope we used up at the lake last summer for the washline?"

"In the cellar in the valise," the old lady whispered. Reles went for the rope and then, a few minutes later, was again kneeling in the dark. "Hey, Ma," he said. "What about the ice pick? Where the hell is the ice pick?"

"In the pantry," she told him. "The ice pick is in the pantry."

As Pep was stashing the ice pick and rope behind a chair in the living room, a door opened and in came the old lady. "You seem to be working so hard out here, I thought I could fix you something," she said.

"No, thank you," said Pep. "Why don't you go back to sleep?" He said this in a way she understood. As she disappeared into the back of the house, Reles turned on the radio, something soft and sweet, perfect for a winter night.

Buggsy Goldstein was driving Puggy around, pretending to look for Tiny Benson. "No, he's not here. Damn, I thought sure this is where he'd be." More than anything, the Brownsville Boys were great actors, con men who knew just the words to put a mark at ease. "Hey, I know where Tiny is," Buggsy said. "He's at the Kid's place. Let's run over and get this done with."

When Buggsy and Dukey led Feinstein into the living room, Pep stepped from the shadows and got Puggy around the neck. Here is what Puggy must have been thinking: What kidders! Or: What a story this will make! Or more likely: I'm fucked. He probably did not realize he was already half-dead. As Pep held Puggy, the Kid poked him with the ice pick. Buggsy and Dukey were beating on Puggy, punching and kicking. And Puggy was fighting back, trying to get Pep's hands off his neck. He sank his teeth into Pep's left hand. Pep screamed. Reles turned up the radio. Pep pulled Puggy to the floor and sat on his chest. He looped the rope over Puggy's neck, legs, hands. Over the years, this became Pep's specialty. The more Puggy moved, the tighter the rope got. As the Kid, Pep, Buggsy, and Dukey watched, hands on their knees, huffing and puffing, Puggy strangled himself to death.

"Look at this," said Pep, holding up his hand. "That bastard bit me."

As Buggsy and Reles carried the body to the car, Pep went to the bathroom for iodine. The men then grabbed a can of gasoline and got in two cars: kill car, crash car. They decided to take the body to the municipal dumps. There was always something burning on the dumps, so who would notice one more fire? But Buggsy got all turned around, and they instead wound up in one of those residential colonies in the flats near Canarsie, a city in the weeds. They dragged the body into a field, doused it, threw a match, and drove away.

A woman living in the development spotted the fire and came running with a bucket of water. She put out what she thought was a nuisance fire set by neighborhood kids, only to see a charred face looking back at her. Bad dreams. When the cops came all they got was a watch and some teeth, but that was enough to identify Puggy.

All the while, Puggy's friends were waiting around the candy store. At midnight they decided Puggy probably got a ride home from his new pals. But when they reached Borough Park—no Puggy. So they went back to Brownsville, where Buggsy, Pep, Reles, and Dukey were again in back of the candy store, playing cards. After most murders, the killers went back to the store. They watched, with narrowed eyes, everyone who came through the door. "Have you guys seen our friend Puggy?" one of the kids asked.

"No," said Buggsy. "He left. You know what, fellas? It's late. You should be in Borough Park."

News of Feinstein's death made the morning papers. Another body in the weeds. Another Mob killing. Criminals killing criminals. A few days after that, the *New York Daily Mirror* ran a letter from Sydney Levy, a lawyer who had grown up with Puggy:

> Dear Editor:
>
> I desire to write a few words concerning Puggy Feinstein.
>
> Puggy and I played punchball together in the neighborhood. He was a small fellow and wanted to be a big shot. So, we took different paths. But both paths are so closely entwined that we should understand those who take a path that we just miss. He, too, had a fine background.
>
> Last year Puggy enthusiastically told me how he was going straight. . . . The cause of his return to his proper environment was that he was in love with a respectable Flatbush girl.
>
> But after he had bought the furniture and planned the wedding, a neighborhood boy went up to the girl's folks and told them of Puggy's past. This broke up the match and broke his heart.
>
> He reverted to type. And now I read Puggy was a torch-murder victim.
>
> He was a swell punchball player.

Most of the killings were done out of town, in some city clear across the country. Some gangster in a place like Chicago or Detroit would call Lepke or Lucky or Lansky with a problem, a rival who wouldn't fall in line. If the big boys agreed to take care of the problem, the phone in back of the candy store would ring. All you see is a hand holding the phone, the side of a face, lips pursed. A few days later one or two killers are on a train, heading west, rails clicking under the wheels, platforms singing by. Arriving in town, the killers were met by a member of the local mob. Probably they did not hold a sign reading "Abraham 'Kid Twist' Reles, Syndicate Killer." Who needed it? The local thug would spot someone like Abe Reles right away. Into the small, unsophisticated Depression-rocked farming towns of Middle America came the gangsters, in dark cashmere coats and hats, leather gloves, silk scarves.

The local thug came to welcome the killer, but also to help. The gangster was to kill a man he had never seen, so the local was to finger the mark. He usually pointed out the mark from a distance, across a crowded street, coming out of a store or restaurant("That's him! That's him!")—the poor unsuspecting bastard. Over the next few days the killer made a study of the mark's habits—*Where does he go? Who does he see?*—laying down a murder plan. His nights were spent in a hotel or rooming house by the train tracks, the kind of place that caters to transients. When the moment was right, the killer packed his bags, checked out, made his move.

They called the men they were about to kill "rats" or "bastards" or "no good rat bastards." They convinced themselves all marks are guilty, have it coming, that they are bringing not some random death, but a kind of justice. In this way they took the sting out of their crimes, turning the mark from person into object. The last thing the mark sees is the face of a stranger, his last minutes a mystery. Men were killed in fields, hallways, alleys. Harry Strauss killed a mark in a movie theater in Jacksonville, Florida, as the picture played. While the killing was taking place, the local hoods, everyone with a motive, made sure they were somewhere in public, witnesses all around, an iron-tight alibi. Before the cops even found the body, the killer was on a train heading east, the country turning red out the window.

In the coming years, Harry Strauss killed more than thirty men in over a dozen towns and cities, including Boston, Chicago, Philadelphia, Miami, Detroit. He traveled with a small leather case that held pants, silk underwear, a white shirt, a gun, and a rope. He was in the tradition of the Jewish peddler, the ambitious immigrant who moves west with the country, traveling dirt roads, like Levi Strauss, hoping to sell canvas tents but instead cutting and sewing them into the first pairs of jeans. Pittsburgh Phil was like that, only it was all reversed. He was the aggressor, not the victim: a killer in a strange land. "Like a ball player, that's me," he later explained. "I figure I get seasoning doing these jobs here. Somebody from one of the big mobs spots me. Then, up to the big leagues I go."

The Syndicate had invented contract killing. A stranger arrives, kills, is gone. The local cops are left with nothing—no motive, no suspect—nothing. By the mid thirties the contract killer had become a national character, like the frontiersman or logger, who embodies aspects of the American personality. To some he was a kind of existential cowboy, riding the line between being and not, the mysterious stranger of Mark Twain who carries death in his pocket. To others he was a city-spawned monster, a Catholic or Jewish immigrant who has broken free from his slum to ravish a Protestant countryside.

Ernest Hemingway anticipated the emergence of this character in his 1927 story "The Killers," which tells of big-city mobsters entering a lunch counter in a small midwestern town, waiting for a mark named Ole Andreson. The killers pass the time with George, who owns the counter, Nick Adams, and Sam, the black cook. The killers are Jews; they could be members of the Reles troop.

> Their faces were different, but they were dressed like twins. Both wore overcoats too tight for them. They sat leaning forward, their elbows on the counter. . . . Both men ate with their gloves on.

After a while, George asks the men: "What are you going to kill Ole Andreson for? What did he ever do to you?"

"He never had a chance to do anything to us. He never seen us."

"And he's only going to see us once," Al said from the kitchen.

"What are you going to kill him for, then?" George asked.

"We're killing him for a friend. Just to oblige a friend, bright boy."

"Shut up," said Al from the kitchen. "You talk too goddam much."

"Well, I got to keep bright boy amused. Don't I, bright boy?"

"You talk too damn much," Al said. "The nigger and my bright boy are amused by themselves. I got them tied up like a couple of girl friends in the convent."

"I suppose you were in a convent?"

"You never know."

"You were in a kosher convent. That's where you were."

A few pages later the killers are shown as the strangers they are in this town:

> The two of them went out the door. George watched them, through the window, pass under the arc-light and cross the street. In their tight overcoats and derby hats they looked like a vaudeville team.

Damon Runyon, working with the same material, came away with a different story. From New York City, where Runyon lived, these men seemed less objects of scorn than amusement, even pride. Some Americans have always felt a kind of pride for their gangsters—men who cannot be broken. In his 1932 story "Delegates at Large," which first appeared in *Cosmopolitan* magazine, Runyon writes of some Brooklyn boys, led by a man named Harry the Horse, who headed west to fill a contract: "There is no doubt that Harry the Horse has a wild streak in him and is very mischievous," Runyon writes. "[Harry] is always putting Spanish John and Little Isadore up to such tricks as robbing their fellow citizens of Brooklyn and maybe taking shots at them, and sometimes Harry the Horse personally takes a shot or two himself."

Little Isadore, telling his story, then gives a pretty good description of contract killing:

> We go to Chicago by special invitation of some very prominent parties out there. I will mention no names but these parties are very prominent indeed, especially in beer, and they invite us out there to take care of a guy by the name of Donkey O'Neil, as it seems this Donkey O'Neil is also in beer in opposition to the prominent parties I speak of.
>
> Naturally, these parties will not tolerate opposition, and there is nothing for them to do but to see that Donkey O'Neil is taken care of. But of course they don't wish him to be taken care of by local talent, as this is a very old fashioned way of transacting such matters, and nowadays when anybody is to be taken care of in any town it is customary to invite outsiders in, as they are not apt to leave any familiar traces such as local talent is bound to do.

When reporters first got a sense of what was going on, of just what the Brownsville troop specialized in, they gave the boys a nickname: Murder Incorporated. And that's what they were, a corporation dealing in death, who had organized killing along the lines of modern business. In the thirties the troop killed dozens of men across the country. Bodies turned up in fields, lakes, dumps. The details of these murders must have run together in the minds of the killers, creating a single, perfect murder the killer could go over in his head just before sleep. Street, sky, pistol, approach, getaway, the car running past vacant lots and dark houses, out to some lonely railroad platform, and the long ride home.

I don't want to glamorize what these men did. They were killers. They killed as if there were no consequences, so for a lot of them there weren't. Just errands between vacations. Their development had jumped the rails. And yet, looking at how Jews were everywhere being treated, the abuse they took and would continue to take, I cannot help but admire some part of their story. Here were men who had no idea Jews are supposed to be weak, so they weren't. This was the 1930s, the last years of the European part of Jewish history, an era that saw Jews leave their ghettos, cut their beards, give up their God, deny their uniqueness. And maybe the gangster was the dark side of that story, an instinctive twitch from something that was dying.

"When all was said and done, they were nothing more than professional assassins," Albert Fried wrote in *The Rise and Fall of the Jewish Gangster in America*. "They were too crude to come within miles of the gangland summit occupied by Lepke and the Syndicate leaders, by those who presided over vast business concerns. In that sense they were a monstrous throwback to the old Lower East Side gangsters from Monk Eastman to Little Augie."

A few years later, Burton Turkus, the assistant district attorney who prosecuted many of these men, asked Reles how he could kill with such ease. "Did it ever bother you?" asked Turkus. "Didn't you feel anything?"

"How did you feel when you tried your first case?" Reles replied.

"I was rather nervous," said Turkus.

"And how about your second case?"

"It wasn't so bad, but I was still a little nervous."

"And after that?"

"Oh, after that I was all right. I was used to it."

"You answered your own question," said Reles. "It's the same with murder. I got used to it."

A few months after Reles joined the Syndicate, Louis Capone came by the candy store. He asked Rose to send out the Kid. The men talked on the corner in the early fall, leaves falling around them. "Listen here," said Capone. "Tomorrow you be in front of Albert A.'s place in Ocean Hill."

"What for?" asked Reles.

"Albert will tell you what for," said Capone.

The Kid drove to Ocean Hill the next morning, Pitkin to Van Sicklen, the kosher butchers giving way to Italian bakeries. Two of Albert's gunmen, Joe Coppola and Jack Parisi, were waiting in front of the clubhouse with a car. They told Reles to get in. They drove along the water. "Where are we going?" asked Reles.

The men up front looked at each other. Maybe one of them smiled. "Target practice," said Parisi, who was small and dark.

"Target practice?" asked Reles.

"Sure," said Parisi. "The boss wants to make sure you can shoot. If you can't, we gotta teach you."

"Oh," said Reles. He must have fallen into his seat and sighed. Target practice. Well, he was part of the Syndicate now. A local boss. A torpedo. So he had to go through Syndicate training, the same way a manager of the Home Depot must go through Home Depot training.

A few hours out of the city, the road began to climb through the trees. From the top of a rise, they could see fields, houses, silos, barns. Newburgh, New York. The valley had attracted immigrants. Italian could be heard in the stores and fields—a Sicilian town hiding upstate. They could see the road rise on the far side of the valley and disappear into the hills.

A few miles on, they turned from the highway onto a dirt road with tall grass growing between the tire tracks. The road ended at a house. An old man was sitting on the front porch. He raised pheasants. He was a mysterious old man. People in town said he had once killed someone in New York City. He had been hiding up here as long as anyone could remember. The only person he still knew from the old days was Albert Anastasia. Albert would sometimes come up to the farm, the kitchen light burning late into the night. Other times the farmer hid Albert's or Lepke's men on the lam.

The old man led the gangsters to a beat-up building that sat on the edge of a field. He opened the padlock on the door. The building was filled with weapons: rifles, shotguns, pistols. "Enough ammunition to fight a war," Reles later said.

The old man took down several weapons and led the gangsters out back, where he had set up a crude shooting range. The old man would pick up a gun and say something like "If you have to shoot a person from a window across the street at this distance, here's the gun you want to use." He then showed the men how to aim and fire the weapon. The gangsters took turns. They shot until the sun went down.

They spent the night at the Italian hotel in town. They went back to the farm the next morning and shot guns until they ran out of ammunition. When the last bullet was fired, Parisi looked at Reles and said, "Well, I guess you're a pretty good shot."

The Brownsville Boys were being brought, step by step, into the Syndicate. There were phone calls, meetings, jobs. Each encounter, whether they knew it or not, was a test. They were being gauged for skill, intelligence, loyalty. With each test passed they moved further into the fold. Secrets were revealed. By the mid-thirties Lepke was even sharing his gunmen with the Brownsville Boys. It was sometimes hard to tell the gangs apart, as Reles, Goldstein, Strauss, Maione, and Abbandando were seen everywhere with Lepke's best torpedoes, underworld legends, the toughest Jews in America: Albert Tannenbaum, Charlie Workman, Mendy Weiss.

Not only did the killers work well together, they liked each other. They had more in common with each other than they did with the big *machers,* like Lepke or Albert A. They were foot soldiers, doing the dirty work. Some of them did this work as a means to an end, but others did it because they liked it. They did not want to be in some office, playing businessman. They wanted to be on the street, chasing shadows. Lepke's boys were soon honorary members of the Reles troop. Some took vacations with the Brownsville Boys. Some even moved to Brooklyn and hung around the candy store. As much as Reles had joined the Syndicate, the Syndicate had joined Reles.

Of all the new gang members, maybe of all gangsters everywhere, my favorite is Albert Tannenbaum. I like Albert because his experience makes the most sense to me. Most of the other gangsters (Kid Twist, Pep) lived lives that now seem as mysterious and archaic as stories in the Bible. When I try to imagine their world, I can see it only in black and white. They went into crime out of necessity or boredom, or maybe it was in their nature. They were vicious men. But Tannenbaum was different. He fell in with criminals in a way I can imagine happening to me. He hung around gangsters—at first, anyway—because he was young and they were the coolest people around. Being exposed to someone too cool at too young an age is dangerous. The too cool person can act like a strong magnetic field, screwing up your bearings, ruining your compass. When he was around these gangsters, Tannenbaum, then in his teens, was so excited he talked and talked. He talked so much they called him Tick-Tock; they said his mouth went like a clock. He is the only gangster I know of whose nickname is entirely benign.

Albert had a dark, narrow face, a comically long nose, sad eyes, and a tightly furrowed brow. Over the years, the choices he made seemed to turn up on his face. Flipping through his mug shots is like watching time-lapse photos of a city going to seed, weeds coming up through the sidewalks. He was five feet nine and weighed just 140 pounds. Born in Nanticoke, Pennsylvania, on January 17, 1906, he had three siblings: Irving, who would later move to Georgia and become a lampshade salesman; Solomon, who would make his name in motion picture supplies; Jean, who would wait tables at Enduro, a restaurant on West Thirty-ninth Street. In 1908 Albert's father, Sam Tannenbaum, who ran a general store in Pennsylvania, moved his family to Orchard Street on the Lower East Side.

Sometime before the First World War, Sam Tannenbaum got together enough money to buy a resort in upstate New York. Many immigrants dreamed of doing this—buying a piece of land in the country. In much of the old world, Jews were forbidden to own property. So, for many of them, land became a kind of grail, a dream, something worth fighting for. After all, they had come from places like Russia and Poland, where governments and currencies rose and fell, where land was the only thing worth a damn. My father used to quote an ad for a land development firm that summed up the views of many of his ancestors: "Banks may fail, women may leave you, but good land goes on forever." In the first years of the century, lots of Jews withdrew their faith from God and reinvested in a parcel of land. Sam Tannenbaum put his cash first in a campground in Rock Hill, New York; then, when he sold that, he bought the Loch Sheldrake Country Club.

The land around Loch Sheldrake is all hills, valleys, gorges, and woods full of deer and beaver and hunters on trails, straight or curved, that open on moonlit or sun-dappled lakes. By car it is about three hours north of the city. I am not sure what the grounds of the country club looked like, but I have a pretty clear picture in my head, a picture formed by old stories and ghostly snapshots my grandparents took at similar resorts in the Catskill and Pocono Mountains. I see the club as a clearing in the woods; lights on a green hillside; a cavernous mess hall ringing with accents; a life guard standing at the edge of a rocky shore; a gloomy bathhouse smelling of dead fish. Going to the bathhouse with a bar of soap was a ritual, a pleasant memory, which made later talk of European Jews being gassed in bathhouses only more horrible.

The Loch Sheldrake Country Club, and other resorts scattered upstate, were just full of Jews. They drove up after Memorial Day in wagons loaded with luggage. Crossing the Willis Avenue bridge, they could feel the road open, the sky unfold. And soon they were rolling over a narrow gravel path to the lodge, where they were met by friends from summers before. At night they sat smoking on porches, looking at the woods. Fathers, who worked all week in the city, drove up each Friday night, a ritual better observed and with more meaning than the lighting of the candles. These places were teeming with Communists and Zionists and anarchists and Socialists and Democrats and even a few Republicans. At night, after the kids were asleep, the discussions were lively. It must have sometimes seemed less like they were upstate than at some Black Sea resort, with pious old men and preaerobics, full-bodied *balabustas* in huge, one-piece, cover-all bathing outfits pinching daughters, calling them real bathing beauties and their sons little Romeos. "What a little Romeo my son is, romancing the bathing beauties." There were dozens of such upscale resorts, like the Concord, the Nevele, the Royal, Grossinger's. Other families stayed at *kochalayns,* cottages with communal kitchens. And those poor souls stuck sweltering in the city were left to dream of a weekend in the Jewish Alps.

By the time I was a kid, all that was left of this world were summer camps for Jewish kids scattered around the lakes of the upper Midwest. These camps had Indian names, like Ojibwah, Kawaga, Apachee. I went to Camp Menominee, in Managua, Wisconsin. We had a cheer: "Easy, Izzy, Jake, and Sam, we're the boys who eat no ham. Matzoh, matzoh, that's our cry; matzoh, matzoh, 'til we die. Yeah, Menominee!" Looking over the names of these camps, which advertised each Sunday in the *Chicago Tribune,* my father would shake his head and say, "You think Indians send their kids to Camp Goldberg?"

When he was old enough, Allie began spending his summers at the resort. Probably he waited tables in the dining hall or set up beach chairs at the lake. It must have been fun for him, being the son of the owner, having the run of the place. And Sam Tannenbaum must have been happy with the connections his son could make. The club serviced a ritzy clientele. It was not cheap. Almost everyone on the beach represented a success story. But Allie looked past all these men, seeing instead those other success stories, men who were the loudest in every room, took the best tables, were impressed by no one, and carried with them a cloud of laughter. Even in the woods, where the life of the city was just a noise in the distance, the most glamorous men were criminals.

Each year, in the first days of summer, the gangsters would pile into sedans and drive north. Reles had a summer home in White Lake, New York. A lonely little shack, a light in the woods, a path to a lake, a line holding colorful clothes. In the winter this same line was used to strangle men. The gangsters spent afternoons reading magazines or comic books or else ran around the woods trying to kill animals with handguns. At dinner they introduced themselves to other guests as labor organizers or said they were in the garment industry or trucking or importing. Away from the dining hall, the respectable clientele must have whispered, "Guess what he does in the city?" Among the Jewish success stories who spent summers at Loch Sheldrake were Greenie Greenberg, Louis Lepke, and Gurrah Shapiro. For most kids, summer vacation meant the beach, sand castles, cookouts. For Albert Tannenbaum, summer vacation meant gangsters.

Allie met Gurrah at the resort in the summer of 1925. Gurrah, with his gruff voice and hard eyes, must have been easy to spot among the regular clientele. Allie was drawn to him the way most young men are drawn to power. He was impressed. Gurrah introduced him to Lepke and Greenberg, who saw in the kid someone they could teach, who would reflect their greatness. Allie also had something concrete to offer: intelligence. Over the years, he had come to know the terrain around the camp, paths and roads, caves and gulches, shortcuts.

There must have been a moment when Sam Tannenbaum realized his son was rejecting his example. But what could he do? Lepke and Gurrah were teaching the boy something new: to be tough. When Allie found himself in a tricky situation, when he felt threatened physically, he must have swallowed his fear and asked himself, "What would Gurrah do?" For a lot of young men, the idea of the tough Jew was something you could hold in your pocket, something to keep you calm, like a religious icon. Of course, Allie did not know the gangsters could lead him only halfway: they could take him away from home, but how could they get him back?

One afternoon in the late twenties, Allie was in the city, walking along Broadway, killing time. He was going to be a senior at Bushwick High School in Brooklyn and worked part-time at the College Shop, a haberdashery on 113th Street in Manhattan. As he crossed 32nd Street, someone called to him. It was Greenie Greenberg, who worked for Lepke. Greenie asked Allie if he needed work. *Sure. Who doesn't?* So Greenie sent Allie to a dress factory downtown, where the workers were on strike. Lepke had charged Greenie with breaking the strike leadership. Allie was to go to the factory, say he was a worker, and sit in the sewing room. When members of the leadership turned up, he would tell them to leave. If they refused, he would use force, saying he was doing it for Lepke and Greenberg.

Allie liked the work. It was more fun than selling hats, and he was good at it. He quit school. His three years at Bushwick High still made him one of the best educated members of the Mob. He was well spoken and had the kind of perfect penmanship taught in public schools before World War II. He wrote in clear, concise sentences. Brains were always an asset to the gang, and Allie rose through the ranks. He was soon moved from the street to the Perfect Coat Company, a downtown factory where Lepke had an office. He was put on the payroll at $125 a week. Allie was just like other young, ambitious personal assistants, only he did not go out for coffee or salads or take dictation; he went out stink bombing or strike breaking or schlamming. And he was soon running with other Lepke guns, like Mendy Weiss and Charlie Workman. And, bit by bit, he was becoming a killer. Over the years, he had a hand in at least six murders. How he went from a worker at his father's resort to an East Side killer is a mystery. Somewhere in that mystery is wrapped the secret and allure of crime.

Albert Tannenbaum also did some freelancing, hiring himself out to whoever had the cash. In 1931 he went to work in Brownsville for some brothers who were fighting a war with young upstarts. When Meyer Shapiro shot up Buggsy Goldstein's pool hall, Albert was driving the car. It was Albert whom Reles saw at the wheel. Louis Capone later introduced the men, making them shake hands like a couple of kids after a schoolyard fight.

By the time Reles and Lepke were working together, everyone was friends. When Albert's sister got married in the thirties, Reles was on the guest list, as was Charlie Workman, Buggsy Goldstein, Harry Strauss, and Mendy Weiss. In the coming years, the bond among the gangsters, Jews and Jews, Jews and Italians, was strengthened at such parties. They were like underworld summits. The guest list alone could give you a sense of how things were going, of alliances and feuds.

Things probably peaked in 1935, at the *bris* of Charlie Workman's son, Solomon. The Workmans lived on Avenue A and Fourth Street, in what is now the East Village but was then still the Lower East Side. They lived in an apartment house: a few rooms, window, airshaft. Guests began arriving in the afternoon. It was midwinter, so the ladies probably wore fur, their coats piled high on a bed. The living room was full of shoulders, smiles, hairdos. Some of the most important criminals in America were crowded into the apartment: Lepke, Gurrah, Moey "Dimples" Wolensky, Longy Zwillman, Reles, Strauss, Goldstein, Dasher, Maione. Good gangsters don't talk business around wives, so if there was anything important to say, one gangster probably took another to the bedroom and talked next to the coats. Maybe they felt the pile, making sure no one was hiding there.

In the other room, everyone was drinking or had just finished a drink or was about to have another. Stories were told, jokes. The boy was hugged, pinched, kissed. And at the center of it all, taking gifts and coats, was Charlie Workman. In pictures, most midcentury gangsters look like ancient, spectral figures, something from mythology. Charlie was not like that; Charlie looked modern, like someone you see at a Superbowl party, a big hit with the ladies. His eyes were black and deep as pools, something you try to find the bottom of. Neighborhood girls called him Handsome Charlie. Neighborhood boys called him Bug. In the twenties, in a bootlegging war, he was shot in the shoulder. The bullet pierced a nerve that ran down his arm, a wound that affected him until the end. If he held anything in his right hand for more than a few minutes (a beer, a gun), that hand would quiver and shake. It was one of those external injuries that mirrors something crippled within.

Charlie Workman's may be the saddest story in organized crime. He would live to see his best friends betray him, his friends and enemies die, his way of life rebuked. He grew up on the Lower East Side, had a sister and two brothers, quit school after ninth grade. Though he worked for a time at his father's bakery, he could not escape his nature. He had the gangster spirit. On fire escapes and tarry roofs, he grew accustomed to the simple logic of crime. Do or get done. When he was eighteen, he was arrested for stealing a twelve-dollar bundle of cotton off a truck on lower Broadway. A year later, while still on probation, he was charged with shooting a man behind the ear in an argument over ten dollars. He came to Lepke's attention a few years later, during the summer strikes of 1926. He was a gifted schlammer. Lepke put him on the payroll at $125 a week.

Workman was often sent to kill rival bootleggers, assignments he especially liked. A successful bootlegger might carry as much as ten grand in cash, and Charlie was always cool enough in the siren-filled aftermath of a hit to go through the pockets of the corpse. When the cops got him, he would give his name as Jack Harris or Jack Cohen or whatever came to mind. He told people he was a Brooklyn undertaker or that he sold cars.

Workman was openly admired even by the top bosses. When he moved with his wife to Long Island, housewarming gifts came from around the country. His fireplace was a gift from Ben Siegel. A police report on him reads, "Charlie was on Lepke's payroll as a triggerman. He was considered one of the best in the line. He can, if he will, give more information to the DA than all the other songbirds put together. Charlie's wife was extravagant, keeping him constantly out of funds."

Workman had spent many years in the Syndicate. By all accounts he should have climbed the ranks, from alley to boardroom, but he liked the street, so that's where he stayed. When Lepke hooked up with the Brownsville Boys, Workman started killing with the troop. He was soon friends with Reles, Buggsy, and Strauss. He dressed in slick, downtown suits, beautiful shirts and hats, and was known as a dandy. He was someone you might make fun of (behind his back), then go imitate. Though he did not want to lead, people followed. He was an elder statesman to the troop, teaching by example. A few years later, a prosecutor asked Reles how often he would see Workman. "Whenever the occasion arose," said the Kid. "When we had business together."

"What is that business?" asked the lawyer.

"The murder business," said the Kid. "The extortion business. All kinds of business."

Workman was never very far from Albert Tannenbaum. When you looked for one, you found the other. They were best friends. They met in Lepke's office, when both were salaried young gunmen. The friendship blossomed over a month spent together at the Park Beach Hotel in Miami. Each man was there for his own reasons. They spent days at the track or at illegal casinos in Broward County. In Manhattan they played craps each week at the Lincoln Republican Club on Allen and Forsythe streets. They moved with their wives into houses a few doors from each other on Ocean Parkway in Brooklyn, an underworld version of *I Love Lucy.* Wacky neighbors. Surprise drop-bys. Joint vacations.

The couples went north each summer, to the Ambassador Hotel in Fallsburgh, New York, or else to Edgemere in Rockaway, Long Island, where they took adjoining bungalows. In the winter they went to Florida, which is where they were when Charlie and his pregnant wife decided it was time to go home, that the baby would come soon. The Tannenbaums saw the Workmans off at the station, the train rolling through rail yards, signal towers cutting the sky into patches of color.

The Tannenbaums were home in time for the *bris.* Allie probably slipped an envelope into his best friend's pocket—something for Solomon. Things seemed to be going well for Charlie. Here were his friends: Reles, Strauss, and Goldstein wandered the room, telling jokes. Here were his bosses: Lepke and Gurrah wandered the room, being told jokes. Here was his wife, whom he obviously loved. When he lived at 441 Ocean Parkway, he once beat up the superintendent for looking at her wrong. And here was Solomon Workman, about to be marked, the wound that begins every Jewish boy's commitment to God.

At some point, the *mohel,* who conducts the *bris,* said the prayers. Prayers in Hebrew always sound so sad, songs of a lost people. Then the knife. The baby cried. Drinks were served. Music played. And slowly, glass by glass, the men gave themselves to the moment, rolling up sleeves, hugging, smiling. It was a frozen instant, the kind of afternoon people look back on. Outside, the sky turned black. Cars ghosted down the avenue to lower Manhattan, where, in courtrooms and offices, decisions were being made, decisions that would affect everyone in the room. In one way or another, all these men were marked by the violence that made them. Though they steered clear of the law, the harder they ran, the closer to it they came, running, to the very thing they were trying to escape—obituaries spread across front-page headlines.

Corners

FOR THE BROWNSVILLE troop, and for a lot of other Brooklyn boys of that era, life centered around the corner. In the thirties and forties people had favorite corners the way people have favorite cities today. For more than a few kids, trouble was something first encountered on the corner. Established gangsters recruited from corners, and it was from corners that young men went into gambling, extortion, killing. When you went to the corner, you didn't have to go anywhere else. The world, sooner or later, came to you. Each group of kids had their own corner. If they went to a strange corner, they took their chances. Some corners were friendly, some not so friendly. In Brooklyn every cool kid had in his head a map of friendly corners stretching from here to home. On summer nights a group of pals might make their way clear across the borough, friendly corner to friendly corner, until they reached their home corner, where nothing could touch them.

Sometimes, late at night, a dark sedan would glide up to the corner. A window would roll down. The kids could barely make out a figure, but they recognized the voice. Someone who once hung out here, who went from this corner to underworld power, a local celebrity. Picking out one of the kids, the gangster would say, "Hey, you! Get over here."

The kid races over, nerves tight. And now his friends see him in the streetlight, bent to the window. The gangster whispers something. The kid gets in. The car drives off. Those left behind are excited, and sad.

Their friend has gone into an adult world, leaving them behind. A curtain has dropped. What's on the other side? Before they can answer, they are again lost in the trivia of a summer night.

In 1941 a prosecutor asked a Jewish gangster about this aspect of underworld life. "You say you hang around corners?" he asked.

"Yes, sir," said the gangster.

"What were the corners you frequented in 1937?"

"New Jersey and Pitkin; Linwood and Pitkin; Saratoga and Livonia," said the gangster.

"Now, when you talk about the corner of Saratoga and Livonia, what do you call it?" the prosecutor went on.

"Well," said the gangster, "we call it 'the corner.' "

Saratoga and Livonia was the intersection in front of the candy store. By the thirties, when the Brownsville troop came to power, it was one of the most important corners in Brooklyn, where members of Murder Inc. came to smoke, talk, unwind. At night it was a collection of dark shapes, hats, cigarettes, shoulders. It had an eerie eye-of-the-storm quality. What happened to the gang in these years, the good and bad things, is really just the story of what happened on Saratoga and Livonia, the history of a New York street corner.

Like a plant, a corner needs certain things to flourish. A corner should be remote enough for privacy, yet well enough trafficked for action. You need suckers to practice on. There should be a light nearby: a storefront, a street lamp. A corner should also be well fed, with apartment or town houses, the kinds of places kids loiter in front of. And there must be a brick wall, bench, or street sign, something a kid can lean or sit or lie on, look cool near. The corner of Livonia and Saratoga, though often quiet, was under the elevated, which supplied a stream of businessmen returning from the city; was lit by the candy store window; had a brick wall, bench, and street sign. It was the kind of corner a thug gets one look at and says, "There's gotta be talent there."

In the thirties, when Pep decided, as things were going so well, it was time to expand, train a new generation of Jews, he went no farther than the corner. Pep was always scouring the corner for neighborhood punks who might turn into studs, artists who stand out from the other dingy faces in police lineups. Pep could spot them the way a Brooklyn Dodger scout would later spot Sandy Koufax throwing a baseball in Prospect Park. He was looking for kids still young enough to fall for the great practical joke that a criminal life really is, an up-front promise so great it hides the back end: prison, execution. He was looking for kids who were floating, who had rejected their parents' way and had yet to find a way of their own, who could be tricked into accepting someone else's vision of the world. Pep's vision.

Pretty Levine quit school when he was fifteen and had been floating ever since. He had dirty blond hair, gray eyes, hawk nose, big smile. When Pep met him, he was drifting job to job, working as a printer, in a radio repair shop, in his father's grocery in East New York. Then his drifting ended. "Hey, you," said Pep, spotting him on the corner. "Get over here." Soon Pep was sending Pretty out on errands, small jobs all over Brooklyn. And he gave him a partner: Dukey Maffeatore, another discovery of Pep's.

Dukey was a fuck-up. Today a school counselor might call him spirited. And he might be right. But he would still be a fuck-up. And as there was no failing up in those days, Dukey spiraled down, down, and down, until he reached a depth where criminals could get him. At a crap game in 1934, he was approached by a well-dressed older man. "Hey, kid, you like this?" the man asked, flashing a bankroll.

"Sure," said Dukey.

"Well, stick with me, you can make big money," the man said. "All you need is to drive a car."

A few days later, Dukey was chauffering the man and his friends around Manhattan. The man had Dukey pull up before an office building. When the passengers left the car, Dukey was told to wait with the engine running. Soon after the men went in the building, Dukey heard alarms. He realized he was parked before a bank. He tried to think. What name did the man give him? Sutton? Shit. This is Willie Sutton, the most wanted man in America, who said he robs banks because "that's where the money is." Dukey jumped from the car and ran. From then on he decided to associate only with crooks from the neighborhood.

A short time later he was standing on the corner when he heard someone call to him. "Hey, you!" said Pep. "Get over here."

And there were other recruits working for the gang: Blue Jaw Magoon, Sholem Bernstein. To Strauss these kids were more than just order takers: they were the future, the next generation, the gangsters who would one day look to him as he looked to Lepke. America is all about moving up, and one way to get higher is to build something beneath you. That's what Pep was doing. He set the boys up in business. "When I was twenty, I got in with the Mob," Dukey explained. "I went into the shylock business. Pittsburgh Phil gave me the territory. He made me borrow the money to start out from his brother Alex."

Pretty and Dukey became experts in auto theft, giving the troop a steady supply of kill and crash cars. Every few weeks Pep would call over Levine. "Hey, Pretty," he would say. "Go clip me a black car."

Levine would grab Dukey and off they would go, scouting the streets. Pep usually had the boys steal a sedan. Blue. Brown. Black. Not flashy. A car that falls into the background, another man off to work. And four doors. It must have four doors. Getting into a two-door getaway car, you would get tangled up and confused and flustered and maybe even caught.

The cars were usually swiped from a lot on the other side of Brooklyn. The boys would sneak into a garage in the early morning, as some overworked nightwatchman snoozed in the office. After choosing a car, the boys would search for keys above the visor, on the dash, beneath the floor mats (*got it!*), release the parking break, and roll into the street. With the sky going gray, they let the car glide down some hill and then, slowly slipping it into gear, turn the key, and the engine cuts the silence. Pretty, who had been behind the bumper pushing, would run for the other car, the one that got them here, Dukey's beat-up, mud-splattered maroon Pontiac, and pull behind the hot car. And off they'd go, ghosting through Greenpoint, Flatbush, Crown Heights, all the way back to Brownsville.

Every time Dukey pulled up to a stop sign or traffic light, Pretty pulled right behind, hiding the license plates so no suspicious do-gooding smart boy could take down the numbers and call the cops. As the sun appeared above the church spires, they would drop the car in the garage behind Pep's house. They then swung by the candy store—morning now, only stragglers and lunatics here—and tape the keys under the toilet in back.

The next morning Pretty would again go to the candy store, talk about the mean piss he's got to take, walk back, feel under the toilet, retrieve the stolen license plates some other thief has left there. Then on to the garage, where he removes the old plates, busts them with a tire iron, and puts on the new plates. He then leaves the car at a drop, a side street or alley, with guns in the glove. Then he waits, checking the papers each day, waiting to see what body turns up in the car he stole.

And in another part of Brooklyn, some poor bastard gets a call from the cops: *Your stolen car has been found, only covered with blood and carrying a dead gangster.*

That's how it was with at least a few of Pretty Levine's acquaintances, Brownsville kids he knew from the corner. One day they are hanging around, talking about this or that, the next day they turn up dead in one of Pretty's stolen cars. Did Pretty feel bad? Probably not too bad. It was just part of the job. Dukey and Pretty were small cogs. They didn't look at the big picture. They didn't think about it—not even a little. A few years later, when Dasher was on trial, a lawyer asked Pretty about a car he stole for a crime. "When Strauss asked you to get a black sedan, for what purpose do you think he wanted that sedan?"

"I did not even want to think," said Pretty. "I didn't ask any questions. I would not ask any questions. I would be crazy to ask questions. He told me to get it and I just got it."

A lawyer later asked Reles why Levine never inquired about the use of the stolen cars. "He did not have to ask," Reles explained. "He could read the papers and see for himself what happens, who is found in the car."

Know-nothing recruits like Pretty and Dukey were a crucial part of the equation, leaving cops with a murder committed in one place (Brownsville) and a body found somewhere else (Canarsie) in a car stolen in still another place (Greenpoint) with license plates stolen from another place (Red Hook). It was as though the killers were mocking the cops, and the system did frustrate the authorities. The cops knew they would never solve any of these crimes until someone on the inside began talking. And the cops hated a rat almost as much as the gangsters.

With the stolen car delivered, Pretty and Dukey would go for breakfast. They would often eat in the diner my grandparents owned in Brownsville. Sitting at a corner table, they would speak in hushed tones, like athletes after a victory. Dukey had glittering green eyes and would call for coffee without saying a word. When the businessmen started wandering in, stripping off coats and opening papers, they would call for the check. They always left a lot more than the bill called for. They were valued customers. "Tell you what," Pretty might tell Dukey. "Take me to the baths. I think I'll take a steam." Other times Pretty would take a car out on the highway, driving like a madman, until the engine rocked and rattled, steam poured from the hood, the wheels smoked. When the car was spent, he would run right out and steal a new one. The American dream.

These were the glory days of Murder Inc. If the gang were a rock band, this is when they would record most of their hits. If they were the Beatles, this would be 1967 to 1970. If they were Bruce Springsteen and the E Street Band, this would be the eighties. If they were Wings, well, the troop could never be confused with Wings. But if they were the Rolling Stones, these would be the years of *Beggar's Banquet, Exile on Main Street, Sticky Fingers.* Bodies turned up all over the country, and what could the cops do? Nothing. The boys had developed a system of killing as groundbreaking, as effective, as influential, as Henry Ford's assembly line. And they had in the process become perhaps the most important part of Lepke's operation, making them among the most important criminals in America.

Though the troop had been heading here ever since they killed the Shapiros, what really put them over was another killing: the Ambergs, a crime family out of Williamsburg, Brooklyn. The Ambergs were successful neighborhood bullies who had been robbing, extorting, and killing since the early 1900s. They probably resented Reles: his power, his relationship with Lepke. And they were the only gangsters in Brooklyn willing to challenge Kid Twist. Sometimes they even extorted money from merchants in the troop's territory. Whenever this happened, Pep wanted to go right out and take care of it. But these matters were instead settled by the courts Lansky and Luciano had created to prevent just such gang wars. The Ambergs had powerful friends (Joe Adonis, Red Levine) who were always able to smooth things over. But they kept pushing—pushing and pushing. And when the boys at last pushed back, it was like one of those bloody civil wars that finally brings a raucous territory (Brooklyn) under the leadership of a single power.

The Williamsburg gang was led by Joey Amberg, a thirty-two-year-old Russian immigrant. Joey had brown eyes and wore his curly brown hair slicked back. He was five four, weighed 135 pounds, and wore size seven shoes. His police record went back to 1908, when he was charged with petty larceny. He was arrested a dozen more times over the years, for everything from selling narcotics to robbery. His body mapped his troubles. A four-inch knife wound snaked across his belly. A grooved .38-caliber slug was a lump in his back. He was a tough Jew, but probably not as tough as the Jews in Brownsville. You have to be a certain shade of foolish to pick a fight with assassins.

In 1935 Amberg gang members had a dispute with Hy Kazner, a small-time thug working for Murder Inc. According to a police report, one of Joey Amberg's torpedoes—Jack Elliott or Frankie Tietlebaum—owed Kazner $1,100 or $1,600. Whenever Kazner tried to collect, these men stalled. At last, in the summer of that year, Kazner told the troop he was going to get paid. Someone told him not to go alone. He smiled, saying the Ambergs were "but bums," that he could take care of himself. That was the last anyone ever saw of Hy Kazner.

A few days later Pep Strauss went to Williamsburg to find out what happened. Strauss found Amberg at his clubhouse. Amberg said Kazner had not been around in weeks. So Pep went to see Louis Capone in Ocean Hill. Capone was also worried about Kazner. But all he had were suspicions, and Joey Amberg was too well connected to be killed on suspicion. Until something else happened, Kazner's disappearance would be just another Brooklyn mystery.

And it would have stayed that way had it not been for Gangy Cohen. Gangy was a handsome, broad-shouldered, Brooklyn-born thug. He was well liked. His best friend was another thug named Walter Sage. Gangy sometimes worked for the Ambergs, hanging around their clubhouse, joking, plotting, listening. After listening to an especially interesting piece of news, Gangy might go see Pep. That's what he did, anyway, when he learned the fate of Hy Kazner.

A few weeks before, when Kazner had arrived at the clubhouse in Williamsburg, he was asked to state his business. When he said he had come to collect his money, Amberg's men dragged Kazner into a cellar, beat him, tied him up, cut him to pieces, put the pieces in a bag, dumped the bag in a sewer. The sewer emptied into Jamaica Bay, and the tides carried Kazner to sea.

When the troop heard about the killing, they went to see Albert A. and Lepke. They knew what they wanted to do, but they needed permission. Lepke got the go-ahead from other Syndicate leaders. A few days later, Albert A. and Louis Capone ran into Charlie Luciano in Saratoga, New York. They told Lucky the story, and Lucky added his approval: Amberg could be dealt with. There was nothing Red Levine or Joe Adonis could do. Amberg and his guns had killed Reles's partner; Reles was a partner of Lepke. By a transitive property that underlies all Mob business, Amberg and his men had killed Lepke's partner.

The Brownsville troop must have been happy with the way things worked out. Hy Kazner for Joey Amberg was a good trade. A lot of people did not like the Ambergs. When a guy like Joey Amberg turns up dead, people say things like "Karma is not supposed to work that fast!" For years Joey had been back stabbing other thugs in Brooklyn. Now Joey gets his. Maybe Reles even thought, What goes around comes around! Probably not. For this suggests there is a finite amount of shit, and every gangster knows the amount of shit is infinite. It also suggests a degree of cause and effect, and every gangster knows the shit you give and the shit you take are only sometimes connected. And this is one source of the gangster's power: a freedom the rest of suspicious, God-fearing America will never have access to. Gangsters know that even if they stop doing bad things, which they so enjoy doing, bad things will still happen to them. So why not go ahead and break shit before you yourself are broken?

Joey Amberg was killed in a garage at 385 Blake Avenue in Brooklyn. They got him on September 30, 1935, when he went to pick up his 1933 LaSalle sedan. That morning a few gangsters sat around an apartment with a view of the garage, waiting for Amberg's arrival. The apartment, a top-floor, three-bedroom place at 474 East Ninety-eighth Street, belonged to Mikey Sycoff, a thug who wanted to get in good with the troop. His big, round, doughy face was like the moon seen through a telescope—gray and white with small blue patches that were his eyes.

The day before the killing, Sycoff ran into Pep Strauss on the corner of Sackman and Livonia. Strauss asked if he and some friends could use Sycoff's apartment. "When Sycoff asked the purpose of this meeting, Strauss stated it was to talk certain matters over, to iron something out," reads a 1941 police report. "When Sycoff was assured there would be no rough stuff at the apartment, he assented."

At ten A.M. the next day, there was a knock on Sycoff's door. It was two men who, according to the report, were "of obvious Italian extraction."

"Are you Mikey?" one of the men asked.

"Yes," said Sycoff. "Who sent you?"

"Harry," the man said.

The gangsters sat in the living room. More turned up. Louis

Capone. Strauss. Dasher. Happy Maione came by, said a few words, left. Much of the time these men spoke Italian, which Sycoff could not understand. They kept their coats on, fingered their hats. Every now and then one of them went to the window, pushed back the curtain, and looked out. There was a man leaning on a car across the street. This was Walter Sage. Whenever a gangster looked down, Sage looked up, shook his head, and looked back down the street. At around eleven-thirty A.M. Sycoff went to the window. He saw Sage waving his arms. Looking out, one of the gangsters said, "There he is."

"The entire group immediately left the apartment," reads the police report. "About an hour later, when Sycoff left the house, he learned from gossip on the street that Joey Amberg had been killed."

Sage waving was a signal—it meant Joey Amberg had entered the garage. He was not alone. Morris Keossler, his thirty-year-old chauffeur, was with him. Killing Keossler was not the plan, but here he was, a presence that had to be dealt with. The men entered the garage. Across the way a race car was propped on blocks, and two men, passing tools, worked on the engine. When they reached the LaSalle, Keossler walked to the driver's side and Amberg went to the passenger side. As Amberg reached for the door, a man dressed as a mechanic stepped from the shadows. He wore a greasy coverall. He had a gun. "Turn around," he told Amberg. "This is a stickup."

Amberg seemed to recognize the gunman. It was Happy Maione. Amberg started to say something ("It's—"), but before he could finish, Happy shot him. The other killer, never identified, shot Keossler. The shots must have echoed wildly in the garage. If there had been a convex mirror posted, the killers would have been reflected as squat little men with squat little guns, and the blue flames from the pistols and the blood running across the sloped concrete into a drain.

Amberg had been shot three times in the chest, once in the head. He was wearing a brown tweed suit with red flecks, a brown shirt, green silk suspenders, a white ribbed T-shirt, blue boxer shorts with deep blue vertical stripes, brown wool socks held up by leather garters, which can only be called a luxury, oxford laced Lord & Taylor shoes. He carried two handkerchiefs, one initialed *J.* He had ten dollars and a comb in his pocket.

On the other side of the LaSalle but already an infinity away, Morris Keossler was dying. He had been shot in the back, probably as he fumbled for his keys. He was wearing a green jacket, the right sleeve smeared with blood and grease, a vest, a shirt with a button-on collar, tan shoes. His soft gray fedora was full of blood and brain tissue. The cops found him on his back, a bullet in his arm, another in his head. He was buried a week later in Mount Hebron Cemetery.

A few blocks from the garage, a cop working the school crossing at Sackman Street and Blake Avenue heard the shots. As he arrived on the scene, someone grabbed his sleeve, pointed out two men dressed as mechanics, and said, "There they go!" One of these men, fleeing down Christopher Street, outran the cop. The other ran into a building. When the cop went back to the building, he found the roof door open. On the roof he found a tan coverall, a blue sweater, and a gray salt-and-pepper cap.

A few days later the police arrested Louis Capone. But they had no evidence and had to let him go. The men who had been working on the race car told the cops that they were sorry but had seen nothing, as both were under their car at the time of the shooting.

The troop caught up with Frankie Tietlebaum a week later. They pulled him off the street, shot him, stuffed him in a trunk, and left the trunk under the Manhattan Bridge for a scavenger to find.

And that should have been the end of it. Amberg killed one; the troop killed three: a winning fraction. It should have been the end of it, but it wasn't. There was a loose end: Pretty Amberg. Pretty was five years younger than his brother Joey, and even more hated. He had once worked as a gun for Dutch Schultz. He had a violent temper. He could often be found at the Second Avenue baths, invisible through the steam but for his glowing cigar. He spent his nights at Yiddel Lorber's, a hang-out of Jewish gangsters near the on-ramp of the Williamsburg Bridge. He had grown up in Brooklyn, lived his short, violent life there, and would leave his bones in the soil of a dusty lot where the ash is carried on the wind.

When Pretty learned of his brother's death, he went over to Midnight Rose's candy store. He went to Brownsville the way Hy Kazner had gone to Williamsburg, pledging to take care of it himself. He found members of the troop on the corner. He demanded answers. He said he would avenge his brother's death. He was in a rage. He kept nothing hidden. A few days later he proclaimed, to all who would listen, his intent to kill Louis Capone and Pep Strauss. He didn't stop long enough to ask, "Am I committing suicide?"

Even those who might have supported Pretty backed away. His

anger made him weak. He was out where no one could help him. It was the kind of anger that attracts attention—a threat to everyone. Even law-abiding residents of Brooklyn could feel it, a tension in the air. In 1935 such a citizen was concerned enough to write the police:

> Dear Sir:
>
> Please take notice that you will stop a new gang war for revenge if you will pick up (Dopey) Red Levine and his partner Pretty Amberg.
>
> Red Levine, if he is sweated, will tell you who committed the last few murders in Brooklyn. You can find him any night at Raetner's restaurant on Delancey Street.
>
> Sincerely,
> Dan Seveozza

If the troop did not get Pretty, Pretty would get the troop, or the police would get Pretty and Pretty would get the troop that way. But who gets Pretty? The guy was vigilant. He thought just about everyone in Brooklyn was out to get him, and he was right. He would not go easily. If the troop went in with force, he was sure to take a few of the boys out with him. One day, as the troop mulled this over, Mendy Weiss stepped forward. Mendy was Lepke's top gun and also happened to be an old friend of Amberg's. "Pretty won't go with nobody but me," he said. "He likes me. I'll steer him. He'll never get wise."

Mendy asked Pretty to meet him for dinner at Yiddel Lorber's. Before they sat down, Yiddel asked the men to the kitchen for a drink. Two torpedoes were waiting there for Pretty. For many gangsters, the moment before death is a moment of betrayal. It is the second to last thing that ever happens to them. Looking at pictures of dead gangsters, you can say, "Betrayed, then killed; betrayed, then killed; betrayed, then killed." It happens all the time; it's one of the things that must make this way of life especially hard and isolating. It gives many gangsters an edge, a paranoia that sends them on killing sprees: betray before being betrayed. And it also makes gangster life a powerful metaphor for life in general.

The killers tied up Pretty Amberg. Then, using small knives, they cut him to pieces. The boys had decided Pretty's death should be especially painful. He was the last of the Ambergs. With this killing, the troop was not just taking out a rival, they were wiping out a people. They were stealing everything from Pretty: traditions, stories, dreams his grandparents carried from Russia, the children and grandchildren he was to pass those traditions on to.

Mendy loaded what was left of Pretty into a car and drove the car out near the Brooklyn Navy Yard. He parked on North Elliot Place, facing a field called City Park. The boys met him out there, looked at Pretty, mingled. They talked about their girlfriends and wives. The women in the underworld were dolls, ornaments. Of course, they could sense the dread that surrounded their men, the menace the boys shed like light. Maybe it's what attracted them in the first place. But they had no idea how the boys earned that aura. Wives and girlfriends were insulated by many layers of ignorance. A man who tells his wife everything is a romantic, a fool. Ignorance protected the boys from the wives and the wives from the cops. If you know nothing, there is nothing to give away. And still the women asked: Where do you go at night? What do you do? Who do you see?

They want to know what we do? Well, let's show them. So that night the boys went across the borough, helping ladies into sedans, having pleasant conversations as they made their way back to City Park, where they all stood looking in at Pretty, a piranha in glass. Bloody limbs. Someone doused the car in gasoline. The women drew straws. Pep's girl, Evelyn, the bombshell of the group, drew the short straw. She crossed the field and dropped a match on the car. The faces of the girls and their gangsters flickered in the flames. Looking back, the boys would say, "Yeah, that was ladies' night."

With their most powerful rivals gone, the troop carried on as never before. Most of them had a regular job, a means of support, something to tell the cops. Tannenbaum was a cutter. Pretty Levine drove a garbage truck, which he sometimes used to haul dead bodies. But their real moneymaking came from extorting merchants, bullying bullies, running scams. Reles hosted a crap game on State and Court streets in Brooklyn. When a gambler lost his money, Reles lent him more, often at 25 percent interest. To pay back Reles, the gambler might borrow from Strauss or Pretty Levine or Dukey Maffeatore. Before he knew what had happened, the gambler owed everything he had to the troop. Some of this money the boys invested in local businesses. Happy Maione bought a flower shop in Ocean Hill. Sholem Bernstein opened a bar and grill in Bensonhurst. Abe Reles started a rental car agency in Brownsville. The rest was spent on clothes or trips or cars or girls. They were what grandmother would call "big spenders."

And all of it—vacations, cars, stores—was paid for by the killings. Killing for the Syndicate gave the boys the right to run eastern Brooklyn. And there was always killing to be done. If these killings could be given names, they would sound like Edward Hopper paintings: *New York Pavements, Two on the Aisle, Conference at Night.* The killing of Frankie Tietlebaum would be called *Manhattan Bridge Loop.* The killing of Pretty Amberg would be called *Girlie Show.* And the killing of Walter Sage would be called *Road and Trees.* It would be painted in blues and blacks, and the figures in the foreground would have the same vague shape as the hills in the background. It would be a gloomy painting, but also funny.

A few years before, Sage had been given control of the troop's Long Island slot machine operation. Over time, a problem developed. Sage's books did not balance. He was stealing from the troop. In the Mob, one bad deed wipes out a lifetime of good work. Stealing is a capital offense. Sage had to be killed. And who should kill him? Gangy Cohen. He could steer Sage without making him suspicious. They were best friends. A few years before, they had lived, along with Pep, in an apartment in Brooklyn, a hit man's bachelor pad. Their relationship would now reach a proper underworld conclusion.

Getting the men together was easy enough. It was the middle of summer, and everyone was up in the Jewish Alps. One afternoon Gangy phoned Sage and suggested a nighttime ride through the woods. A good way to relax. From there it was just a matter of getting some of the boys together. That afternoon Strauss went resort to resort, recruiting a crew.

Pretty Levine was staying with his wife at the Evans Hotel, near Loch Sheldrake. They were taking in the vistas—the mountains sloping out the window—when there was a knock on the door. It was Pep. "I heard you were in town," he said, leaning in the doorway.

"Do you want to come in?" said Pretty.

"No, I just decided to come by." Pep paused, then said, "Hey, Pretty, you got a car up here?"

"Yeah, I got it parked downstairs. Why?"

"Look, meet me down at your car at seven o'clock tonight. Don't be late. Okay? Good to see you. So long."

Pretty met Strauss that night in front of the hotel. Allie Tannenbaum was there, too. The three men got in Pretty's car, drove a few miles down the road, and pulled onto the shoulder. And they waited. Hours went by. It was one of those lonely country roads that winds through the trees. When Pretty asked what they were waiting for, Pep said, "Just wait."

At midnight a car came down the road. The headlights flashed once, very fast. "There it is," said Pep. "Follow that car. Not too close. Just follow."

Pretty was driving the crash car. The car ahead was being driven by a man he did not know. Also in that car were Gangy Cohen and Walter Sage. Pep watched the kill car closely as Pretty drove.

This story comes from testimony later given by Levine and Tannenbaum, so our point of view is the crash car, which, like a camera on a dolly, follows the action. We see a dashboard, a hood, a piece of road, and then the car ahead, where shapes move. Things are revealed. Noises. Sage is in the front passenger seat. Gangy is directly behind, a seat reserved for the mark's trusted friend. When a gangster rides shotgun, he looks at the man in back and asks himself, Will he kill me?

As the men in the kill car talked, Gangy, leaning forward, drove an ice pick into his friend's chest. Then, holding Sage tight with his left arm, he stabbed him thirty-one more times.

Pretty could see the struggle in the car ahead, arms flailing. In a cartoon, the air would be filled with jagged lines. He heard a scream. He saw the car swerve left, right, left, then off the road. As the nose went into a ditch, the back wheels came off the ground. Levine saw the back door open and a figure race into the woods.

When the crash car pulled up, the back wheels of the kill car were still spinning. As Pretty walked over, he saw the driver wiping off an ice pick. Every now and then he looked at the woods and shouted, "Come on, Gangy! Come back!"

No one knew why Gangy had run into the woods. Was it a joke?

The boys waited on the road awhile, then left. No one saw Gangy again. He had just disappeared. It was a great mystery.

The boys put Sage's body into Pretty's car and drove to Loch Sheldrake. When a lawyer later asked Pretty, "Were you in the car with Sage?" Levine thought a moment, then asked, "Alive?" They carried Sage into a boat, lashed a slot machine to his chest, rowed him out, and dumped the body. A few months later, when the corpse and the slot floated up, the message was clear to those who could read: Here's what happens when you steal.

A few years later, Pretty Levine and Dukey Maffeatore went to see a movie at the Loew's Pitkin in Brownsville, *Golden Boy,* a classic boxing picture written by Clifford Odets and starring William Holden and Barbara Stanwyck. In one scene, as the hero fights in the old Madison Square Garden, the camera sweeps the crowd, landing on a heckler. "Hey!" said Pretty. "That's Gangy Cohen!"

"Where?" asked Dukey.

"Up there—in the picture. The guy waving."

"That's him all right," said Dukey.

"Wow," said Pretty. "Wait till the troop hears this."

They left the movie and went to the corner. When they told the boys about Gangy, few believed them. There was an argument. Bets were made. Then everyone went to see *Golden Boy.* They were sitting side by side—Reles, Pep, Capone, Blue Jaw Magoon, Pretty, Dukey—when Gangy came on. "Well, I'll be damned," said Pep.

The troop later found out what had happened. After killing Walter Sage, Gangy had an epiphany few gangsters experience in time: *If they have me kill Walter, then, sooner or later, they will have someone else kill me.* By the time the kill car had pulled over, his mind was made up. He would run. He went for miles through the trees. The night closed in. The stars came out. He found a train station in a clearing. He bought a ticket and went as far west as the train would take him. Upon reaching California, he looked for work. He started in the movies as an extra. He worked his way up. He changed his name. He was now the actor Jack Gorden. A few years later, a police officer, who had long been looking for the missing Gangy Cohen, found him on screen in the movies, playing a cop. Gangy was brought back from California in handcuffs. He was tried. He was acquitted. He was a hero to the boys. If things got too rough, they could always go to Hollywood and become movie stars.

Here is what confused the troop about Gangy: Why quit such a great job for the whims of Hollywood? By the mid-thirties the boys were among the highest paid men in Brooklyn. Each was making around a hundred thousand a year. This money came partly from the retainer paid by Lepke for contract killing, partly from the odd jobs they did around Brooklyn. This was not Lepke or Lansky money. They were not millionaires. They were not capitalists. They had to work with their hands. Still, they were bringing home more cash than they probably ever dreamed possible. Most of them never made it past eighth grade. Most had been told, by teachers and cops and parents, that they were bound to fail. And here they were, in the midst of the Depression, the only men around who could afford to vacation, sleep late, drive new cars.

Of course, success brought new worries. They were hit hard by ambition. With their first taste of power they knew only that they wanted more. Members of the troop were trying to climb, which meant winning the favor of Lepke and his guns. And they soon came to see their rivals not as other gangs or cops, but as each other. Old friends came to resent old friends, as each encounter became a test, an establishing of position. They were riven by the kind of politics that sets worker against worker. Speaking of Reles, Blue Jaw Magoon once said, "He was mean and cheap. When he was with his superiors in the Mob, he wined and dined them, and made a show at splurging. With his equals or subordinates he would argue when it was his time to pay a check. But not with Mendy Weiss, Charlie the Bug, or other mobsters of a higher grade."

One night Blue Jaw went to dinner with Reles and Strauss. They ate lobster. After the meal Pep and the Kid argued over who should pay. So there they sat, old friends glaring at each other. Three hours passed before they agreed to split the bill. It is probably not unfair to say this argument was about more than money.

I suppose it is logical that once the troop had whipped their enemies (Shapiros, Ambergs) they would turn on each other. They were cantankerous men and needed someone to fight. I also suppose that once they began fighting each other, their downfall became inevitable. The system of killing they had designed was so sophisticated that maybe the only thing that could topple them was the rivalry that followed their success, a success that changed not only the dynamic of the group, but also the character of its members.

Even friends said Reles was changing. He had once been seen as an underdog. He was becoming just another bully. He swaggered around Brownsville, kicking in doors, roughing up punks. When his brother testified against him in court, he stabbed him. He was a great small-time hood, like a ball player who breaks all the minor league records but still cannot make the majors.

He was twenty-five. Twenty-five is the age of plans, of looking ahead, of the next moment and the moment after that just coming into focus. When he visited the future, he probably saw only himself: how he would come to dominate every situation, defeat every foe. He was riding on a kind of high-octane confidence, a belief that he could get out of any jam. Nothing struck him as fatal. That's how it was when he met Jake the Bum. Anyone else in that situation would say their prayers and wait to die. Maybe Reles was just too dumb to give up like that.

Jake the Bum was a criminal hack who had strayed into the troop's territory. Late one night, in a crowded club in East New York, he had words with Reles, who said something like "Next time I see you, I'll kill you."

"Not if I see you first," said Jake. "Not if I got the drop on you."

"Think so?" said Reles. "Well, even if you get the drop on me, even if you have every advantage, I will still kill you. That's a promise. I am telling you now."

"You little loudmouth bastard," said Jake. "Let's see how tough you are dead."

A few months later Jake ran into Reles in Red Hook. "Hey, Kid," said Jake. "Ready to die?"

Reles didn't have his gun. The cops were on him for every little thing, so he had to travel unarmed. And here he was, far from home, looking into the snub-nosed .38 of Jake the Bum. "You win," said Reles. "I'm a loudmouth. You proved it. And now I'm good as dead. You win. But look, Jake. What's it going to get you? The Combination will take care of you eventually. They will have to. You can't kill one of them without yourself being killed. You know that. And what's the percentage in both of us getting rubbed out? But together? Together we might do business."

Jake frowned. It made sense. The men went into a saloon. They talked for hours, drinking as Reles explained a future where Jake and

Kid Twist are partners, running rackets, getting rich. As they walked out, arm in arm, Reles told Jake about the problems he had been having with the cops. "You know, if you're my partner, you shouldn't carry the gun so much," he said. "The cops shake me down every time they see me. They will do the same to you. Besides, if you're with me, you don't need the gun. The threat of the Combination is all you need. Hell, give me the gun and let me get rid of it."

When Jake handed over the .38, Reles said, "You stupid fuck. I told you I would kill you."

Jake's body was found in the weeds a few days later. Shot twice in the head with his own gun.

Reles thought he could get himself out of any jam, and usually he could. It was his strength. Confidence alone can often win the day. It was also his weakness—a fatal flaw. Success had taught him the wrong lessons: that there were no limits, that his temper could be trusted, that he would never let himself down, that he was important. He could probably not picture a world big enough to shake him off. When I read about the bad things that later happened to Reles, I can't help but think he had been set up: by circumstances, by success, by the fates, which were about to withdraw their favor.

In 1934 Reles pulled his sedan into a parking garage in midtown. He honked. No one came. His friends were griping in the backseat. He honked again. Nothing. He laid on the horn. Finally an attendant appeared, a black man named Charles Battle. Battle told Reles to pipe down. The friends in back broke up laughing. Stepping from the car, Reles told the man to watch himself. There was a threat in his language, something the attendant could not hear. Or maybe he just didn't care. Battle told Reles to go to hell, that he was not here to make him look the big man in front of his friends.

Reles had a violent temper. He searched every sentence for the insult. When he closed his eyes, he must have seen shapes and colors, red, black, orange. Maybe, just before he lost control, he saw blood or flames or sparks. Probably before he knew what he was doing, Reles was punching Battle. He hit him again and again. When Battle fell, Reles went on kicking until the attendant was just a bloody thing on the floor. His temper, which always got him out of trouble, was getting

Arnold Rothstein, the Moses of the underworld. [UPI/Corbis-Bettman]

Jacob "Gurrah" Shapiro, one of the Gorilla boys. [UPI/Corbis-Bettman]

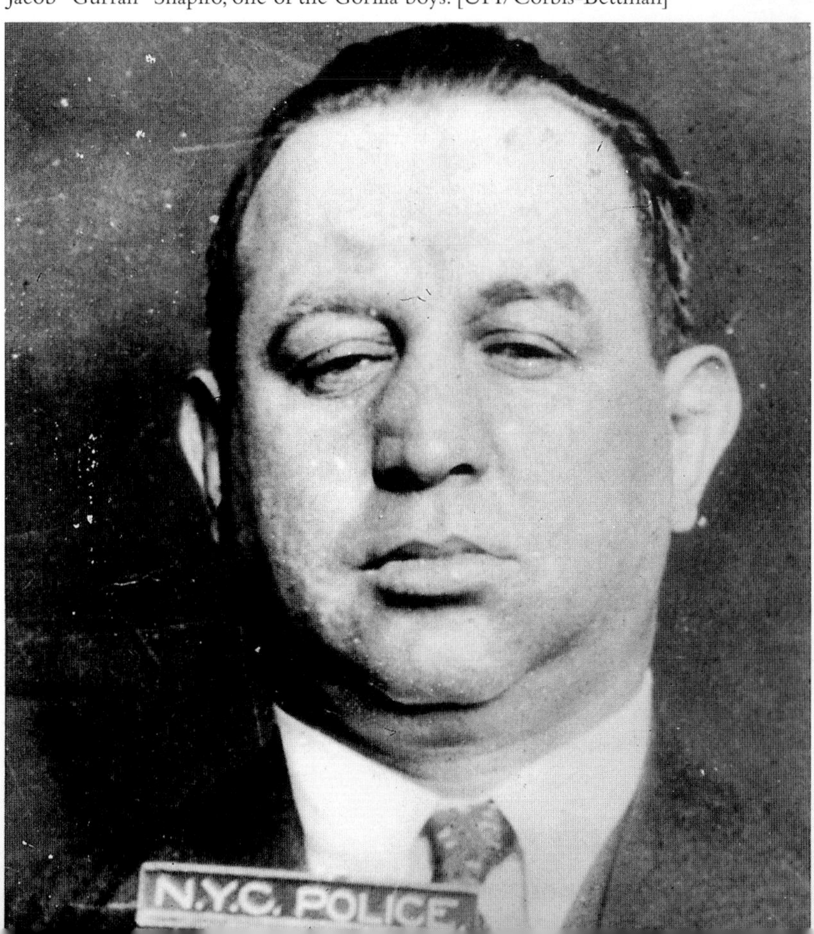

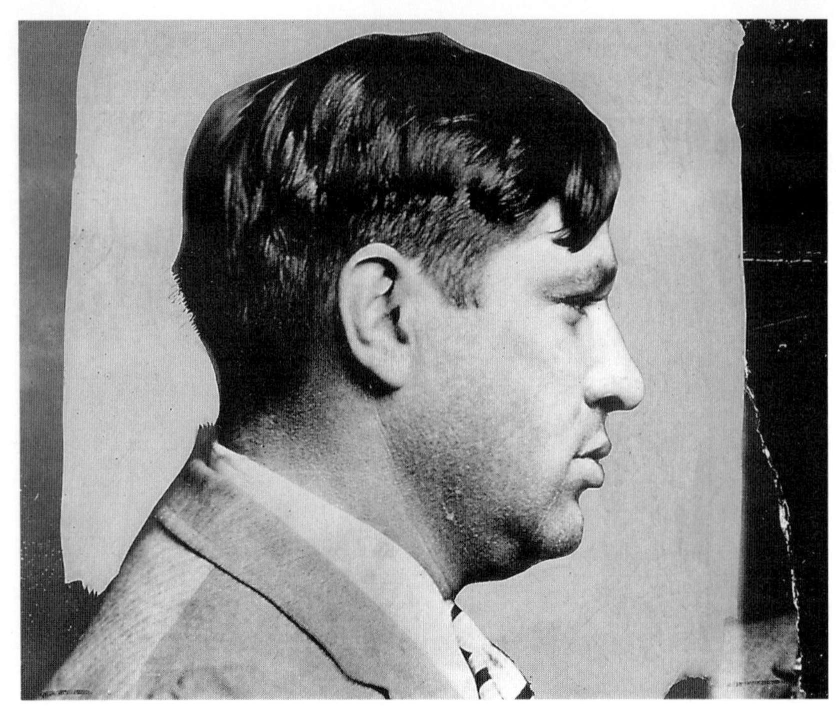

Emmanuel "Mendy" Weiss, always beating, stealing, and smoking cigars. [Culver Pictures]

Albert Anastasia, who ran the daily operations of Murder Incorporated. [Culver Pictures]

Benjamin "Bugsy" Siegel in 1940, the best-looking thug in the underworld. [UPI/Corbis-Bettman]

Me in 1972, dressed like Bugsy Siegel.

Abraham "Kid Twist" Reles, searching each sentence for the insult. [UPI/Corbis-Bettman]

Dutch Schultz found "Not Guilty" in Malone, New York. The star-struck crowd followed him back to his hotel. [Associated Press]

Mayor Fiorello LaGuardia in 1934, busting up underworld slot machines. [UPI/Corbis-Bettman]

Thomas Dewey, the straight-arrow boy prosecutor who took on the mob in the 1930s. [UPI/Corbis-Bettman]

Burton Turkus (with witness), the Brooklyn prosecutor who sent the boys, one after another, to the death house. They called him Mr. Arsenic. [UPI/Corbis-Bettman]

DETECTIVE DIVISION
CIRCULAR NO. 11
AUGUST 8, 1939

POLICE DEPARTMENT
CITY OF NEW YORK

CLASSIFICATION

$25,000 REWARD

DEAD OR ALIVE

TWENTY-FIVE THOUSAND DOLLARS will be paid by the City of New York for Information leading to the capture of "LEPKE" BUCHALTER, aliases LOUIS BUCHALTER, LOUIS BUCKHOUSE, LOUIS KAWAR, LOUIS KAUVAR, LOUIS COHEN, LOUIS SAFFER, LOUIS BRODSKY.

WANTED FOR CONSPIRACY AND EXTORTION

The Person or Persons who give Information Leading to the Arrest of "LEPKE" will be fully protected, his or her identity will never be revealed. The information will be received in absolute confidence.

RIGHT HAND

LEFT HAND

DESCRIPTION — Age, 42 years; white; Jewish; height, 5 feet, 5½ inches; weight, 170 pounds; build, medium; black hair; brown eyes; complexion dark; married, one son Harold, age about 18 years.

PECULARITIES—Eyes, piercing and shifting; nose, large, somewhat blunt at nostrils; ears, prominent and close to head; mouth, large, slight dimple left side; right-handed; suffering from kidney ailment.

Frequents baseball games.

Is wealthy; has connections with all important mobs in the United States. Involved in racketeering in Unions and Fur Industry, uses Strong-arm methods. Influential.

This Department holds indictment warrant charging Conspiracy and Extortion, issued by the Supreme Court, Extraordinary Special and Trial Terms, New York County.

Kindly search your Prison Records as this man may be serving a Prison sentence for some minor offense.

If located, arrest and hold as a fugitive and advise the THE DETECTIVE DIVISION, POLICE DEPARTMENT, NEW YORK CITY, by wire.

Information may be communicated in Person or by Telephone or Telegraph, Collect to the undersigned, or may be forwarded direct to the DETECTIVE DIVISION, POLICE DEPARTMENT, NEW YORK CITY.

LEWIS J. VALENTINE, Police Commissioner

TELEPHONE: SPring 7-3100, SPring 7-2722, SPring 7-1366 or CAnal 6-2000

Lepke Wanted Dead or Alive: The poster tacked to lampposts and post office peg-boards around the world sent Lepke into hiding. [UPI/Corbis-Bettman]

Kid Twist Reles (center) and Tick-Tock Tannenbaum (left), rats ready to hang old friends. [UPI/Corbis-Bettman]

Charlie "the Bug" Workman in 1941, charged with the murder of Dutch Schultz. [UPI/Corbis-Bettman]

Abe Reles (right) and Allie Tannenbaum on their way to court in 1941, dressed like a vaudeville team, in matching hats and coats. [UPI/Corbis-Bettman]

Harry "Pittsburgh Phil" Strauss on trial for murder in 1941. The beard was to convince the jury he was crazy. At his right sits Martin "Buggsy" Goldstein. [Culver Pictures]

Pep Strauss (left) and Buggsy Goldstein seemed to enjoy their last trip, a train ride to the death house at Sing Sing. [Associated Press]

During the trip, Strauss threw his shoe at a photographer as Goldstein hid behind his newspaper and cops laughed. [Culver Pictures]

Louis Capone passing a quiet moment in the police station. [UPI/Corbis-Bettman]

Louis Capone (left) and Mendy Weiss cuffed together for their last ride up the river to Sing Sing. Dopey sightseers look in the car windows. [UPI/Corbis-Bettman]

Louis "Lepke" Buchalter, surrounded by G-Men, is still the only boss in mob history to suffer execution. [UPI/Corbis-Bettman]

Herbie Cohen (my father, top row center), Larry King on his left, and the boys in the Bensonhurst clubhouse tried hard to look like gangsters. Note the hat-wearing cigar-smokers in the bottom row.

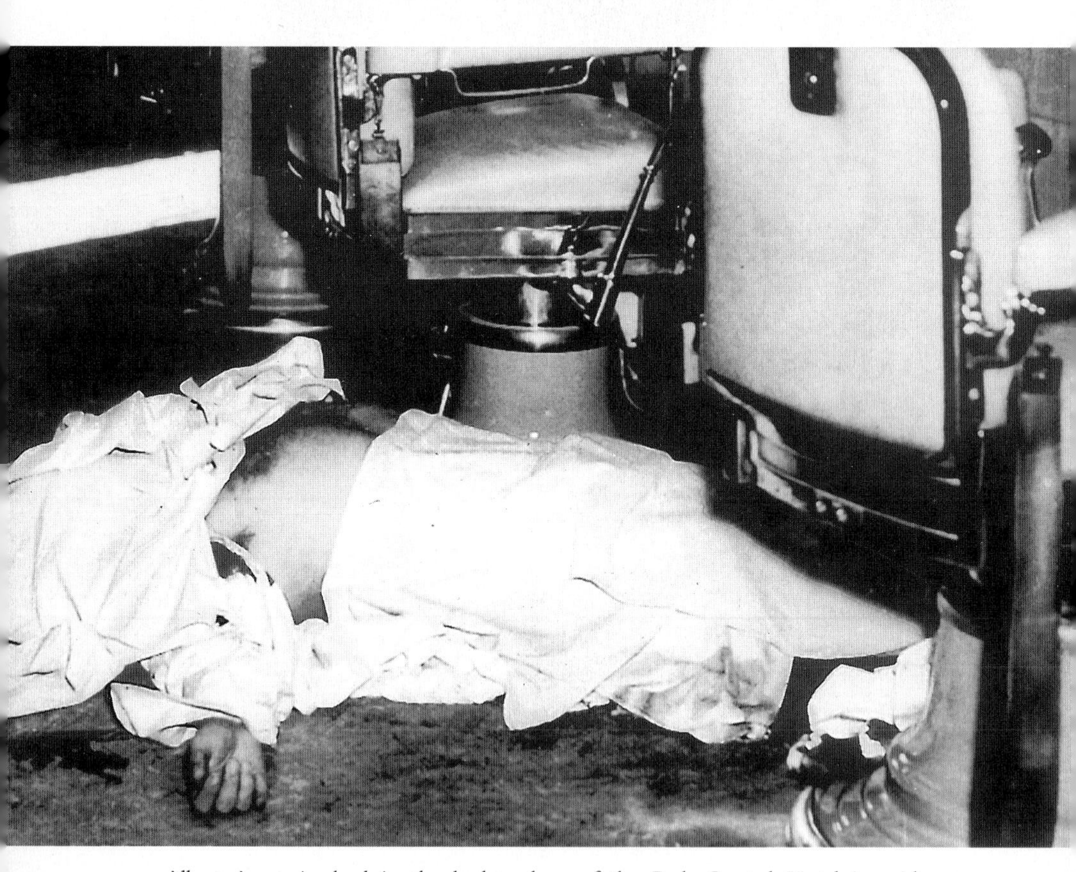

Albert Anastasia dead in the barber shop of the Park Central Hotel in midtown Manhattan. [Daily News, L.P.]

The Warriors on the stoop. My father is at the top right. Larry, as always, is at his side.

Army of Occupation. My father (far left) and his pals in a West German forest in the fall of 1954.

Charlie "Lucky" Luciano in exile in Italy in 1955, where he wore smoking jackets and dreamed of Delancey Street corned beef. [UPI/Corbis-Bettman]

Meyer Lansky in Miami Beach in the 1970s, just another schnorrer out for a walk with his dog. [Historical Museum of Southern Florida]

Me in a junkyard in Illinois, a suburban high school student pretending he's in Brooklyn.

My father, my brother, and I (left) at my sister's wedding in 1990. "Remember, Richie, nothing is more important than the family."

Sid Young, Asher Dann, Herbie Cohen, Larry King (left to right) in 1996, still hanging out, still talking about Jewish gangsters.

him into it now. As careful as he was while killing for the Syndicate, he was just as careless here. He was beating an attendant in a garage where he was known. The next day the man who came to relieve Battle, a man named Snider who looked a lot like Battle, was found dead behind the garage, stab wounds in his chest and neck. The cops figured Reles had come back later that night and killed Snider, whom he must have mistaken for Battle—who was himself recovering at home. Reles was charged with the murder.

It was a scandal in Brooklyn. A lot of people hoped Reles would die in the electric chair, or at least spend his life in prison. But the evidence wasn't there. Reles was instead convicted of assault, a misdemeanor. The judge was angry. He felt the system had been cheated. He gave Reles the maximum sentence: three years. "I had hoped for a felony conviction," said the judge. "I could have sent him away for ten years." Then, giving Reles a kind of backhanded compliment, he added: "Why, this man is the worst character in greater New York. He's worse than Dillinger!"

Reles was sent to Sing Sing. It should have been easy time. He read, wrote, talked to guards. A visitor came each week with an envelope—his share of troop proceeds. Yet this experience broke something in him. He forever after seemed haunted by the idea of again losing his autonomy to the grid of prison life. Most of the Jewish gangsters had been to prison as young men. It occupied a small, almost romantic place in their minds, a part of their education. They did not go to jail in the twenties or early thirties. They had by then perfected a system that kept them on the street. So when they were again sent away, many realized prison was worse than they remembered. It was harder now that they were older, fatter, slower, more successful. Jail was a place for young men, a place to learn—not a place to pass your middle years. Starting in 1935, Lepke and Gurrah learned the same lesson, serving two years in a federal pen for racketeering. Like Reles, they probably realized they could not go through it again, a realization that would go a long way toward explaining their future decisions.

When Reles was released from Sing Sing in October 1936, he had just $1,600 put away. He went to Florida to relax. When he came back to Brownsville, he found the troop going as before, only in all capital letters: MORE BEATINGS, MORE KILLINGS. Like many successful people, the members of the troop were becoming caricatures of their youthful selves, imitating now what came naturally then. Strauss was running things, and the business was touched by his brazen style. Reles was slow getting back in the swing. Prison had changed him. He was not sure where he fit in. "I had nothing to say," he later explained. "I just came out of the pen. I was no big shot then. I was a bum. They were the big shots when I came out."

Most people have never heard of Jewish gangsters. They do not believe they ever existed. The very idea of a Jewish gangster goes against basic stereotypes of Jews, stereotypes that explain the place of Jews in the world. Jews are physically unthreatening office creatures. I once heard a comedian refer jokingly to the Jewish Mafia. The very idea seemed absurd. The mere mention of a Jewish gang broke up the audience. "You know why the Jewish Mafia never worked," he said. "Because the nicknames weren't tough enough. There was Matzoball Goldberg and Hanukkah Harry Fishbein." Sometimes, when I see this comedian's bit rerun on cable, I imagine Pep Strauss entering stage left and cutting him belly to chin.

Even the few Jewish gangsters who are widely known are viewed through these stereotypes. They are seen as number crunchers, financial geniuses who could have worked their craft as easily on Wall Street as on Hester Street. When paging through one of the many true crimes books I own, like *World Encyclopedia of Organized Crime* or *Blood Letters and Badmen,* I look up "Jewish Gangsters," and the paragraph usually opens with a picture of Meyer Lansky above a paragraph that describes him as a kind of accountant to the Mob. How can people believe in violent Jewish mobsters? Jews don't do that.

Jews themselves have suppressed the memory of Jewish gangsters. It was once seen as a major community problem. There were conferences. Now, less than two generations later, even Jews find the idea unbelievable. They have kept before them the image of Holocaust: Never forget. Never forget when you were victims. They have pushed aside the image of the gangster: Forget. Forget when you were bullies. When I tell old Jews about this book, they change the subject. The blood drains from their faces. Sometimes they argue with me. When I told a friend about my book, he was upset. He said it would be a self-hating book, a book to make Jews look bad. I would not mind Jews sometimes looking that kind of bad. I want the freedom to be a bully.

Without that freedom, my decision to *not* be a bully doesn't mean very much. I am a Jew. What choice do I have?

My friend's reaction may have to do with his upbringing. He grew up in Manhattan. His ancestors were uptown Jews, and for uptown Jews the downtown gangsters were a shame, a *schanda*. They tried hard to disassociate from that rabble. My father grew up in Bensonhurst, among the rabble, those descendants of Eastern European immigrants. Of course, there is not really a class consciousness among most Jews. There is no rabble in Jewish history, only the lucky and unlucky. And now we are all the elect in America.

But even among those who claim to know the story of the Jewish gangster, one thing you never hear about are Jewish drug runners. They are off the map, beyond the pale even for the Brooklyn-born rabble. Even Jews who love to romanticize criminals don't talk about it. They just didn't exist.

The first major American drug dealer was probably Arnold Rothstein. "It became increasingly obvious to us that dope traffic in the United States was being directed from one source," a late twenties federal crime report reads. "More and more, our information convinced us that Arnold Rothstein was that source." For Rothstein, drugs did not have the fall-of-civilization taint they carry today. When he was growing up, drugs were just another colorful aspect of downtown life. Opium dens were strung along the harum-scarum Chinatown intersection of Doyer, Mott, and Pell Streets, which was called the Bloody Angle. More people were killed on the Bloody Angle each year than anywhere else in the world. The killing was done mostly by Chinese hatchet men, who carried knives up their sleeves and fled into the Chinese theater, which was underlain by secret passages that led killers to the safety of the crowded market.

East Side gangsters met in the dens, where they could plan and schmooze as they got high. They sat hollow eyed in the gloomy basements, smoking in the half-light of some old Chinaman's idea of luxury, laundry strung wall to wall, a bed or couch creaking beneath their weight. As a kid, Rothstein spent hours there, coolly watching as thugs wandered up from Hester and Delancey Streets, slipped off their shoes, picked up a hookah. "Many of these guys were opium smokers," John Cusack of the Federal Bureau of Narcotics told me. "Luciano was an opium smoker. I'm almost positive Lansky smoked opium. A lot of these Jewish guys smoked. It kept them calm."

This aspect of East Side life was captured in the Sergio Leone film *Once upon a Time in America.* It is interesting to me that the only movie that makes a real effort to portray Jewish gangsters was made by an Italian director best known for westerns. It also seems fitting. Whenever I read one of Isaac Babel's stories about the Jewish gangsters of Russia, they remind me of westerns: in a world where normal, bourgeois morality has been inverted, the hero rides the void in outline against the sun, which is always just going down or coming up. Within this world Leone shows the opium den as a temple, a reprieve, a sanctuary from where the chaos of the street can be seen through a sheen of smoke.

At the end of the movie, one of the gangsters, played by Robert De Niro, comes into a lavish den, slips off his shoes, and takes the pipe. And for a moment, as his eyes lose focus, you sense that maybe the whole thing is a dream. And maybe the story of the Jews is also a dream—bondage in Egypt, destruction of the Temple, exile, shtetl, pogroms, crossing the ocean, America—all just flickering patterns in the smoke. For the Jewish gangsters, and for a lot of other people, too, drugs offered a way to believe things could have happened a different way.

For much of America's history, there was no such thing as an illegal drug. That was a silly idea, like an illegal apple. Then, in the mid–nineteenth century, when the government started to ban certain narcotics, drugs were smuggled in from Europe and the Far East. But it was a slapdash affair—not a business. Rothstein changed that. He saw Repeal coming and knew drugs could fill the void left by alcohol. Here was another vice that seemed victimless, where the government was legislating morality, where society had lost the capacity to give grown Americans what they desired. So in the late twenties Rothstein retooled a mechanism he had built to carry booze. It would now carry, among other things, heroin and cocaine. It was as natural as a car factory retooling, on the eve of war, to make weapons. And it was yet another of the shameful, unintended side effects of Prohibition, which built a system that remains a blueprint for smuggling drugs into America.

Rothstein put together a team, a group of young men to operate his narcotics empire. His first lieutenant was Louis Lepke, who hired dealers to move the drugs and make sure no other wiseguys hijacked shipments. Rothstein also hired a field agent to take care of supply. In those years drugs were easy to come by. Cocaine, heroin, and morphine were made legally in pharmaceutical plants in Europe. "Every country had eight or ten drug factories," John Cusack told me. "You could go to certain regions of France, and just breathing the air would get you high."

Rothstein's field agent spent several months a year in Europe, going factory to factory, cutting deals. He was a kind of criminal Willie Loman, out there on a shoeshine and a smile. His name was Yasha Katzenberg, and he was one of the great mysterious figures of the Jewish underworld.

When Rothstein died in 1928, his drug operation was taken over by Lepke. Then, in 1931 the League of Nations drafted a treaty prohibiting much of the world's drug production. Each country could now produce only as much of a narcotic as was needed for domestic medical use. In the coming years, as country after country signed the treaty, which was fully ratified in 1934, Lepke's drug supply ran dry. In the mid-thirties, in a last-ditch effort to get something going, he sent Katzenberg east.

Yasha vanished into China, leaving behind a trail of letters. He turned up months later in the hills around Shanghai, surrounded by an army of Chinese thugs. He taught them how to make heroin. He built a factory in a river valley. Heroin was soon flowing back to the Lower East Side. On the eve of the Second World War, as Japanese soldiers stormed Manchuria, Yasha kept on. In a time of chaos, he functioned smoothly. He was like some ancient Mongol warlord, with his kingdom and his army. In the late thirties his operation netted Lepke around $10 million.

Katzenberg was Russian born and grew up on the East Side. I do not know what he looked like, but I have tried to imagine him. I see his eyes as mirrors, reflecting not what he is looking at, but what he will see: mountains, rivers, wars. I imagine him tall and slender, wearing a hood, taking his time—something long prophesied, a nomad who has crossed wastes to get here. Or maybe he was completely unremarkable, just another curly-haired Jew boy in back of Hebrew class, saying the words but thinking only of the presents his bar mitzvah will bring. To me, Yasha Katzenberg was the ultimate example of the wandering Jew, going country to country, east to west, always on the other side of the glass, lost in the wilderness.

In the late thirties, when officials at last figured out what

Katzenberg was up to, the League of Nations declared him an international menace. A few years later Yasha was indicted, along with Lepke and twenty-eight others, for violation of narcotic laws. I don't know what happened to him after that.

As trade in narcotics grew, so did the mechanism to fight it. In the twenties the government created the Federal Bureau of Narcotics to go after smugglers and dealers. At first the FBN, the forerunner to the Drug Enforcement Agency, was like a group of men working in the dark, hoping something would catch their eye. Lepke was then operating an opium plant on Seymour Avenue in Brooklyn. In 1935 it blew up. It was hard to miss. From then on Lepke, whether he knew it or not, was being watched, his drug shipments tracked and followed. In the end, drugs gave Lepke what they give so many serious users: a short, intense high followed by withdrawal and ruin.

Before the creation of the FBN, few in law enforcement understood organized crime. Local cops knew about gangsters in their own city, but how could they know about the national Syndicate? These were state and municipal cops: they could see only the part of the picture that was under their feet. National trends were a mystery. Even the best cops, those who wanted the truth, knew little of the conferences where people like Lansky and Lepke governed the underworld. And when cops found a gangster who would talk, they still learned little. For gangsters, talking can be just another way of saying nothing, of distracting cops as truth slips out the door. For police, it was like adding up a column of numbers and still coming up with zero. Some experts said the criminals were just being true to the Omerta, the code of silence that the Mafia had brought from Sicily.

For a long time the only organization in any position to map the underworld was the FBI. Founded in 1908, the bureau was to go after criminals (kidnappers, smugglers) who crossed state lines. Big-time gangsters, who ran drugs and booze state to state, should have been prime targets. But for some reason, J. Edgar Hoover, who then headed the FBI, was not interested in the Mafia. He didn't even believe the Mafia existed. He thought it was a fairy tale, the kind of goblin mayors cook up to explain away problems. When investigators came forward with evidence of the vast criminal conspiracy, he dismissed the idea as absurd. He told reporters, "There is no Mafia in America."

Why did Hoover deny the existence of organized crime? Some say he just didn't want to believe it. If he admitted there was an American

Mafia, he would have been obligated to fight it—a daunting task with no assured outcome. The gangsters were well connected politically, with access to the best lawyers. "The Mafia is so powerful that entire police forces or even a Mayor's office can be under Mafia control," William Sullivan, a top FBI official, wrote in his memoir, *The Bureau: My Thirty Years in Hoover's FBI.* "That's why Hoover was afraid to let us tackle it. He was afraid we'd show up poorly. Why take the risk?"

Others say the Syndicate was just low on Hoover's list. He was too busy attacking those he considered a real threat: civil rights leaders, Communists. After all, what was so bad about gangsters? They were really a lot like Hoover—men who know the power of information. "He thought organized crime constituted no danger to the established order," wrote Albert Fried in *The Rise and Fall of the Jewish Gangster in America.* "Syndicate members were in fact pillars of the status quo. They had a vested interest in the free enterprise system, in America's triumph over Communism, over anything that threatened their specific opportunities."

Others sense something more sinister in Hoover's indifference to organized crime. What if the mobsters had something on him? What about all those afternoons he spent at the track? What about the betting tips he got from Frank Costello? And what about the recent revelations? Hoover in a dress. The Mafia knew everything else, why wouldn't they know this, too? Information is power. Maybe it was like the scene in *The Godfather, Part II* where the senator from Nevada wakes up next to a dead prostitute. Maybe Hoover was beholden. For some, a high official in a dress is just too fantastic not to explain a lot of other things. How could Hoover's cross-dressing not have affected American history? To such people I say this: J. Edgar Hoover wore a garter belt for the same reason as everyone else—to hold up his stockings.

Or maybe it is more simple. Maybe Hoover just underestimated the gangsters. Maybe he saw them as little more than brutish thugs, clearly not smart enough to create a national Syndicate. Maybe he felt about Italian and Jewish gangsters the way many Americans felt about the Japanese before Pearl Harbor—a bother, not a threat.

The work of the FBN changed all that. FBN agents were the first to glimpse the sophistication of the underworld. Tracking narcotics showed them how the Syndicate worked, how it was built. For agents, drugs were like a radioactive dye injected into a heart that shows doctors how the blood flows. Watching shipments move through all kinds of valves and arteries, they came to understand the system assembled by Rothstein in the first days of Prohibition. "We at the Narcotics Bureau were the only ones who really knew about the Mafia," John Cusack told me. "Why did we know? Because we took the time to study it; because we knew how smart these men were; because we were working in Italy as far back as the thirties; because we followed the drugs through the maze."

For over twenty years Hoover ignored this work. "There is no Mafia in America." He ignored it in the thirties, forties, and much of the fifties. He ignored it right up until 1957, when two cops in rural New York made a bust that changed everything. It was a flash of lightning that illuminates a landscape: fields, hills, telephone poles, and over sixty gangsters conspiring in the dark.

The local cops had received an anonymous tip: Keep an eye on Joseph Barbara's place. Something is about to happen. Barbara had come to America from Castellammare, Sicily, in 1921. After early trouble on the East Side, he moved upstate. He prospered. By 1957 he was said to run the Buffalo Mob. He was also president of the Canada Dry Bottling Company in Endicott, New York. He remained friends with many of the East Side gangsters. He lived in a ranch house outside Apalachin, New York.

The house was large and secluded and had been host to many Syndicate meetings. When the cops drove by in 1957, it must have been like stumbling on a car dealership in the trees. Everywhere black sedans with out-of-state plates. Inside, the owners of the cars were attending a meeting that had been called by Vito Genovese. They were discussing the future of the crime family set up by Lucky Luciano. Genovese was making a grab for power. The cops turned into the driveway.

The men inside had spent the afternoon talking around a table. Paunchy old gangsters. Chins had fallen, eyes lay hooded, but the threat was still there—you just had to look for it. These were still the most dangerous men in America. From New York, in addition to Genovese, there were, among others, Carlo Gambino, Joseph Bonanno, Joseph Profaci, Gerardo Catena, Paul Castellano. Meyer Lansky and Doc Stacher had been invited but did not attend. Santo Trafficante Jr. had come from Florida; Gabriel Mannarino from Pennsylvania; Frank DiSimone from Los Angeles; Joseph Civello from

Dallas; James Colletti from Colorado; Frank Zito from Illinois; John Scalish from Cleveland; Joseph Ida from Philly; Sam Giancana from Chicago. When they talked, the room was full of double meanings. When they did not talk, the room was held in the kind of silence it takes more than one person to make. But what you would have most noticed were the men who were not there, those who had died or were sent to jail or into exile. More than anything, a life in organized crime is a war of attrition.

Looking out the window, someone spotted the patrol car heading up the driveway. He shouted to the others. Never before had these men been found in the same place. What would happen if the cops realized they worked together? They panicked. They fled the house like high school kids fleeing a party when that word hits the room: Cops! From above, you would have seen gangsters pouring out doors on every side of the house and others coming through windows; you would have seen hats and arms moving in patterns across the grass; you would have heard that metallic jangle—change and keys in pockets—that fills the air whenever old men run.

Some made it to cars, got a key in the ignition, and coasted along country roads. Others scrambled down trails, raising dust and dirt. As they ran, not wanting to be caught with too much cash, they set bills in the wind. Others busted through bushes and brambles and danced off into cathedrals of pine. They were at first running, then jogging, then walking, then standing, hunched over, getting their breath.

Some cops gave chase, shouting, shooting in the air. Others called for backup. Blocks were set on all the local roads. So one by one, state troopers stopped the gangsters in sedans. Most of those who had gone into the woods came back. Where could they go? Within a few hours the cops had rounded up almost sixty men. When they were brought in, the gangsters told the cops they had come to visit a sick friend. Barbara had suffered a heart attack a few months before, but no one believed this story.

Sam Giancana was one of the few who got away. Walking through the woods, loafers crunching twigs, sleeves rolled up, he must have looked like a lunatic, the remains of a crazy businessman. He was built like wire, with bristly black hair. He wore dark glasses, Panama hats, and pin-striped suits. Looking back from a distant hill, he would have seen police lights, cars, cuffed gangsters, cops, disaster. It later turned out that Lansky had tipped off the cops. He had been fighting a low-grade war with Genovese. How better to discredit a foe than have his party guests locked in jail?

The cops charged the gangsters with conspiracy. They were tried and convicted—a conviction later overturned. But none of that mattered. What mattered was how elected officials and the public reacted when the story hit the papers. No Mafia in America? Never again would the gangsters get a free ride from the FBI.

"Apalachin was the grand council of the Mafia," said John Cusack. "Over the years, there had been national meetings in Chicago, Colorado, Florida, Las Vegas, Atlantic City. This one just happened to be in upstate New York. And it at last convinced the FBI we had been telling the truth all along: that there was a Mafia that organized crime not just within the cities, but throughout the country and the world. How else could they explain all these men, notorious in all their local cities, coming together in a small town in upstate New York? That meeting changed the way Americans looked at crime forever."

A few months after the arrest, the New York State Legislature scheduled hearings. When state senators asked Hoover for information on the gangsters, he referred them to the FBN. When hearings began that fall, the FBN sent a young agent to New York to explain the meeting in Apalachin. The agent they sent was John Cusack.

John Cusack went to work for the FBN in 1947. He was an undercover agent, trying to make buys and bust dealers. Working his way up, he was soon going after traffickers and suppliers. After thirty years with the bureau, and later the DEA, he was forced to retire at sixty-five. He was not ready and instead moved to the Bahamas, where he oversees drug enforcement. He has been very successful. Five years ago, when he took the job, the country was among the top spots for international drug traffic. It is no longer ranked.

Cusack works in a white stone colonial building that sits on a hill above Nassau. Looking out his window, he can see down a narrow brick street to the harbor. In the afternoon, when the fishing boats come in, the street fills with chatter. When I met him one winter morning, he shook my hand and fell back into his chair. His desk was covered with mugs and pens and paper. He has a large, chiseled head, stripped-down features, and lucid blue eyes. He was seventy-three years old. "So you want to know about Jewish gangsters?" he said. "It all seems so long ago. A different world. Sometimes I hardly believe it existed." He frowned, then said, "But other times it seems like yesterday. Some of those men were the most interesting people I have ever met. And, of course, some were not."

When Cusack started with the FBN, there were still dozens of Jewish drug dealers roaming New York City, the remnants of Rothstein's machine. Before our appointment, he had written their names on two sheets of white notebook paper. Next to each name he had jotted a few notes to refresh his memory. Over the next few hours he carefully read each name, then told me what he could remember. Cusack has an expressive way of talking. His voice is low and calm, but his words are full of color, pictures, flashes of light. As he read a name, that gangster seemed to file in, nod at me, and stand in the corner, holding his hat as Cusack discussed him. Rothstein bounded in with his diamond tie clip and gold watch; Lepke stormed in, eyes blazing; Lansky shuffled in, shook my hand, and said something about his ulcer. *Oy, gevalt! This pain in my side!*

"And there were dozens of others," Cusack told me. "So many, and all of them dead. There was Solly Gelb, who lived on West End Avenue and was always into drugs. And Solly Gordon, who was into drugs going back to 1914. And Tudi Schoenfeld, Artie West, Niggy Rutkin, Harry Koch, Sam Haas, Moe Taubman, Harry Hechinger. There is a very famous hardware store in Washington called Hechinger's," Cusack said, looking up. "Harry was the founder's brother. As young men, they had been in the machinery business. They worked in one of those big buildings in SoHo.

"So one brother goes into hardware, the other into opium. We all make choices. Harry was a big-time smoker. A pipe fiend. I arrested him for it. One night, in the fall of 1947, my group leader had information that a guy named Murray Krim, a low-level hustler, was running a drug thing from his place. When we went over, Murray wouldn't let us in. He said he was in mourning—sitting shivah. When we heard that, we said, 'Okay,' and left. Coming downstairs, we ran into Harry Hechinger. He's got this big tray wrapped in cellophane. We figured, Aha! We searched the tray, and it turned out to be a beautiful array of cookies. We apologized and left."

Some of the gangsters were brilliant men. Their restless, inventive minds were lit from within: by poverty, necessity, ambition. "What about Tolly Greenberg?" said Cusack, leaning back. "Tolly did something very smart. In most of the South, there was no heroin, no morphine. And during Prohibition, those people were looking for something to do. Also, there were drug addicts passing through who needed a fix. So Tolly took a piece of pharmaceutical equipment and converted it. He rebuilt this machine so it would turn liquid heroin into pills, which he then sold in the South as morphine pills. He made a killing."

When I think of someone like Tolly Greenberg, I think of my grandpa Ben. The same restless energy drove both men toward invention. Ben worked in a diner and was tired of clunky sugar dispensers and so converted an existing piece of machinery, a tea bagger, creating the first sugar packet. Tolly worked in narcotics and knew there was a southern market for drugs and so converted an existing piece of machinery, creating the first morphine pill.

I would like to say there is some great difference between these men. I would like to say Tolly was working for evil, my grandfather for good, but I don't know if it's that simple. I sometimes think the moment of invention, the flash of insight, is itself the good thing, a reflection of the divine spark. What becomes of that invention, the value it is given by the world, is not the whole story.

And then the question of motivation. Was Tolly excited when he finally got his pill machine to work? Did he rush home to tell his wife? Or did he think he was involved in something wicked? I did not know Tolly at all, but I think I knew my grandfather even less. Tolly's motivations seem clear to me: money, power. My grandfather's remain a mystery. Was it money he was after or something else? I think of his ambition as an Abstract painting: something I don't understand, something that makes me feel stupid. Besides, who can know how their work fits into the greater scheme of things? Who has the imagination to feel how their actions affect others? It seems impossible to know. Well, both Tolly and my grandfather are dead now, so maybe they have the answers. Or maybe not.

Most Jews I know do not believe in heaven or hell. Or they just do not think it matters. How you live this life, that's what matters. Depending on how you live, you can find heaven or hell here on earth, a view most of the gangsters could have confirmed. For them, heaven, hell, redemption, damnation—it was all in Brooklyn. Few gangsters had to reach the next world to be punished. The reckoning began in the parking lots, garages, street corners, and rooftops of East New York, Brownsville, Williamsburg. If anything, God seems more present in the underworld; every time a gangster dies, another judgment has been passed. The punishment that found the drug dealers was often the worst. "That was the curse of it," says Cusack, frowning. "These guys started dealing drugs, and before they knew it, the drugs were dealing them."

They wandered the streets, their elegant suits crumpled like pajamas. Even the most powerful of these men, those with their hands on the levers, could be sucked through the needle. What about Waxey Gordon, who years before had gone to Rothstein with the plan to bootleg alcohol? "Just think about him," said Cusack. "For Waxey, narcotics was the last stop on the way down."

His real name was Irving Wexler. He was first called Waxey on the Lower East Side, where he waxed his fingers to help him slide wallets from the pockets of strangers. In the twenties he was making around $2 million a year. He was like an early underground version of Ralph Lauren: a Jewish city kid who turns himself into a WASP-y country gentleman. He built a huge mansion on the palisades in New Jersey. He filled the library with Thackeray, Dickens, and Scott, every book leather bound, not a binding broken. It was like the scene in *The Great Gatsby* where Nick Carraway comes across a man going through Gatsby's library. Waving his hand toward the shelves, the man says, "Absolutely real—have pages and everything. I thought they'd be a nice durable cardboard. . . . What thoroughness. What realism. Knew when to stop, too—didn't cut the pages."

Waxey went to prison in 1933: income tax evasion. Ten years later, when he got out, he turned to drug dealing: here was a way to rebuild the empire. He was soon running all over town, lit up with the desperation of the small-time peddler. To other hoodlums he became a warning, an after photo. In 1951 he tried to sell heroin to an undercover narcotics agent. When he realized he could not bribe his way out, Waxey asked the agent to shoot him. In his mug shot, Waxey looks worn out and faded. His face hangs in the air like a reflection, something seen in a pane of glass. He was sentenced to twenty-five years in prison. Wexler died in 1952 in Alcatraz.

There is an underworld myth, spread by movies but also by the gangsters themselves: that the Mafia bosses banned family members from dealing drugs. This issue is seen as a debate between bosses in *The Godfather.* When Joseph Valachi, a low-level member of the Gambino family, turned informant, he told prosecutors that some bosses paid capos $200 a week to steer clear of narcotics; he also said members caught selling drugs were sometimes killed. In his autobiography, *A*

Man of Honor, Joseph Bonanno writes, "My tradition outlaws narcotics. It has always been understood that men of honor don't deal in narcotics. However, the lure of high profits tempted some underlings to freelance in the narcotics trade."

Many see such statements as a tactic, something to throw off the cops. Even the most arrogant mobsters knew drugs could be the downfall of the Mafia. Here was an issue where the public would demand results. Gangsters killing gangsters was one thing; gangsters selling drugs in a school zone, that was something else. It was one area where wiseguys could not buy off cops, where even the most corrupt judges would not give them a pass. And if a low-level dealer was somehow tied to the big boys, it could put the bosses in jail. So, in their loudest voice, the bosses told the capos, "No drugs," as they faithfully collected their percentage. Vito Genovese, who was among the first of the modern gangsters, died in jail for narcotics dealing.

"I knew a lot of the big guys had been mixed up in drugs," Cusack told me. "You kept your eyes open, you saw it. But I learned something in the seventies that did surprise me. I found out that Meyer Lansky was, at one point, addicted to heroin. That was a big surprise. It had to do with a time in the old days when he about broke down."

Cusack was referring to a crisis Lansky went through in the early thirties. In the middle of the Castellammarese war, his first child, Buddy Lansky, was born crippled in both legs. "Lansky's first wife was very religious," Ralph Salerno told me. "Yet she married a gangster and spent her honeymoon at the big 1929 Mob meeting in Atlantic City, where she met people like Al Capone. Then her first son has all these problems. I think she blamed her husband; she saw it as the wrath of God. Is it any wonder she later wound up in the booby hatch?"

Lansky was troubled. Who wants to be on God's bad side? One day in 1931 he got in a car and drove north, past towns and rivers, to a hideout the gang kept near Boston. For the next few days he did not shower or change; he let his beard grow. He was Henry Thoreau alone in the woods, getting to the bottom of things; a holy man, locked in the desert, challenging the night. Why had his son been crippled? Were his sins being visited on the boy?

The sun came and went. The wind rattled the windows. There was a knock at the door. It was Vincent Alo, who had been sent by Luciano to look after Meyer. Alo was a broad-beamed Sicilian. Friends called him Jimmy Blue Eyes. "For nearly a week Alo sat with Lansky," Uri Dan writes in *Meyer Lansky: Mogul of the Mob.* "As the grief-stricken Little Man struggled with his emotions, Alo provided his friend bottle after bottle of his own whiskey."

The hours passed. The shadows shifted. Then, one day, Lansky got up, showered, shaved, got in his car, and drove back to New York. Though his week away was never again mentioned, it was understood: Lansky had made his peace.

While John Cusack accepts this story, he says there was another element at play: not only was Lansky struggling with his son's illness, he was going through heroin withdrawal. Lansky had gone north to kick the habit. Alo was there to guide him through hell. Is this true? Cusack says it is. He says agents in the FBN knew about it at the time. And if he's right, if Lansky was up there with the shakes, we now have a new image of the gangster, an image at odds with the constrained, button-down Lansky of the gangster movies: Lee Strasberg in *The Godfather, Part II;* Ben Kingsley in *Bugsy.* It means Meyer Lansky knew something Kurt Cobain and Jimi Hendrix would later find out. And it sets him firmly in the narrative of this century, at the forefront of grunge, just another addict looking for a fix. It also means Lansky was stronger than we ever supposed. Weaker, too.

In the ensuing years, Meyer Lansky and Vincent Alo became best friends. When Meyer at last came out of the woods, having shed the indulgences of youth, Alo was with him. "What Lansky and Alo had was a love affair," Cusack told me. "Even those of us on the other side of the law came to respect what they felt for each other." In the eighties both men were living in Miami, old gangsters walking the beach, eating in diners.

When Lansky died in 1982, Alo kept on, opening a restaurant in South Beach. He's still there, just another white-haired old man haunting the ocean avenues of Miami. He is a slight, stoop-shouldered man in his nineties, yet people are still scared of him. They say it is his connections they fear, but really it is the man himself. They fear him the way you might fear a toothless dog that was once ferocious. A dog that has tasted flesh remains a dangerous dog.

A few years ago I was having breakfast with my father and his friends (Sid, Asher, Larry) at Nate 'n' Al's, and I asked if they could put me in touch with Vincent Alo. "I think we can make a few calls," said Sid. "We know someone who knows him."

"Yeah, but be careful," said Asher. "When Jimmy Blue Eyes don't like something, it's not a letter to the editor he sends."

"Tell him about the espresso drinker," said Sid. His voice was pinched with excitement. "Go on, tell him."

"Sure, I'll tell him," said Asher. "Well, Blue Eyes has a restaurant in Miami Beach. And he has this guy running it for him, a real big espresso drinker."

"This guy's always sippin' espresso," said Sid. "Sip, sip, sip."

"Yeah, always sippin'," Asher said. "Well, anyway, Blue Eyes lets this espresso drinker run the joint. One condition: he's gotta keep a table open for Blue Eyes. Don't matter if Blue Eyes is out of town, that table stays open. It's Alo's table. So, okay. Months go by and no Blue Eyes. The place gets hot. The lines run out the door. One night, the espresso drinker gets greedy. Someone slips him a hundred. He gives 'em the table. An hour later, and who walks in with a bunch of outta-town friends but Jimmy Blue Eyes."

"Whaddya know," said Sid, clapping his hands. "Walks in that very night."

"So, Blue Eyes looks at the table, looks at the espresso drinker, walks out," said Asher.

"Doesn't get mad or nothing," said Sid. "Just walks out."

Asher ate a fry off Sid's plate, then said, "An hour later, the espresso drinker is stretched out in the kitchen, flat as a board, dead."

"Flat as a board, dead," said Sid. "Poison espresso."

This story is not true. No way. A ninety-year-old man does not poison the espresso drinker. But Asher and Sid believe it's true, which shows how good a gangster Alo must have been. As a young man, he crafted an image that seventy years later still has people talking on the other side of the country. My meeting with Alo never did come off. He sent word back that he had no interest in talking about the old days. Before I left that morning, though, Sid grabbed my sleeve and said, "We like you, Richie. If you meet Jimmy Blue Eyes, make nice."

Is it any wonder some of the gangsters turned to drugs? Their lives were made of stress. Things used as metaphors in corporate America (bagman, hit man, hatchet job) were reality here. Living into middle age was itself a kind of victory. They worked under a pressure unknown even to deep-sea divers. They had built their world on a shifting landscape, a riot of feuds, wars, schemes. They learned to see their actions through strange eyes, to refract their lives through the eyes of enemies. Who will kill me next?

They were often awakened in the middle of the night. A pebble on the window. The stores below are shuttered, stoops empty. A man is standing under the streetlight. *Hey, Kid, it's me, Pep. We need you at the candy store.* So they dress in a cold room, in the light of a naked bulb, not knowing if they are going out as killer or mark. If they were dumb, they were soon dead. If they were smart, they were afraid all the time. Afraid of enemies, more afraid of friends.

They joined the Mob when they were young, before they knew what it was about. Only later, after the first robbery, the first killing, did the picture come into focus. *This is a world where no one is trusted, where no one walks away, a world without windows or doors.* And by then it was too late.

Now and then, someone did try to get out. He would go all around the candy store, shaking hands. He had fallen in love or found God or whatever. He had forgotten something, too—that the last person who had fallen in love or found God or whatever had turned up in the weeds.

But when a man makes up his mind, what can you do? You just shake your head and watch him go. A shack in a forest, an apartment in a city, a house in a suburb. For a few weeks the reformed hood is left to live his new life, a routine just beginning to form, a glimpse of a future. But it's an illusion, a dream that comes after the gunshot, before the bullet. Sooner or later there is a knock on the door.

For the boys, someone who quit was a threat. It was someone they had lost control of, like a plane that's gone off radar, and who knows where it will turn up? It did not matter how many promises you made. *Don't worry 'bout me, boys! I'll never tell a thing!* Once you quit, you were carrying around the secrets of everyone in the gang. You couldn't be allowed to walk off with that. That would be like stealing. Sooner or later the boys would track you down. When they did, they would take back what you stole. And the only way at it was through your head. They bled it out. The only person who ever got away was Gangy Cohen, and to do it he had to run to the movies. No. Quitting was something you were not allowed to do. If they let you go, not only were you a threat, you were the worst kind of advertising, a message to everyone with a gripe, an arrow saying, "This way out!"

That's how it was with Tootsie Feinstein. In the thirties Tootsie rode with Charlie Workman on all kinds of errands. He and Workman were friends. They cared for each other. Then one day Tootsie tells Workman that he is going straight. He wants a future as real as his past. Workman drops off Tootsie, heads into the city, and tells Lepke all about it. Yes, he is friends with Tootsie. But a mistake made by a friend is still a mistake. So Lepke gives Workman the job. "Charlie has a tough assignment," Lepke said. "I hate like hell to have to do it, but we have got to take Tootsie Feinstein." When issuing a death sentence, Lepke used the word "take," like a heavenly bureaucrat just following the timetable set down by God.

A few days later Workman told Tootsie he had something on his mind, that he wanted to go for a ride. Did Tootsie know he was going to die? A lot of the gang members killed by friendly fire must have sensed something was up. They had seen it so many times: someone makes a mistake, there is a pause, a passage of time, a knock on the door, a friend wanting to go for a ride. Maybe the mark knows there is no way out and figures, if he has got to go, it might as well be with a friend. At least the conversation on the way to the weeds will be pleasant. Workman buried the body in Lindhurst, New Jersey, in a lime-lined grave the boys kept on the bank of the Passaic River.

A few days later a member of the troop rang Feinstein's bell. When Tootsie's wife answered, he handed her a fifty-dollar bill. He said her husband would be gone for a while. Every week someone came by with a fifty. Some women might tear up the money. Tootsie's widow was a realist. Because she lost a husband, did she have to lose everything else, too? She liked the lifestyle. She continued to spend time with the boys. She even spent a winter with the troop in Miami. Allie took home movies on the beach, the jerky black-and-white film showing surf, sky, and Tootsie's widow goofing with the man who killed her husband. When lawyers later prosecuted Tootsie's killer, she spoke on his behalf. This only added to the legend: When Handsome Charlie kills a man, the widow stands for him in court.

By the mid-thirties the gangsters had built a world of their own. They had friends in every town, towns in every state. No matter the jam, someone could always be contacted. There was always somewhere to go. Entire counties out west had been made gangster friendly: houses bought, cops, politicians paid off. In a few small villages in Michigan, strange men in dark suits and fedoras could be seen on the road from town, groceries in hand, walking back to a house in the woods. They would be seen on the road every day for a week, a month. Then gone. The trouble back east had been taken care of. In 1919, when Al Capone was wanted in Brooklyn for murder, he hid in Bugsy Siegel's place on Fourteenth Street long enough for Siegel to arrange safe passage to Chicago.

If things got especially hot, if there was a dead cop or a dead kid, a gangster might be sent clear across the ocean. For Italians there was Italy, the villages of their ancestors. In 1937 Vito Genovese, wanted for murder, fled to Naples, where he ran drugs and formed an alliance with Mussolini. In 1947 he was brought back to New York for trial. He was acquitted. For Jews, whose past seemed to vanish just behind them, there was Miami, the other holy land. And soon there would be Israel. For Jewish gangsters, Israel's successful war of independence meant partly a victory for self-determination, partly a victory for Jews on the lam.

And if a gangster just needed to get away, if he was waiting for something to blow over, or if maybe he was sick of his wife, he could always head down to the Hotel Arkansas, a spa and casino Owney Madden ran in Hot Springs. Madden was the last of the old old-timers. His youth was lived in another age, an early century world of thousand-man street gangs, of opium dens, of Monk Eastman and Big Jack Zelig and knife fights at dawn. He was like an exotic animal that turns up from the past, a parrot feeding with pigeons. He had a sallow face on which everything was written. He is what might have happened to a Dickens character who lived into the twentieth century, was taken too far from home, had all of the ambition, none of the luck. To childhood friends he was "that little banty rooster out of hell."

Madden came to America from Liverpool, England, in 1903. He lived with his aunt in Hell's Kitchen. When he was eleven he joined the Gophers, one of the last of the old street gangs. He was arrested forty-four times before he was twenty. He took over the gang when he was seventeen. To celebrate, he went out and killed an Italian immigrant, someone who would not be missed. In 1916 he boarded a streetcar and killed a kid who had asked out his girl. Though he killed the kid in front of witnesses, no one came forward. He fired his gun as the trolley, rumbling up Ninth Avenue, crossed Sixteenth Street, a few blocks from where I now live. The streetcar is gone, but you can still go look at the elevated tracks, which run across the tops of newsstands and auto repair shops. Away from buildings, the tracks run on a sort of steel viaduct, the supports rusty. In the summer, cattails grow through the ties. Madden killed five men by his twenty-third birthday. On the street they called him Owney the Killer.

Madden was sent to Sing Sing in 1914. He had been convicted of killing a rival. When he was released in 1923, he found himself in a new world. He had gone to prison in the morning, and now it was night, the racy night of New York in the twenties. Madden was maybe the only old-timer to really make the transition. While legends like Monk Eastman stumbled opium soaked through the East Side, Madden was cutting deals with the new generation, making a fortune in numbers and bootlegging; he owned the Cotton Club in Harlem. Madden worked with Lansky and Lepke for the same reason Frank Sinatra later cut songs with Bono of U2 and Paul Simon: because things change. In 1929, when young underworld leaders (Luciano, Costello, Lansky, Al Capone, Lepke) held a conference in Atlantic City, Madden was there, a historical figure who wandered into the wrong era.

When Prohibition ended, Madden went south. He had ridden atop the New York underworld long enough to know he could not do so forever. If he stayed, he would sooner or later be killed or locked up. People like Reles and Madden lived in a world of diminishing returns, where everything to be had can be had in youth. So Owney took his winnings and bought the Hotel Arkansas, a spa and casino in Hot Springs.

By the mid-thirties the hotel had become a gangster getaway. Thugs took the train from New York, stayed in big, well-lit rooms, were healed by the waters, lost fortunes in the casino. They stayed a week, a month, a season. All paths led to the dining room, where the boys stayed up late, smoking. After dinner they sat outside in chairs, charting the night by the stars. On weekends bands came from Little Rock to play Gershwin and Cole Porter songs. And the wives dripping jewels in the shade. And the boys out on the town, in clubs up and down the strip, leaving a charge in the air. When a warrant was put out for Lucky Luciano, he came to the hotel, where he felt as safe as Vito Genovese in Naples. It took several months, a political scandal, and the state militia to root out Lucky and get him on a train north.

And it was at the Hotel Arkansas, on rainy evenings and balmy afternoons, that gangsters developed that most important part of their style: hanging out, an activity that came to define their way of life. Gangsters were maybe the first common-born Americans who did not spend all their time at work or with families, men with time on their hands; they were among the first Americans to grapple with the great problem of the age: boredom, how to fill the hours between waking and sleeping. It was a problem faced by Abe Reles on the corner of Livonia and Saratoga; by Bugsy Siegel in the lobby of the Waldorf-Astoria; by Frank Costello at the Hotel Arkansas. These were perhaps the first Americans to break truly free of the Puritan work ethic. They stood on corners all day, tracking the sun across the sky, watching commuters go and come. They were pioneer members of a class of aimless adults later portrayed on TV shows like *Seinfeld*. They were men waiting for a bus that never arrives.

Now, all these years later, my father, and a lot of other men old enough to know better, are still hanging out. They lose whole mornings at diners like Nate 'n' Al's, give entire afternoons to the club. A few times each year, my dad and his friends go to La Costa, a spa near San Diego, where they live pretty much like Lucky Luciano lived in Hot Springs. They play cards, take massages, swim. They sit under the stars at night, burning off those extra hours they worked so hard to accumulate. It's a legacy of the gangsters; it's what men do. Whenever I phone Asher Dann, I am taken through the same pleasantly absurd chain of events. Calling his house, I am told, "Asher is at the Friars. Try him there."

When I call the Friars Club, I am connected to the locker room. "Looking for Asher?" asks the attendant. "I'll get him." I hear the phone set down as the attendant goes through the room, shouting, "Asher! Ash! *Asher!*" As his voice trails off, another sound takes its place, the sound of men hanging out. Though I cannot see them, I know what they look like. They wear towels, sit on a wood bench along a row of lockers. Some have towels wound around their faces, an opening where a cigar goes in. Some wear gold chains. Their chins are covered with hard gray stubble. Their eyes sparkle. They are mischievous. At the ends of sentences, their voices rise, indicating the joke. They have mostly New York accents. They talk about a deal they are about to close, a car they are about to buy, an amazing thing their kid just did. They all have the greatest kid in the world. They also talk about the old days, Brooklyn, and how it was when Jewish gangsters were the toughest thing going. "Sorry," says the attendant, picking up the phone. "Asher is taking a steam."

The clientele at the Hotel Arkansas was mostly Italian and Jewish. Regulars included Louis Lepke, Lucky Luciano, Meyer Lansky, Joey Adonis, Frank Costello. These men had forged a bond beyond religion. Jew or Italian, they even looked alike, with dark eyes and dark hair, came from the same ghettos, seemed to want the same things. "You know how you tell a Jewish neighborhood?" Ralph Salerno asked me. "Look for the Italian restaurants."

At Madden's resort, in the shimmering light of the pool, they were one people. "The Italian Mafioso had tremendous respect for the Jews," said John Cusack. "They didn't push them around. Luciano was the first to say, 'Fight these guys? What do you mean? Get with them. Work with them.' " But it was a world fast disappearing. This was the golden age of the Jewish-Italian underworld alliance. These people were thrown together by poverty, and prosperity would soon pull them apart. Back then, Jewish and Italian gangsters looked alike the way seeds look alike. But as they blossomed, with money, with power, differences would emerge. What they wanted, their ambitions, fears, dreams they had for their children, were not the same. Over time, these differences would draw the children of Jewish gangsters away from crime, until a Jewish presence in the underworld was a vague memory, as hard to believe in as the youth of your parents. "The Jews were ahead of the Italians: ahead of them in immigrating here, ahead of them in being organized criminals, and ahead of them in getting out of it," Cusack said.

When an Italian gangster made a criminal score, he usually kept the money in the neighborhood. He might take a better apartment, move up a few flights, buy a new car, a new girl. You might see him cutting down the street in a razor-sharp suit, the sky in his shoes. But the Italians, at least those below the top echelon, rarely left the corner where they grew up. Why make it big if you can't flash it on the street? Who wants to look sharp for strangers? In Italian neighborhoods like Ocean Hill, the criminal hierarchy was there for everyone to see, as naked as the wheeling of the constellations. There were men on the streets, in the doorways, in the clubrooms, in the apartments above. And all this was the best recruiting poster in the world. Here is your bleary-eyed, overworked, dog-tired father. And here, a few doors away, is a cool, well-rested wiseguy who does nothing but hang out. "You know what parents told their kids the first day of school?" Salerno asked me. "They told them, 'Sometimes you get in a fight in the schoolyard. Okay. We understand. But there is someone you never fight with. We know who his parents are. You hurt him, you end up in Gowanus Canal covered with wire. And if you see that man on the sidewalk, step into the street, put your arms out, and say, "Hello, Don Chich." ' "

When Jewish gangsters made their score, in rackets or robbery, first thing they did was get out. They moved from Brooklyn or Queens to lower Manhattan, to the Upper West Side, Central Park West, or West End Avenue, to the suburbs, Westchester, New Jersey, Long Island, and then to Miami, Las Vegas, or Los Angeles. Who knows? Maybe Jews are just more comfortable on the road. Maybe all those years in exile have made them restless. Maybe no homeland meant no home. Maybe something deep in them said, "Get out before the roof caves in." For a successful Jew, a big part of life is visiting the old neighborhood, walking the shoulder-wide streets with a sense of victory. Jews collect hometowns. "The Italians liked the celebrity of that life," Cusack told me. "The Jewish gangsters, when they made it, got out of the neighborhood. They didn't have the bravura of the Italians, who wanted to walk down the street and everyone knows them and they're loved and adored. The Italians wanted to be in the neighborhood, wanted people to know who they are and this and that. But the Jews were different. They married, moved uptown, lived on the park, dressed modestly, and made sure everyone thought they were businessmen."

For Jewish gangsters, crime was not a way out of the system; it was a way in. Jews were mostly not wanted in the white-shoe firms of Wall Street and Madison Avenue. Their kids were not accepted by Ivy League schools. In a society so often closed, is it any wonder guns could seem the best way in, a shortcut to the American dream? But they did not glory in it. Many of the Jewish gangsters did not even like it. When they wore flashy suits, it was not to advertise their wealth; it was because they didn't know better. A gangster in a fuchsia suit is a gangster who wants to be loved.

For these men, the greatest dream, the dream they reserved for their children, was to be a successful, law-abiding American. The Jewish people wanted a future like the one my father and his friends live today: summer in the mountains, winter in the sun, deals in the steamroom, politicians to the house, and nothing to go to jail for. Legitimate power. Doctors. Lawyers. The gangsters knew they could not have this for themselves. They were too rough, too green, not far enough from Europe, the shtetl, the pogroms. They were like the generation Moses led out of Egypt, a generation lost in the wilderness, a slave generation that must die away before Jews can settle the promised land. So they instead got themselves in position to make the dream come true for their children. "The Jewish Mafia was never passed on like the Italian Mob," Cusack said. "Jews didn't recruit. The old-timers did what they felt they had to do; but they did not want the younger generation of Jews mixed up in it."

Most Jewish gangsters said they were importers or mediators or organizers. They rarely even told their children what they did. I have found only a handful of Jews who say they are related to gangsters. And even those found out only years later, long after the grandfather or great-grandfather was senile or dead. It was a family secret, something that slipped out after a few glasses of wine. And there must be others, thousands of Jews who will never know the secrets of just a few generations back. To them, their ancestor is just a kindly old face pasted into a photo album; to others, that face was Knadles or Bugsy or Kid Twist. When Abe Reles died, his wife remarried, changed her name, changed the name of her children. And off they drifted into the mumbling crowd that is Jewish America.

The gangsters made sure their kids lived normal lives, stayed in school, studied, got into college. They had the muscle their fathers didn't, the muscle to take on the schools with quotas. "I knew a Jewish kid who used Bugsy Siegel's gangster money to get into medical school," Salerno told me. "Those schools didn't want Jews or Italians. I don't give a shit how smart you are. All right? But the people who made the decisions, they could be corrupted, too. And who among the Italians and Jews had the power to do that? Gangsters. Someone from the neighborhood would approach a gangster and ask the favor. Do it for your people! And so the gangster would send someone up to one of these fancy schools and they would say, 'Your answer is no? Who do I have to see who will tell me yes?' "

The sons of the gangsters went off to college and grad school and then into medicine, law, business. Lansky's second son, Paul, graduated from West Point. After ten years in the army, he moved to California and became a computer programmer. When he had a son of his own, he named him Meyer Lansky II, which upset the gangster. The idea was to fade into America, not brandish your name. Lansky's other son, Buddy, who was handicapped, remembered the old gangster's reaction. "Dad got mad," he told Robert Lacey in the book *Little Man*. "He thought it was not fair on the kid that he should have to live with that." For later generations, the life of the ghetto, the crime and violence, were just stories, something you forget before you hear. Why should they remember? In the story of the Jewish underworld nothing compares with the Italian dynasties, the Gottis, the Gallos. No one runs out to avenge a family name. That's the last thing the patriarch would want. Even the most violent of the gangsters saw themselves as good Jews, people of the Book. They went to temple on High Holy Days, thought of God when things went bad, had their sons circumcised and bar mitzvahed. Being a Jew was not something they were thinking of all the time, but they were aware of themselves as Jews, as players in a larger story—the Temple, the Exodus. How did they square their criminal life with the life of the Bible? Well, like most people, they made a distinction: this is the life of the soul, this is the life of the body. Next year in Jerusalem. But this is how I live in the Diaspora.

A lawyer asked Reles how he dealt with the contradictions. "Do you have any regrets?" asked the lawyer.

"This is the way I live," said Reles.

"Do you believe there is a God?" asked the lawyer.

"Yes, sir."

"When did you start to believe in God?"

"Always knew there was a God," said Reles.

"You knew there was a God while you were doing these different killings?"

"That is the way my life was mapped out," said Reles. "That was my profession."

"Did you believe in God while you were killing Jake the Painter?"

"I knew there was a God."

Of course, most people in the neighborhood had no sympathy for the gangsters. To people in places like Brownsville, those who worked for everything they had, the gangsters were nothing but cheaters. Probably no one hated them more than other Jews. When federal prosecutors began targeting Jewish gangsters, a large part of each legal team was Jewish; Jews thought it important to be seen fighting Jewish criminals. It's hard enough finding your way in a new world without thugs ruining the name of your people. Other locals ignored the problem, telling themselves gangsters lived somewhere else, Italian areas like Ocean Hill. Not here. When I asked Marty Glickman about Jewish gangsters he gave me a blank look. Glickman, a Jewish athlete who represented the United States in the 1936 Summer Olympics in Munich, Germany, who was not allowed to compete for fear of offending Hitler, who went on to become the first voice of the New York Knicks, who invented the word "swish," grew up in Brownsville in the twenties, when the neighborhood was run by Abe Reles; you couldn't turn around without seeing a wiseguy. Yet Glickman seems convinced Jews were above organized crime. "I don't know how many gangsters there were, but it could not have been very many," he told me. "After all, being a gangster is not a Jewish way of life."

Even when the gangsters did something helpful—made sure Brownsville got its share of government spending, stood up to Irish or Italian bullies—people still asked themselves, "Is it good or bad for the Jews?" And almost always they decided it was bad. The image of the Jews was being tarnished. In movies and fiction, the heavy often had a Jewish last name or a mother with a European accent. Edward G. Robinson, a Jewish actor, earned his fame playing gangsters many people thought were based on Buggsy Goldstein. One of the great turnarounds in movie history, ranking with the rout of the musical, is the way Italian actors have cornered gangster roles; until about 1950, a movie gangster was as likely to eat corned beef as pasta. "Most Jews hated Jewish gangsters," Herbert Brownell told me. Brownell, who managed Tom Dewey's presidential campaigns, prosecuted the gangsters while serving as President Eisenhower's attorney general. "Those people wrecked the image of the Jewish community. It was only the kids that admired them, because those crooks seemed to beat the system. Of course, a lot of them wound up dead.

"I found it remarkable that there even were Jewish gangsters," Brownell went on. "These people had such opportunity, such chances. They could have done anything. And they muffed it. I mean, if you look at what the Jewish people have done for this city—they built it.

And that some of their sons should choose to tear it down . . . I never understood that."

Herbert Brownell, who died a few months after we spoke, was a Nebraska-born Protestant. He came from a different world from that of the gangsters. Silos, grain elevators, cornfields. How could he understand someone named Buggsy Goldstein? Many of the men Brownell worked with came from the same world, small Protestant towns scattered around the West and Midwest. They went east to work in the U.S. Attorney's Office, to go after gangsters they felt had a stranglehold on New York. When I spoke to those still alive—they are in their eighties and nineties now and remember only bits of stories—they had trouble recalling the gangsters in individual detail. They remember them more as a type, a single, sneering *über*-thug. "Nothing but punks," said Edward Lumbard, who served as the New York district attorney, then as a federal judge. "They were hiding behind their people, sapping their community."

Many of the prosecutors did not even see the gangsters as men. They saw them as strangers, a foreign presence, the cause of every social evil; it's the way many white people now see black and Hispanic gangs. To some, the problem wasn't poverty or the ghetto—it was Jews. In some churches there was talk of how the Jews betrayed God, killed Jesus, and were now up to their old tricks in the new world. In my father's neighborhood, at four o'clock every weekday, the streets would fill with Catholic school kids spoiling for a fight. When I asked my dad why they wanted to fight, he said, "Because we killed their Lord." A lot of the journalism of the day carried the scent of the old European anti-Semitism, of blood libel, Jews spiriting away gentile babies. In the twenties, when a reporter for the *Saturday Press* was criticized for linking Judaism to crime, he responded in print: "When I find men of a certain race banding themselves together for the purpose of preying upon gentiles; gunmen, killers, roaming our streets shooting down men against whom they have no personal grudge; defying our laws; corrupting our officials; assaulting business men; beating up unarmed citizens; spreading a reign of terror through every walk of life, then I say to you in all sincerity, that I refuse to back up a single step from that 'issue.' "

All this helped open a rift between the uptown Jews and the Jews downtown. The uptown Jews, educated, prosperous, assimilated, were threatened by such creeping anti-Semitism. And whom did they blame? The anti-Semites? No. They blamed the downtown Jews, who, with their accents and crime, were an embarrassment. The uptown Jews looked at their cousins downtown the way my big brother looked at me when his cool friends came over—as though they had snuck in the back door. Over time, this attitude drove some downtown Jews into sympathy with the gangsters. For people in far-flung Brooklyn, a sense of exclusion led to a kind of unity. The gangsters, at least, were with them.

When Reles and the boys were hanging out at my grandparents' diner and the cops came by, my great-grandmother would hide their guns in the onions. She hated gangsters, but she hated people she thought hated Jews more. Besides, the gangsters did things the cops couldn't. They kept the streets safe, got local kids into college. When my grandma Betty went into labor while working in the diner, who do you think drove her to the hospital? Abe Reles. "The gangsters helped crack barriers," Ralph Salerno told me. "The world was closed to people in their neighborhoods, and the gangsters had the muscle and money to see that it was opened."

The gangsters were fighting a hearts and minds campaign. If they were liked, they would be protected. A gangster fighting for the little guy is a gangster you don't rat on. (Of course, if they weren't liked, they made sure they were feared.) And who liked them most? The kids. Kids in places like Brownsville were starved for role models. They were always on the lookout for someone other than their father, a destiny other than the domestic one they saw at home. They followed Jewish boxers: Benny Leonard, Barney Ross. They knew Jewish actors by their movie names and real names: Kirk Douglas, Jeff Chandler, Tony Curtis (Bernie Schwartz). In Brooklyn, kids made up all-star baseball teams consisting entirely of Jews: Al "Flip" Rosen, Max Fischl, Heine Bloom. "One year, Hank Greenberg, who played first base for the Detroit Tigers, was holding out for more money," Salerno told me. "So he got a pitcher and went to the park to hit flies. It was one of the funniest sights I have ever seen. There must have been two hundred outfielders. Every Jewish kid in the neighborhood wanted to catch a ball hit by the great Hank Greenberg."

My father lived in Bensonhurst, not far from Sholem Bernstein, a junior member of the Reles gang. To kids on the block, Sholem was both familiar and alien. He was a Jew like their fathers; yet he was a mystery. He blew through the neighborhood like a gust of color, in

$300 suits, hair greased back, a cigarette in the corner of his mouth. At fourteen, Larry King, trying to smoke like Sholem, leaned to kiss a girl, forgot about the cigarette, and just about burned a hole in her face. "Sholem was like some kind of a champion athlete," Larry told me. "Everything he did looked cool and easy, but when you tried it, you fell flat on your ass."

Sholem Bernstein owned a store in Bensonhurst. Now and then some of the boys would drive over from Brownsville. If it was a nice day, they might walk through the streets. When my father describes the gangsters walking by, all you see are big meaty hands, gold watches, pinky rings, teeth, very white, thick wrists, and broad shoulders under a green sky. Walking down Bay Parkway, they were followed by whispers. From a distance, people picked them out like Dodgers on a scorecard. "The short stocky one is Reles; the handsome one, that's Charlie Workman; the mean-looking one with blue eyes is Pittsburgh Phil Strauss; and the one who looks like Edward G. Robinson, that's Buggsy Goldstein."

Shoulder to shoulder they walked past dusty bars and concrete stoops where men in shirtsleeves read the *Brooklyn Eagle,* past crowded basketball courts and apartment house windows where mothers were calling children to supper, past side streets where kids were playing stickball. Asher Dann is pitching. He pushes his hair from his face. Sid Young is catching. He calls for the fastball. Herbie is hitting. He waves a broomstick. Larry is down the street fielding, just glasses and a laugh from here, waiting for the pink speck against the green sky. Larry spots the gangsters first. He bites his lip and runs to the mound. He calls for a conference. As the boys pretend to talk, they check out the hoods. Look at them! They live in another world, outside everything the rabbi says on Friday night, our fathers say the rest of the week. And still they prosper. Look at those clothes! I can see my reflection in that jacket!

To kids like my dad, the gangsters were something different from the books and prayers, mourning and wailing, of the Jews. If the gangsters lived in Palestine, there would be no Wailing Wall. It would be the Don't-Fuck-with-Me Wall! A few years later, when kids on these blocks were faced with the image of the German concentration camp, the memory of the gangsters would give them another image: tough Jews, Jews who will not be led to slaughter. What do you think Pep Strauss would do to a guy like Heinrich Himmler? Drill fifteen holes in him, the Kraut bastard! I sometimes think my father's image of himself, how he faces the world, began with those first gangster encounters. Even though he did not follow their lead, they gave him the illusion of freedom. *Who knows? Maybe I will end up like that.* "Here's my tip for the future," one of the gangsters says. "Lose the ball; keep the stick."

"What's the history of the Jews before they came here?" Ralph Salerno asked me. "They were in Europe. Cossacks chopped their heads off. They came here and were not accustomed to defending themselves. Who was it among them who knew how to defend themselves? Who could teach them to fight back? Gangsters. Jews with guns, like Meyer Lansky and Dutch Schultz and Ben Siegel. They proved that Jews can be the toughest guys of all. If you want to mess with them, okay, but you're in for a real fight."

So, in the mid-thirties, when Tom Dewey, working first as a special prosecutor, later as a district attorney, then as the governor of New York, went after the gangsters, Jewish kids all over Brooklyn were transfixed by the fight. They followed the action each day in the papers and tried to read between the lines. Most of them believed the gangsters would come out ahead. From their view, somewhere above the home run leader and the heavyweight champion was the gangster. But the view from Dewey's office was different. He knew the truth about the gangsters: that their strength was the strength of the weak, the terrorist, the man outside the system. With courage and patience, he could topple the leaders of the underworld. And if the Jewish gangsters couldn't give the kids of Brooklyn a victory, they would at least give them a terrific fight.

On the Lam

TOM DEWEY GREW up in Owosso, Michigan. Born in 1902, he passed the first years of the century among the shopkeepers and waitresses of small-town America. Wearing princely little boy outfits, hair parted neatly, eyes wide, he knocked out his small-town teeth playing left guard on the small-town football team. He spent summers in the Upper Peninsula, that overgrown piece of Michigan wilderness where Ernest Hemingway set his first stories. In high school he acted in a minstrel show (*The Dudes of Blackville*) and edited the school yearbook (*The Spic*). And though he delivered papers before school and did odd jobs after, he never missed a single day of school. He was the perfect son of an old Republican family. His father, during a youthful stay in New York, pledged to fight Tammany Hall, the corrupt Democratic machine. So from the beginning, some of Dewey's dreams were political: he would carry on his father's fight, take on big-city corruption. But he had other dreams, too. He wanted to sing opera, the great halls of the East, grown men in tears. So, after a few years at the state university, he went to New York for the same reason Meyer Lansky's dad went to New York: to start his real life.

When his dreams of a life in music began to fade, Dewey enrolled in Columbia Law School. (He was in the same class as Paul Robeson, the black tenor who later turned Communist and moved, for a time, to Russia.) Dewey got his degree in just two years. After a stint in private practice (1925–1931), he was named chief assistant to George Medalie, the U.S. attorney for the Southern District of New York. So began his fight with organized crime—a son taking on his father's obsession, storming the beehive of city corruption. How strange! Tom Dewey, this kid from the sticks, against the underworld! What could he know? More than coming from a different place, he came from a different part of time. How many years lay between Michigan and Delancey Street? A hundred? A thousand? What could he know of the violence of the ghetto? Three thousand people lived in Owosso, the same number that filled a single East Side block. Tom Dewey was grappling with an army of exotics, men who seemed to threaten everything Owosso stood for.

And what did the gangsters stand for? More than anything, even more than money and power, they stood for a style, a way of life. They used the right words (jackpot, beef), wore the right clothes (wing-tips, spats), hit the right clubs (Hotsy Totsy, Stork). Never would they be the dupe, sucker, do-gooder, rule follower. For men like Dutch Schultz and Lucky Luciano, who wanted more than anything to look cool, being taken down by Dewey must have been the greatest insult of all. Dewey was perhaps the most ambitious geek in American history. While Luciano was escorting blondes uptown, Dewey was still back in Michigan, setting a shameful record—perfect school attendance. When his parents suggested he miss a day to see his grandparents, he fired off a Little Lord Fauntleroy note: "Much as I love my grandparents, my job is to be at school learning what I can," he wrote. "It's all part of the preparation for the future."

In the twenties, gangsters had for the first time pushed beyond the cities, running drugs and whiskey into the nowhere towns of America. They came as underworld strangers: Rothstein's boys riding whiskey past sleepy Long Island farms; Reles heading upstate for target practice; Strauss filling contracts in the Bible Belt. The evil of the city had bled the countryside clean through. It's what Hemingway was getting at in "The Killers"; what Iowa-born artist Grant Wood gets at in paintings like *Death on the Ridge Road,* which shows black sedans burning through lush green countryside. With the arrival of Tom Dewey, small-town America would at last return the favor, visiting judgment on the city. "Dewey came along at just the right time to ride the issue to fame," Herbert Brownell told me. "Previously gangsters were known as a city problem, and people despised the city. As the gangs got more powerful, though, this became a national problem, and Dewey was the hero taking them on." By going after gangsters, Dewey would also acquire some of their luster. Whether he liked it or not, he would forever be known as half an equation, a player in the story of American crime.

Tom Dewey tried his first major Mob case in 1933; it was the trial that brought down Waxey Gordon. By the thirties, Gordon was one of the richest gangsters in America. Like all rich gangsters, he was suspected of not paying his taxes. In the end he was tripped up, not by the feds, but by underworld rivals. When Lansky and Luciano grew tired of trading shots with Waxey, they let some documents find their way to Dewey's office. The documents showed Gordon had not paid taxes for ten years, in which time he made something like $5 million.

The trial made Dewey a star. As he cross-examined witnesses, his face worked like an accordion, folding and unfolding, drilling the gangster with rapid-fire facts and questions. His attack on Waxey seemed personal. It was not just organized crime Dewey was after; it was the impudence of the criminals, how they looked and dressed, trying to pass as real Americans. Dewey was not content to convict Waxey; he wanted to expose him for the crass thug he knew him to be. Gordon was sentenced to ten years in a federal prison.

Dutch Schultz was next. A more formidable foe than Gordon, Schultz, whose real name was Arthur Flegenheimer, grew up in Jewish Harlem. He borrowed his name from a legendary member of the old Frog Hollow Gang. In the early twenties he rode shotgun on Rothstein's whiskey trucks. He later put together his own gang, a collection of uptown Jewish toughs, with skills as specialized as the members of a SWAT team: Bo Weinberg, a proficient killer; Abbadabba Berman, who processed numbers like a computer; Lulu Rosenkrantz, a freewheeling sharpshooter. After Prohibition the gang entered the rackets, extorting money from the swankest restaurants in Manhattan: the Brass Rail, Rosoff's, Lindy's. They also moved into the Harlem numbers game, a primitive form of the lottery. "Schultz asked the black gangsters who ran numbers to a meeting," Ralph Salerno told me. "When they came in, Dutch set his forty-five on a desk and said, 'I'm your partner.' "

Unlike Lansky or Luciano, Schultz didn't fancy himself a businessman. He knew his power lay in the threat of violence. He was a tough, a sharpie, trouble in a crowd. He was dark eyes, tight mouth, bent nose.

A chorus girl said he looked like Bing Crosby with his face bashed in—a great description. What is a gangster if not a grotesque version of a pop star, a celebrity gone punk, one feature sounding an off note? Schultz knew this about himself; he had an uncanny ability to see himself as he believed others must see him—an unrefined, bent-nosed Jew. "What's the matter you don't want to come in with me?" he asked a Harlem gangster. "You think maybe you'll find a man with horns on his head?"

By the thirties Schultz was perhaps the most visible gangster in New York. He had twice been tried for income tax evasion. He was acquitted first in Syracuse in 1933; when charges were again brought in 1935, in a case put together by Dewey, Schultz's lawyers had the venue changed to a small town upstate: Malone, New York. Church. Street. Stop sign. Schultz went up a few months before the trial. On the advice of a PR firm, he moved into a small hotel, introduced himself to strangers, gave to local charities, wore modest suits. When asked why he did not wear more elegant clothes, he said, "I think only queers wear silk shirts. I never bought one in my life. Only a sucker will pay fifteen dollars for a shirt."

He was seen at church socials, block parties, bingo games. A week before the trial, he went into a local church and converted to Catholicism; he was not the first or last Jew who, looking to play in the sticks, shed his faith. By the time the jury was asked to deliberate, Schultz had fooled or bribed the entire town. There is a picture of him just after acquittal, the broad smile of a kid who has stolen a student council election. "This tough world ain't no place for dunces," he told reporters. "And you can tell those smart guys in New York that the Dutchman is no dunce, and as far as he is concerned, Alcatraz don't exist. I'll never see Alcatraz."

In the wake of the trial, word came to Schultz from Mayor Fiorello La Guardia: *You're not wanted in New York City! Don't come back!* To avoid arrest, Dutch settled first in Connecticut, then across the river in Newark. Each night his gang met at the Palace Chop House, a steak place a few blocks from Newark's Penn Station. In photos the restaurant is gloomy, with dirty white tablecloths and wobbly chairs, a place where a cook stands in the kitchen door, frowning. There was a room up front with a dozen or so tables and the kind of long, always empty oak bar you today see in Bennigan's. The gang always took a table in back, maybe a dozen paces from the bathroom. There was a mirror behind the table, and a gunman facing the mirror could keep an eye on the hall leading from the bar. The gang was still collecting thousands each week from the numbers game.

Dewey filed fresh charges against Dutch Schultz, going after his restaurant rackets. Mayor La Guardia was going after Dutch's gambling empire, having his slot machines confiscated, dumped on barges, busted up. The papers ran photos of the mayor, ringed by the East River, sledgehammering the machines. And all the trials, the days in court, had loosened Schultz's hold on his other rackets, too. Hoods were moving on his territory. No one had believed he would return from his trial in Malone. "The loudmouth is never coming back," Lucky Luciano had said. These must have been dismal days for Dutch, weeks without Sundays, years without holidays. He caught Bo Weinberg conspiring with Luciano. Weinberg was fitted with cement shoes and dumped in the East River. In 1936 Schultz called a meeting of the Syndicate board, the criminal body that ran the underworld.

The board met in a hotel in Manhattan. I picture the men (Lepke, Gurrah, Lansky, Luciano, Siegel, Adonis, Schultz) seated around a long table, waiters bearing silver trays. Out a window the chaos of the city. For years Schultz had been able to work in the face of uncertainty, which must be a definition of courage. But the struggle had at last caught up with him. He had grown shabby in exile. With a fedora pushed back on his head, he must have looked like a small-town merchant putting up a sign: "Everything Must Go!" He asked the Syndicate to kill Tom Dewey, who he said would not quit until every important New York criminal was in jail. The gangsters decided to investigate, seeing if Dewey could be killed. The matter was turned over to Lepke, who turned it over to Albert Anastasia, who ran the day-to-day affairs of Murder Inc.

Anastasia came to America from Italy in 1917. He came ashore illegally in the night with nothing but what he wore. He had sad, swollen cheeks. As he spoke, his pupils wandered into the corners of his eyes. His nose spread out across his face. He had huge hands. He was known in the underworld as Lord High Executioner. He was said to have personally killed fifty men. He was Lepke's most trusted aide, the man Louis turned to when there was trouble.

Anastasia borrowed a baby. It was a friend's kid, and I wonder where that kid is today. Some adult out there was perhaps the most realistic prop in underworld history. (Send me a postcard.) Albert took the kid in a stroller to Dewey's apartment building at 214 Fifth Avenue. Over several mornings that week, Anastasia, strolling the kid around the block, mapped Dewey's routine, the path he followed through life. Hidden in this routine, between the newsstands and car rides, was the prosecutor's death.

Dewey came out of his building each morning at around eight. Flanked by bodyguards, he climbed into a car and headed downtown. A few minutes later he stopped at a drugstore. As Dewey went in, got a cup of coffee, made a call from a phone booth in back, the bodyguards stood sentry outside. Dewey was checking his work messages before the long ride to Center Street. Albert A. figured he could be waiting at the counter when Dewey came in. When the prosecutor went to make his call, Albert would follow, silence his pistol, shoot the DA through the glass. He would kill the counterman and any customers before slipping into the street. By the time the bodyguards got suspicious, he would be long gone. "Sure, Dewey got all kinds of death threats," Edward Lumbard, who worked in the U.S. Attorney's Office, told me. "But he was never afraid. He was very courageous and forthright. Nobody was going to get in his way. He thought he was doing the right thing. We all did, and we were young and heaven knows what the future was going to be."

Anastasia presented his plan to the board the following week. I like to imagine him holding up pie graphs and using an overhead projector. I know this never happened, but wouldn't it be funny if it did? When Albert A. sat down, Schultz was sent from the room. That's how it worked. When the board was discussing your future, you waited outside. Who wants to be yelled down by an out-of-his-mind gangster?

The men decided against the plan. Even if it went without a hitch, everyone would know it was a Mob hit. And the resulting heat would be more than anyone cared to imagine. It might buy Schultz a few months, but everyone would suffer. It was like taking arsenic to cure a cold. Not everyone agreed. Gurrah Shapiro wanted Dewey dead. He thought the DA would sooner or later lock up everyone. But in the end, the plan was voted down eight to one. "I suppose they figured the National Guard would have been called out if Dewey was killed," said Frank Hogan, who later served as Manhattan's DA. "And I guess they wouldn't have been far wrong."

When Schultz heard the decision, he flew into a rage. "You guys stole my rackets, and now you're feeding me to the law," he yelled. "Dewey's gotta go! I'm hitting him myself in forty-eight hours."

"That meant his death warrant was signed," Doc Stacher, one of the old East Side Jews, later told Uri Dan. "All of us agreed he had to die. He had been ranting and raving. He thought Lansky, Luciano, Bugsy Siegel, and all the rest of us were combining against him and were going to steal his money. At first Albert Anastasia, the most efficient killer of all, was supposed to do the job," Stacher went on. "But even though Dutch Schultz had become a Catholic, our Italian partners looked at us and we all knew this was an internal Jewish matter. It was the understanding we had with each other. And the Italians like Charlie Luciano respected our wishes to keep this in the family."

So all of a sudden Lepke had a new assignment. Take out Schultz before Schultz takes out Dewey. And they had to work fast; Schultz was a time bomb ticking in everyone's ear.

Crime bosses contracting the murder of another crime boss—as rare as the rooking procedure in chess. Lepke tapped Charlie Workman for the job: Charlie the Bug, Handsome Charlie. "We all agreed we should step aside and let Workman organize the execution," Stacher later said. "The Bug had been in the organization from the beginning, and in my opinion he was just as cold and ruthless as Anastasia."

Mendy Weiss was chosen to work with the Bug. A rising star in Lepke's machine, Weiss was a throwback, an echo of the old days, Plug Uglies and killings on the docks. It was as if some gene, the old-time gang gene, proved recessive, skipping the generation of Lansky and Siegel but reappearing in Weiss. A police report later said of him: "While he is the generally recognized successor to the throne of Lepke, it is alleged that he has a very low intelligence quota, bordering on ignorance. He is of the gargantuan type and is given to the use of ruthless brutality to squelch opposition."

Mendy wore the cheapest suits from the cheapest stores. His coats were roomy, and his pant cuffs dragged on the street. When he pulled his hat over his eyes and smiled, he was nothing but teeth. When he pulled his hat over his eyes and frowned, he was nothing but nose. He had a big, what-the-fuck-you-looking-at snarl. Describing him in the thirties, a detective unknowingly penned a great sketch of the Jewish gangster in general: "From information received, it would appear Weiss is not addicted to gambling, does not drink to any great extent, does not make a habit of associating with women other than his wife, in whose company he is invariably seen when he goes out socially, and is perpetually smoking cigars."

Two nights after the Syndicate meeting, Workman and Weiss were driven to the Palace Chop House in Newark by a man called Piggy, a member of a New Jersey outfit who knew the streets. Piggy was like one of the guys Jack Kerouac gets a ride from in *On the Road:* colorful, then gone. At 10:15, as Piggy waited outside, Charlie and Mendy went in the door. The front room was empty, just a bartender and some waiters milling around. Weiss opened his overcoat, flashing a sawed-off shotgun. "Everyone quiet," he said. "Get down on the floor."

As Mendy handled the people up front, Workman followed the voices to the back room, where Schultz's men were at their regular table, going over receipts: Lulu Rosenkrantz, Abe Landau, Abbadabba Berman. Workman raised his .38 and began firing. Landau slid to the floor and reached for his gun. Lulu kicked over the table and returned fire. Berman probably settled his mind on a beautiful algebraic equation and waited to die. Mendy then walked back, his shotgun blazing. *Bang. Bang. Bang.* Bullets filled the air. Lulu was shot seven times. Berman was shot six times. Two bullets smashed the mirror above the table. "It was like a Wild West show," Workman later said. Five bullets lodged in the restaurant's mint green walls.

Landau, hit once in the neck, once in the arm, kept firing. Mendy had him pinned in a corner. But where was Schultz? Workman let his .38 fall to the floor, took out a .45, and went into the bathroom. There was no one at the urinals, and the mirror above the sink was empty. He killed Dutch in a stall, hitting him below the chest with a .45 slug that went through his stomach, large intestine, gall bladder, and liver before landing beside him on the floor. A second bullet lodged above his head in the wall.

Workman came out to see how Weiss was doing. Everything was okay, so he went back into the bathroom. Bending over, he felt through Schultz's pockets. This was his specialty: heisting the mark. A guy like Dutch might be carrying ten, twenty grand. No. All Schultz had was a three-inch switchblade. Things were quiet when Workman came back to the dining room. The walls were covered with blood. Berman was crawling across the floor. There was a siren in the distance. Where was

Weiss? When Bug came through the front room, the waiters were still on the floor. The whole thing had taken maybe four minutes. Workman could not find Mendy or Piggy or the car outside. He heard a shot behind him. Landau, bleeding from his neck, had reeled after him, firing wildly. Workman shot back, and the bullet spun Landau like a bear in a shooting gallery. He fell onto a garbage can. Workman ran.

Dutch had gotten to his feet inside and made it to the front room. "First thing I noticed was Schultz," the bartender told police. "He came reeling like he was intoxicated. He had a hard time staying on his pins, and he was hanging on to his side. He didn't say a cockeyed thing. He just went over to a table, put his left hand on it to steady him, and then he plopped into a chair, just like a souse would. His head bounced on the table, and I thought that was the end of him, but pretty soon he moved. He said, 'Get a doctor, quick.' "

This story has been told before, always from Schultz's perspective. On my bookshelf I have maybe six different renderings, like different artists' versions of the same event—*The Last Supper.* "Oh the air is bad burned air and humid with blood," writes E. L. Doctorow in *Billy Bathgate,* his fictional portrait of Dutch Schultz. "Mr. Berman slumps forward on the table, his pointed back stressing the material of his plaid jacket in a widening hole of blood." The story always ends with Landau's last heroic shot, playing for pride alone. And the killers racing into the night. "A speeding car without lights a half block away fishtails and wavers a moment and in another moment it is lost in the shadows of the street," writes Doctorow. But what happened next?

Realizing he was alone, Workman ran from the chop house, through a little park, where he dumped his bloodstained overcoat, through a swamp, and into a dump. He walked all night, his shoes full of rain on the shimmery blacktops of New Jersey, looking for the way into Manhattan. He found some train tracks and followed them east. He got angrier as the night wore on. Here he was, doing all the work, killing the big man, and what was Mendy Weiss doing? Running at the first sound of sirens. Mendy had left Workman to die. No way around it. Did everything but put a gun in his mouth. Workman must have been thinking this all the way home, railroad tie to railroad tie, stepping aside to watch a train blow by, the wheels throwing up sparks and water. He followed a tunnel under the Hudson River. When he got to the Lower East Side, the diners were full of businessmen, papers twice folded to read the sports. As

Charlie walked past the corners filling with young hoods, he caught the buzz: Mendy Weiss has killed Dutch Schultz.

Workman went to sleep at a friend's apartment in Chelsea. He woke in the afternoon and sent a message to Lepke. He wanted to kill Weiss. Ditching a partner during a job is a capital offense.

Lepke met Workman and Weiss a few days later at Weiss's house at 400 Ocean Avenue in Brooklyn. Lepke heard out Workman. He then called in Weiss. "I claim that hitting the Dutchman was Mob business," said Mendy. "And I stayed until hitting Dutch was over. But then the Bug went back in the toilet to give the Dutchman a heist. I claim that was not Mob business anymore—that was personal business."

As Lepke listened to the killers, he probably asked questions. Maybe he asked them to repeat things, to say everything a second time. Maybe he spoke softly, so the men had to lean in to hear. Probably he took his time, pausing between sentences, between words. Hearing him talk on such occasions was probably like hearing someone read a key to a crossword puzzle out loud. WELL-GENTLEMEN-DIFFICULT-PROBLEM. Tricks to slow things down, calm tempers; tricks I learned from my father, who learned them on the street as a kid, spying on gangsters.

Lepke told Workman his grudge was not worth more killing. "Forget about it," he said. "It was a mistake, and tell everybody not to talk about it."

What about Weiss taking credit for hitting Dutch?

"What's the difference who shot him?" said Lepke. "He's shot. Let's forget about him. It doesn't make a difference. Why don't you fellows forget the whole thing?"

Workman was sent to Miami to cool off. Luciano was down there, too, and Bug went to see him. He needed to borrow cash. Workman was still complaining when he got to Lucky's hotel. "Here's the money," said Luciano. "Now stop talking about that other thing."

After getting hit in the Palace Chop House, Schultz and his men were taken to Newark City Hospital. Over the next few hours, Landau, Berman, and Rosenkrantz all died. Schultz lived longest. Nurses passed in and out of his room; blood passed in and out of his body. Five thousand cubic centimeters in transfusion. I have a photo of Dutch taken a few hours after he was shot. He is flat on his back in a hospital bed, a blanket pulled to his waist. His face is covered with creases, his hair greased with blood. He looks as if he's trying to sit up, to see who is coming through the door, but really he is just looking at his body. There is a hole in his side, blood running to the sheet. His mouth is locked in a frown, less of disappointment or pain than concentration—a man surveying the damage. He slipped in and out of consciousness. When he came to, Newark detective Luke Conlon asked questions. Schultz probably answered as best he could, but he was dying. The exchanges were cryptic, like late night conversations I have with my girlfriend when she is mostly asleep but I don't know it.

"Who shot you?" Conlon asked.

"The boss himself," said Dutch.

"What did he shoot you for?"

"I showed him," said Dutch. "Did you hear me meet him? An appointment. Appeal stuck. All right, Mother."

"Was it the boss who shot you?" Conlon persisted.

"Who shot me? No one."

"We will help you," said the detective.

"Will you get me up?" asked Schultz. "Okay, I won't be such a big creep. Oh, Mama, I can't go through with it. Oh, please, and then he clips me. C'mon, cut that out! We don't owe a nickel. Hold it. I am a pretty good pretzler."

"Why did they shoot you?"

"I don't know, sir," said Schultz. "Honestly, I don't. I don't even know who was with me. Honestly. I went to the toilet. The boy came at me."

"The big fellow gave it you?" said Conlon.

"Yes, he gave it to me."

"Do you know who the big fellow was?"

"No," said Dutch. "I will be checked and double-checked. Please pray for me. Will you pull? How many good ones and how many bad ones? Please, I had nothing to do with him. He was a cowboy in one of the seven-days-a-week fights. No business. No hangouts. No friends. Nothing."

As the hours passed, Schultz became even less intelligible. His temperature had climbed to 106 by the following afternoon. He slipped into a fever dream. In his last hours he was talking nonstop, a ramble of names and places, snapshots from a dying mind. At four P.M., hoping to gather clues, the cops put a stenographer at his side. The result was gangster prose, mostly nonsensical, but here and there shot through with beauty. "There are only ten of us and there are ten million fighting somewhere in front of you, so get your onions up and we will throw up a truce flag," said Schultz. "He eats like a little sausage baloney maker . . . the sidewalk was in trouble and the bears were in trouble and I broke it up . . . my gilt-edges stuff and those dirty rats have tuned in . . . Please, Mother. You pick me up now . . . a boy has never wept, nor dashed a thousand kiln . . . please crack down on the Chinaman's friends and Hitler's commander. Mother is the best bet, and don't let Satan draw you too fast. I am half-crazy. They won't let me get up. They dyed my shoes. Give me something. I am so sick. Give me some water, the only thing that I want."

Schultz fell into a coma at six P.M. He died a few hours later. In the coming weeks, his empire was divided among the Syndicate board, with Lepke and Gurrah taking the restaurant rackets. In the coming years, Schultz's final words, that great mystical document, were shared by fans of organized crime. Like the writings of Nostradamus, people see things in it, hidden meanings, portents, portents of portents. I suppose the amateur sleuths who once went again and again through the transcript are today tuned in to police scanners.

The gangsters had done Dewey no favor. The death of Schultz may have boosted his life expectancy, but it also set back his career. The Schultz case was to cement Dewey's fame. Now he would have to find another big score—not good news for the gangsters. Tom Dewey, so long occupied with Schultz, would go after the other bosses.

Dewey's ambition soon found Charles Luciano, who was living as Mr. Ross in room 39D of the Waldorf-Astoria. With Schultz gone, Luciano was the big gangster on the New York scene. He was one of the most powerful men in the city, with full control of the docks: what went in, what came out. Each night he showed up in the swankiest clubs with the swankiest girls; each morning he showed up in the gossip columns. Why did Tom Dewey go after Lucky Luciano? Because he was the fattest thing on the menu.

In 1936, with voters convinced the city was run by gangsters, Governor Herbert Lehman, an uptown Jew, appointed Dewey special prosecutor of organized crime. It was a new office, created for a man many believed fated to save New York. Though just thirty-two, Dewey already had the cold stare for which he would be remembered. At times his features seemed to fade away until only a mustache remained, the reedy little mustache that came to mean Tom Dewey. Maybe he is what happens when a mustache takes over, wresting power from the eyes and nose, gaining free reign over a face. On certain Brooklyn streets, the mustache became an object of hatred, the embodiment of all that was wrong with the Republicans: arrogance, contempt for immigrants. In my father's neighborhood, when Dewey came on screen during newsreels, the audience booed. "To many people, he was known only as the man who went after gangsters," Herbert Brownell told me. "He was seen as an object of punishment, something wrathful. He lost his identity and became just another piece of bad news."

Dewey rented office space on the thirteenth floor of the Woolworth Building, a white tower a few blocks from the courthouse. For the first time in New York history, the prosecutors would go after the bosses instead of the soldiers. Dewey turned his office into an anticrime factory, as intent on turning out convictions as Motown was later on turning out hits. Temptations, Four Tops, Supremes; Lucky, Lepke, Gurrah. *We're gonna be famous, boys! Famous!* He refused to underestimate his prey; his office was soundproofed and routinely checked for bugs. Afraid cops on the beat could be bought off, he hired his own police, an enforcement wing. He also hired a crack team of investigators and prosecutors. He wanted only those obsessed with crime, convinced they were the agents of Good. *Tom Dewey, what a righteous man!* He was the spirit of his small-town father come back to finish a task: rid the city of evil, starting with the rackets—illegal cartels that seized control of entire industries. He would even go after those rackets that controlled outlaw industries, like gambling or loan sharking, where crooks muscled crooks. And he had a plan, a way to deprive gangsters of the tricks that kept them in power. Instead of making arrests here and there, he would take the underworld by surprise, locking up hundreds of crooks in a single day. If he was going after gambling, his cops would lock up every bookie, runner, and shylock, preventing them from comparing stories or muscling informants. Dewey's best attacks on the underworld were as unexpected and devastating as Pearl Harbor.

On January 31, 1936, Dewey went after the prostitution racket. At eight P.M., after the police reporters had filed their stories, Dewey's cops began arresting call girls and madams and pimps and bringing them back to the Woolworth Building. For the world of prostitution, it was a complete rout. By midnight there were over one hundred girls in the office. So no one working late in the building got wise (they might unknowingly tip gangsters), the hookers were brought to the thirteenth floor in the freight elevator. Every few minutes the doors clanged open, sending another wave of color into the halls. Girls sat smoking in dark offices, filling the air with smoke and echoes. Some of the most legendary prostitutes in New York were here: Polack Francis, Sadie the Chink, Jennie the Factory. Together they held the secrets of the street, fetishes and crazes, what every man was hiding from his wife. The women sat in the office all night. By dawn they were tired, confused, ready to talk. Looking bleary-eyed across the desk at Dewey (frown, mustache), they spoke of money they made and where it went. In story after story one name came up: Mr. Ross. Sooner or later some part of every score made its way to Mr. Ross, a big shot who lived in the Waldorf. Once Dewey identified Ross as Luciano, it was easy to build an equation: If Lucky is paid by pimps, then Lucky must be the pimp of the pimps, the force behind New York prostitution. In just a few months in his new job, Dewey had brought an indictment against the most powerful gangster in New York.

In 1936 a warrant was issued for Luciano's arrest. Lucky would not surrender. He instead went down to Owney Madden's resort in Hot Springs. Madden paid off enough cops and judges to delay arrest for months. Men like Lucky rarely fled the country; they were American, and by God if they would be run off by some glee club squirt like Tom Dewey. In any other situation, Lucky might have turned himself in, and gotten it over with. But the charges caught him by surprise. Prostitution? Since the early twenties, when he was just the brightest of the East Side rats, Lucky had been involved in every form of devilment—theft, bootlegging, shylocking, drug running, racketeering, killing. Maybe the only thing he never touched was prostitution. "Charlie had the same revulsion about running brothels that I did," Meyer Lansky later said. "He believed no respectable man should ever make money out of a woman in that horrible way." That fall twenty Arkansas Rangers came for Luciano. He was cuffed and put on a train, green fields giving way to the parched brown autumn of the North.

The trial lasted three weeks. Judge McCook's courtroom overflowed with spectators. Gangsters in candy-striped suits cut the room into neat squares of color. Lucky, in somber grays, was full of hope, of action. There is a picture of him in court, surrounded by lawyers. They look straight ahead. He looks off to the side, into the camera. Cameras understood the gangsters in a way the cops never could—the camera knew these were the brightest men in the room, shedding light as they walked.

Dewey called dozens of witnesses, prostitutes who flashed the name "Mr. Ross" like a mirror, something to catch the jurors' eyes. The case looks flimsy in retrospect, a construction of fragments and half-truths. The hookers spoke of their lives, how they had been degraded, their innocence sold for a dollar, which often found its way to Mr. Ross. Of course, by paying Lucky, the pimps were really just paying the Syndicate, a tribute that bought protection from cops and judges, the very system that was now judging Luciano. Lucky did not help himself on the stand. He was picked apart, his manners as much on trial as his actions. The *Daily News* claimed: DEWEY RIDDLES LUCIANO.

One of Dewey's final witnesses was Molly Brown, a chambermaid at the Waldorf. Brown identified Lucky as Mr. Ross. She said Lucky's room was often the last to be made up, that he almost always slept in. I suppose this showed Luciano as a man without a clear means of support, or maybe it just showed him as a loafer, but it strikes me as an attack on late sleepers. If sleeping late is a crime, I and a lot of my friends belong in jail. I'm not saying Luciano was innocent; he was probably the least innocent man alive. I just don't think he was convicted for the crimes he committed; he was convicted for being considered a criminal. It would be like getting Al Capone for tax evasion if Al Capone had paid his taxes. There was something un-American about it. Just because you're a crook doesn't mean you should be railroaded. To the underworld, Dewey had broken the rules. "With the gangsters, we had a certain understanding," Ralph Salerno told me. "The gangsters said to us: Don't frame me. Don't drop a little envelope in my pocket, then run up and say, 'I caught you with narcotics.' That's a frame-up. That's a no-no. That's what I demand of you, Ralph. But what I give you in return is, if you ever catch me right, I go to jail and do my time. And they don't drag me out of the courtroom saying, 'You son of a bitch, you and your family are dead.' None of that crap. I'm a professional. And if you be a real professional, too, and catch me right, then it's not personal."

The day the verdict came in, Foley Square in front of the courthouse filled with people, mostly Italian immigrants rooting for Lucky. Faceless old men, features worn down by life; broad-shouldered sons, their boots caked in mud; daughters drawn in a single stroke, dark steady eyes; frock-coated Betties, facial hair dark and coarse. They stood all morning in a sky cut by buildings. At noon the verdict ran in whispers through the crowd: Guilty. The jury spent an hour reading the verdict: Guilty on 558 counts.

There are reasons you should never let your friends call you Lucky, reasons entirely too obvious to discuss. Charles Luciano was sentenced to thirty to fifty years in prison, the longest penalty ever given for prostitution. "After sittin' in court and listenin' to myself bein' plastered to the wall and tarred and feathered by a bunch of whores who sold themselves for a quarter, and hearin' that no-good McCook [the judge] hand me what added up to a life term, I still get madder at Dewey's crap than anythin' else," Luciano wrote in his autobiography, *The Last Testament.* "That little shit with the mustache comes right out in the open and admits he got me on everythin' else but what he charged me with. I knew he knew I didn't have a fuckin' thing to do with prostitution, not with none of those broads. But Dewey was such a goddamn racketeer himself, in a legal way, that he crawled up my back with a frame and stabbed me."

When Luciano went to prison, he left behind stories for the public, lessons for the gangsters. For Lansky, his friend's fate was best read as a fable, a moral waiting patiently at the end. From Luciano's fall, Lansky took away the prize of anonymity. He came to cherish the shadows, the background. A gangster in the papers is a gangster headed for a fall, a piñata every cop in America wants to bust open. In the future, Lansky would steer clear of the flash bulbs. He would live a humble life, a tract house in North Miami Beach, just another retired peddler, a shrug and smile saying, "Forget me. I'm just a schnorrer."

Lepke took away a different lesson. It's nothing new: two men read the same text and hear different stories. To Louis, Lucky Luciano was just another example of what the bastards will stoop to. Here was a man who did everything right, paid off cops, bought politicians, hid the money, distanced himself from violence, paid his taxes. And what happens? The government cooks the case, gets low-level crooks to send him away for the one thing he never did. For Lepke, the story had a bloody moral: You only beat the prosecutors if you destroy the case; you only destroy the case if you steal the witnesses—an errand he would run long after Dewey left for the governor's mansion, and the fight was taken up by Frank Hogan in the Manhattan DA's Office, William O'Dwyer in the Brooklyn DA's Office, and J. Edgar Hoover at the FBI. To meet such threats, Lepke remade Murder Inc. from the enforcement arm of the Syndicate to his own private army, a troop that would act on his every fear, every suspicion. He was forever looking for loose ends, anyone with a gripe, who might fall into the wrong hands, a tool in a prosecutor's plan. He was looking for people like Joe Rosen, a garment industry trucker whom Lepke drove out of business.

When he took over Rosen's company, Lepke promised to take care of him. A few weeks later Rosen was fired by his new boss. He went to Lepke's office to see a man named Rubin. "Lepke and you promised I would be taken care of," Rosen said. Lepke got Rosen a job driving for Garfield Express, a local trucking company. Again Rosen was fired. He was out of work for eighteen months. He opened a candy store in Brownsville, but almost no one came in. Like all men who have seen their prime brush past, Rosen began talking of the old days, back before that thug Lepke ruined him. In 1936, when Dewey began investigating the garment rackets, Rosen was an obvious problem. He was just the kind of loose end Lepke wanted tied down. Lepke got Rosen another driving job, but he soon quit, complaining of a bad heart. This upset Lepke. "Rosen is going around Brownsville shooting off his mouth," he said. "He is saying that he is going down to Dewey's office."

Rubin told Lepke he would take care of it. He sent a few dozen union members to Rosen's candy store to buy things they probably didn't want. I like to think of them there, truckers and cutters, ruddy faces peering through frosted glass—*Yeah, give me five dozen ring-dings*—like something from O. Henry, where beneficence rains down. A few days later, when Dewey's men began asking around Brownsville, Lepke sent Rubin to the candy store. Handing Rosen an envelope, Rubin said, "Here's two hundred dollars. Lepke wants you to go away until things cool down." Before he left, Rubin turned and said, "You better do what he says."

Rosen went to see his son in Reading, Pennsylvania, a coal town in the Allegheny Mountains. Rosen was one of the first of many possible informants Lepke gave the ultimatum: Dead or out of town. It was Lepke's version of a witness relocation program: relocate the witness so he cannot testify. Louis moved them to the hinterlands, the West or a drowsy southern street, where they could lead a new life, far from prying prosecutor eyes. For a lot of people, dead or out of town was not such an easy choice. Out of town meant away from the smells, memories, streets, friends, family, plans, promises, appetites, comforts of home. Dead or out of town. What's the difference?

Within a week Rosen got a note from his wife. She was sick. Seizing on the excuse, he rushed east, the Manhattan skyline rising up in his train window. He was soon back on the street, his silhouette visible in the candy store, the small-town sight of a merchant checking inventory. Lepke had a reputation for calm; his manner was cool and direct, but there was an edge to it. A man who loses control is a man who makes mistakes, gets killed. Lepke knew that. But this was too much. *Of course this pathetic little guy can't hold a job. He can't even stay out of town.* Lepke's eyes flashed when he heard Rosen was back. Albert Tannenbaum was in the next room. Why should Allie, who was in to see Lepke several times a month, remember this particular day? Because this was the only time he ever heard Lepke lose his temper. "I stood enough of this crap," yelled Lepke. "That son of a bitch Rosen, that bastard, he's going around again and shooting his mouth off about seeing Dewey. He and nobody else is going any place and do any talking. I'll take care of him."

A few days later Sholem Bernstein saw Pep Strauss on the corner. Pulling Sholem aside, Strauss said, "Go clip me a car." Soon after that, Sholem and Louis Capone went for a ride. As they spoke, the storefronts of Brownsville ran past. Taking a right onto Sutter Avenue, Capone, his wide, somber face caught in profile, pointed to a small candy store and said, "That is where somebody is going to get killed." He drove on, past parched lawns and run-down houses, stopping when they reached a siding near some train tracks. Pulling over, Capone said, "This is where you will dump the car." And that's how Sholem found out he would be driving getaway, following a route as carefully plotted as a distant star system. Capone had figured this the best way to the drop, where the men would dump the kill car and make their escape. Pointing out each landmark ("Watch this," "Make sure here"), Capone took Bernstein again and again from the candy store on Sutter, left on

Wyona, right on Blake, left on Pennsylvania, right on Snediker, right on Livonia, and then on to Van Sinderen, a dusty half road that runs along the BMT tracks, the course forming a neat line, a constellation in the Brooklyn night. "He showed me the route again and again," Sholem later said. "Seven or eight times we went over it. I learned it by heart."

As he left Sholem on the corner, Capone said, "Go steal plates. Take them where they won't be missed right away. Put them on the hot car and bring it over at about half-past ten."

The triggermen would be Pep Strauss and Mendy Weiss. Jews to kill a Jew; experts to erase a glitch. A few nights later the men drove by the candy store but did not like the setup. It was across from an ice-cream shop, a haunt of some local shylocks. Pep was afraid some of the sharks might recognize them as they fled. Why kill one rat just to create another? They decided to fill the contract early the next morning, before the ice-cream place opened.

Strauss showed up at the candy store at 7:30 A.M. Weiss was just then in the shadows near Rosen's house. When Mendy saw Rosen step into the street, he ran around the corner, where Sholem was waiting. "That rat just come out," he said. "Go over and get the car and stop in front of the candy store. Be sure the motor is running."

When Rosen got to his store, he undid the locks, switched on the lights, began setting up for another day of not much business. When he saw the men coming through the door, he maybe thought, Customers! Probably not. Weiss and Strauss, the look in their eyes was probably not the look you see in the eyes of those off to buy candy. Before Rosen could say a word, the killers were shooting. Smoke drifted from the barrels of the guns. When their time came, marks often saw nothing but the flash of guns. A few months before, when Dasher killed a thug named Spider Murtha, the woman with Murtha told the cops she remembered not faces or clothes or voices, but only "the blue flames from the pistols." Hit twice in the chest, Rosen streaked blood on a glass candy case as he fell to the floor. In the street, Sholem was just another commuter riding car pool, waiting for his passengers. When he heard the shots, he leaned across the seat and pushed open the door. Strauss and Weiss walked from the store, smoothing their coats. When they got in the car, Sholem hit the gas, lurching off into early morning Brownsville. He followed the getaway route turn by turn, as easy and inevitable as a chain of events in a dream.

When Sholem reached the BMT tracks, two cars were waiting. Louis Capone was at the wheel of one; Little Farvel Cohen was at the wheel of the other. The killers rumbled off in Capone's car. Sholem took a last look through the kill car, like a man searching a hotel room before he checks out, then got in with Little Farvel and was gone, streets just stirring to life. "When did you learn the identity of the murder victim?" a prosecutor later asked.

"When I picked up the paper that night," said Bernstein. "I seen a picture of the killing and the name. I didn't know the man."

A few months later one of the boys came across another loose end. Whitey Rudnick, a low-level member of the troop, was seen meeting with a lawyer on Dewey's staff. Being seen with a cop or a prosecutor—not good. Whitey was a heroin addict, a junkie who sailed the rough spots on water and cocaine—a weakness that made him vulnerable to cops, prosecutors, anyone who might cut a deal. He was what the boys called a floater, a solitary figure who rambled each night through Brooklyn. "He used to drift on all the corners," Reles said.

"See, I told you the bastard was a stool pigeon," Pep said one day.

"Who?" asked Reles, having just arrived at the corner.

"Your pal Rudnick," said Pep. "I seen him coming out of Harry Browser's car." Browser was a prosecutor in Dewey's office. "You know what that means," Strauss went on. "That bum has to be taken."

Reles had known Whitey for years on the corner and before that at Elmira Reformatory upstate. Before the boys decided to kill Whitey, they would have done him almost any favor. Everyone liked him.

"Well," said Reles, "if he has to be taken, we will take him."

To let the world know why Rudnick was being killed, the boys decided to plant a note on him, something to identify him as a rat. "I'll have Sholem grab us a typewriter," said Reles. "He'll bring it to my place and we'll write the note over there." The typewriter must have looked funny in the Kid's house, an oddly cerebral touch, an off note in a bawdy song.

The gangsters got to work a few nights later. They would forge a letter, Browser thanking Rudnick for the helpful information. When the note hit the newspapers, the boys figured, the headlines would do the rest: RUDNICK KILLED FOR TALKING TO DEWEY.

The typewriter was broken. Reles held the ribbon as Pep hacked away. They began: Freind George.

"No, you got it wrong," said Reles. "You got 'friend' spelled backwards."

"What the fuck?" said Pep, looking up. "Does it start with a D?"

"No, Pep. It's spelled f-r-i-e-n-d."

"What are you, a genius?" said Pep. "How the hell should you know anything about this shit?"

"I don't know shit about shit, but I know you're wrong."

They couldn't decide. It was a terrific fight. I imagine them going at it, a Brooklyn living room, figures in a window, yelling, hands waving, grunts, sighs. I see them in a long line of great comedy teams: Abbott and Costello, Gleason and Carney. "All right," Pep finally said. "I'll try it your way."

He rolled in a fresh sheet of paper and typed: "Dear Friend."

Both men looked at the page. "Yeah, you were right," said Reles. "That ain't it."

"See, jackass," said Pep. "What'd I tell ya?"

Pep put in another page and typed:

> Freind George:
>
> Will you please meet me in NY some day in reference to what you told me last week. Also I have that certain powder that I promised you the last time I seen you. PS I hope you found this in your letter box sealed. I remain your freind. YOU KNOW, FROM DEWEY'S, THE DISTRICT ATTORNEY'S OFFICE.

Handling the note, Reles wore gloves. When finished, he sealed the envelope and slid it to the back of a drawer. He then burned the wasted paper in the bathroom, flushing the cinders down the toilet.

For the next few nights Reles waited on the corner, note in pocket. Dasher was with him. When they got Whitey Rudnick, they would take him to Happy Maione's garage in Ocean Hill, where Strauss and

Maione would be waiting. When a lawyer later asked Reles if the boys had any more definite plan, he said, "We didn't need any plan. We are experts."

For three nights Reles and Maione waited on the corner midnight to five A.M. They watched traffic, heard kids brag, saw lights go off and on. They went out early the fourth night, May 25, 1937. At around four-thirty A.M., Reles saw a figure stealing along the building line. "It's him," he said. "It's Rudnick."

"You're crazy," said Dasher. "That ain't him." Then, when the figure got closer: "Shit. You're right. That is him."

Dasher ran for his car. Rudnick was probably familiar enough with the routine to know what it meant when Dasher, seeing him, went off the other direction. Turning on his heels, Rudnick went the way he came. When Dasher came by in his car, he rolled down his window. "We have to take him tonight," he told Reles. "If I have to drag him in the car, I will get him tonight."

A few minutes later Reles got in his own car and drove to Ocean Hill. Across from Maione's garage was an apartment where his grandparents lived. Happy's grandfather was very sick, a bedridden old man surrounded by relatives. Now and then there was a rap on the garage door: a cousin telling Happy how the old man was doing. He was dying up there, warped wood floors, shadows, priests. It must have been a strange night for Maione, death, violence, old age, murder, the same note rung again and again.

Reles took his time getting to the garage. He was growing tired of the life, the struggle of every night. By the time he showed up, the job was mostly done. Coming through the door, he saw Dasher pinning Rudnick to the floor; Pep tying a rope around Rudnick's neck; an ice pick on the ground next to Pep. "We don't need you," said Happy, holding a meat cleaver. "The work is all over."

Stepping into the driveway, Happy wiped his hands. "You would not think a skinny bum would put up a fight like that," he said. "It was not as easy as it looked."

A few minutes later a neighborhood kid showed up with a clipped sedan. As Happy directed, the kid backed the car into the garage, next to the body. Dasher took Rudnick by the feet and Pep got him by the shoulders; they pushed him into the backseat. "Was there difficulty putting Rudnick's body in the car?" a prosecutor later asked.

"He was too long," said Reles. "Dasher crumples his legs up; you know what I mean? That makes a guy shorter."

As they folded the body, it let out a groan. It must have been like some spooky Isaac Bashevis Singer story, where the dead cry out, a reproach from the other side: *Why have You forsaken me?* "This goddamn bum ain't dead yet," said Strauss, pulling the body onto the running board. He reached for the ice pick and punched some holes in Rudnick. "That oughtta finish the bum," he said. The killers slid Rudnick back into the car. Leaning in, Happy said, "Let me hit this son of a bitch for luck." And he took a few whacks with a cleaver. "One of them butcher things like you hit bones or meat with," Reles later explained. "All I know, I hear the dull noise."

The boys got in the car and lit out for the far reaches of Brooklyn. Reles followed in the crash car. They left the kill car, which had been stolen in East New York, on a residential street in Bushwick. After switching off the ignition, Happy slid the fake note into Rudnick's pocket. Settling into the crash car, he said, "When they find the guy with the note in his pocket, there's going to be some big splash."

When cops found the body the next morning, they were more impressed by the carnage than the prose. "As he [the cop] looked inside he made a ghastly find," a prosecutor later told a jury. "Propped up against the door, in the rear compartment of this car, was the mutilated body of a dead man. His head was gashed; his hair was matted with blood; his shirt was bloody; there was a rope tightly knotted around the throat of the corpse at the level of the larynx or Adam's apple. The neck and face above this constricting rope were intensely blue. The tongue protruded between the lips." The boys had stabbed Rudnick over sixty times.

When Happy got back to his garage, the sun was just coming up. The street was full of sour-faced men and teary women. The men held hats and touched handkerchiefs to their eyes. Their coats fell into the shadows, leaving their heads suspended, a magician's trick. Happy rolled through the faces, eyes, mouths. Stepping from the car, he was surrounded by relatives. *Your grandfather died tonight, Happy.* Looking across the crowd, he must have realized the gift the old man had left him: an alibi. *No way. Happy Maione had nothing to do with this. What kind of sick bastard kills a junkie the very night of his grandfather's death?*

Lepke went into hiding in the summer of 1937. Things had been getting increasingly difficult for the boss. The feds were closing fast with a narcotics rap, the business he inherited from Arnold Rothstein. William O'Dwyer, the Brooklyn DA, was looking into Lepke's racketeering. Heading the investigation was Burton Turkus, a young prosecutor who would soon prove more dangerous than the Ambergs, Shapiros, or Schultz mob. "He doesn't conform to the general pattern of the prosecutor," wrote Sid Feder, a reporter for the Associated Press. "He dotes on the theatrics of the courtroom and the criminal trial. But he is neither politician nor publicity hound. He looks like the movie version of a DA—suave, dynamic in conversation, sharp." To gangsters, Burton Turkus was "Mr. Arsenic."

Lepke was tipped a few days before the first indictment came down. Rather than wait for the knock on the door, he decided to vanish, to go off somewhere, to orchestrate from the shadows, destroying the government case before it could be made. When all the talkers had been silenced and all the sinners bought off, he would come in alone, a smile and a suit ready to be judged. Until then he would be gone, as vague as smoke in a bottle. Where would he go? Well, he would not make the same mistake as Luciano. He would not go somewhere like Hot Springs, a not very well kept secret, where lawyers could extract him like a splinter. And he would not follow the lead of Vito Genovese, who fled with money to Italy. For Jews, Europe was becoming the worst jail of all. Lepke would instead do what Anne Frank and so many other European Jews would do just a few years later. Disappear at home, moving from this world into a parallel of hidden stairs and false doors, a phantom gangster.

Before Lepke went on the lam, he called a meeting of underworld bosses. Lansky was there, and so was Bugsy Siegel, Albert A., Moey "Dimples" Wolensky, who worked for Lansky, and Longy Zwillman, the boss of Newark. These men had all known Lepke since he was a kid, and it was as though they had come to say good-bye. Louis was going off the map, where he could not be seen or heard. He wanted the blessing of these men before he went. After all, it was other members of the Mob who would have to hide and protect him; and when the cops got frustrated, they would take the heat. Lepke explained his plans, how he and Gurrah would split, both lamming it but not together, how Albert A. would keep them hidden, how Mendy Weiss would take over the troop but still follow Lepke's command. The other gangsters agreed this was the only way: *What the hell, Lep, we don't want the feds should fry ya!*

Louis Lepke was the most wanted man in American history. When the cops realized he was missing, they acted as though a drum of plutonium were gone. Their investigation swelled into a massive manhunt, with more cops out looking for Lepke than ever beat the brush for Jesse James. As Mussolini, Tojo, and Hitler were just hitting their stride, J. Edgar Hoover called Lepke the most dangerous man alive, Public Enemy Number One. Over one hundred thousand Wanted posters were printed and sent to post offices and police stations, passed out at ball games and schools, tacked to phone poles and grocery pegboards, hung in train depots, embassies, and consulates around the world: a dark, melancholy face seen at two angles; low forehead, tired, spaniel eyes. He was soon being spotted everywhere. There were false Lepke sightings in England, upstate New York, on a yacht off South America, in Warsaw, Poland, where he was said to be planning a kidnapping, in Puerto Rico, Cuba, Canada, Vermont, the West and Northwest, in bars, hotels, casinos, swimming pools, restaurants. People hoping to find Lepke probably saw themselves in the newspaper under the headline HERO! For those hoping not to find him, that same headline was MISSING! For those with not much going in their lives, the idea of Lepke, the criminal at large, supplied a harmless diversion. In the years before the Second World War, Lepke was a drama here at home, a national treasure hunt: Where is the gangster?

Where was Lepke? Off radar, moving place to place, house to house, surfacing for a meal, a drink, a talk. Even now his whereabouts in those days remain mysterious. What we do know comes from talkative gang members, like Reles and Tannenbaum. Putting the pieces together, we are left with a herky-jerky film shot on super-eight, full of jumps and skips, some frames missing, others burned at the edges.

Lepke hid first in Newark, New Jersey. Gurrah was in Newark, too, a basement room across town. They sometimes met late at night, a Romanian-Hebrew restaurant for goulash. They would sit long after the plates were cleared, talking, playing cards. A lamster should never stay too long in one place; his path through the world soon makes a pattern, and patterns can be detected. When fall came, Gurrah left for the Midwest, some safe town where a wanted man can melt into the trees. Without Lepke to watch him, Gurrah began acting up. The silence of underground life was too much for him, and he was soon turning up in clubs, at bars, making phone calls. Mendy Weiss got in touch with Lepke. He wanted to reunite the gangsters, hoping Louis could pacify his old friend, the mind could ground the body. But Gurrah wanted more than a familiar face; he wanted his old life back. Gangsters of a certain sort, wild, physical gangsters, wilt in hiding. Like certain species of vine, they die without constant exposure to the sun. Gurrah complained of chest pains, shortness of breath. On April 14, 1938, too sick to go on, he turned himself in on a racketeering charge. He was sent to prison for life.

Lepke spent a few months out west, a ranch in the hills. Lansky went to see Lepke, to tell him to break up his gang. The Syndicate would keep Workman on salary; the other boys would go their own way. Lansky said the gang would run out of money, then become a burden on the other bosses. It was the first sign of discord, the first suggestion that Lepke in hiding was trouble. "Nothing doing," he told Lansky. Without his boys, Lepke knew he would be just another old man holed up in an apartment, hiding from the world.

When Lepke got back to town, he put himself in the charge of Albert A., who moved the boss place to place, a step ahead of the cops. Lepke lived for a time above a nightclub in Coney Island, Cavitola's Oriental Danceland, 2780 Stillwell Avenue; Cavitola was related by marriage to Louis Capone. From there, Lepke went to live in the house of a friend's friend on Ninety-first and Avenue A, a few blocks from Reles. For the Kid, a rock star had moved to the neighborhood. He spent a lot of time over there, becoming close to Lepke, someone who shared his secrets. Reles was one of Lepke's few links with the street, with everything exciting. When the Kid walked through a doubled-locked door, down a dark hall, his face coming in and out of the light, Lepke must have felt a kind of envy, the jealousy the dead have for the living. Reles would sometimes take Lepke on ghostly, late night drives, the boss gazing at the flat, unwinding roads of Brooklyn. He rarely got to see his family. The world came to him through newspapers only or else on the words of those sheltering him, gangsters who brought him news in dribs and drabs, each with his own motives, each coloring the facts with his own ambition, his own desires.

Of course, all the boys wanted to see Lepke. Being taken to the hideout was like being entrusted with a national secret. One night

Mendy Weiss ran into Albert Tannenbaum. *Hey, Allie? Want to see the boss?*

Sure. Who doesn't?

"Well, if you're a good boy, you'll get to see him," said Weiss.

A few weeks later Weiss met Tannenbaum at Yiddel Lorber's, the joint near the Williamsburg Bridge where Pretty Amberg was killed. Little Farvel Cohen was there, too. The three men got in a black sedan and went to a deli, where they picked up sandwiches and champagne. It was New Year's Eve 1938. From there they drove through Brooklyn like guys in a cop show trying to ditch a tail: the wrong way down one-way streets, cutting through alleys, doubling back. They reached the hideout at eleven. They came through the door one at a time, hugged the boss, smiled. Corks were popped, coats draped across chair backs. They talked into the early morning, legs shuffling past the cellar window. Though he rarely left his room, Lepke said he needed new suits. He was like an iron-willed British colonial wearing dress reds in the jungle. Tannenbaum took Lepke's measurements; a few days later he would bring over the clothes.

At three A.M. the boys got up to leave. Lepke pulled Weiss aside. The boss said he wanted to see his wife; he had not spoken to her in months. "Don't worry," said Mendy. "I'll take care of it." Mendy must have liked having control over his boss. Here was the most powerful man anyone knew, and he couldn't walk out the door; he was as beautiful a piece of wasted work as a ship in a bottle.

Keeping Lepke hidden was not easy. For Albert A. it was almost a full-time job. He was like a man playing chess, always five moves ahead, guessing when neighbors would get wise, when the cops would show up. A hideout is like a carton of milk; it should be marked with a date of expiration. If you get three months out of a hideout, you're satisfied. Even the best spots, the back room of some old lady's house, could go bad in an instant. When it did, Anastasia had to have the next move planned, and the move after that. At one point, perhaps tired of the basement-to-basement shuffle, he tried to build Lepke a more stable existence. Calling in Tannenbaum, Anastasia explained his plan, how Tick-Tock would move to Elizabeth, New Jersey, start a business, buy a house. In a few months, when Tannenbaum was established, Lepke would move in. Work hard, he told Allie. Keep regular hours, dress simple. Tannenbaum would be working closely with Longy Zwillman, the boss of Newark.

Longy's boys asked Tannenbaum what kind of business he would start. A haberdashery, said Allie. Zwillman at first said okay, then changed his mind. He wanted Tick-Tock to sell bottled mineral water. He gave Allie $300 to get started. Allie went alone to Elizabeth, an entrepreneur looking into dusty For Rent windows. In town he used his wife's maiden name, Milburn, and told people he had moved from St. Louis. Who could believe him? He had a tight little gangster mouth and the war-torn features of a man whose boss is on the lam. He called his store the Union County Mineral Water Company. From a distributor he bought water at twenty cents a gallon, which he would then sell for thirty-five cents. He opened a bank account with his gangster money, bought a Ford, and hired a seventeen-year-old kid to run deliveries. For a week he took orders and wrote checks, glimpsing the life his father must have wanted for him.

Tannenbaum found a house, eighty dollars a month for a wood-frame, two-story, one-family corner of suburbia. It was surrounded by tall shrubs, as he was told it should be. There were three bedrooms, a glassed-in porch, heated garage, living room, dining room, pantry, kitchen. When he was on his way out for furniture, he got a call from Zwillman: FBI agents are going around Elizabeth asking questions; return to New York City. For Anastasia, one of a dozen plans had gone bad; for Allie, an errand had been wasted. But what about the delivery boy? Did he get another job? Does he still tell the story? Somebody knows; not me.

Anastasia at last found the perfect hideout: a basement apartment on Thirteenth Street in Brooklyn. The building was owned by Mary Porzia, an old lady from the same part of Calabria, Italy, as Anastasia. In the winter of 1939 Reles drove the boss to his new home. Lepke had grown a mustache and wore a fedora pulled low over his eyes. He had gained twenty pounds and had the haggard look of a fugitive; he left some of his defiance in each vacated hideout. Next to Lepke sat a red-haired woman with a baby: Buggsy Goldstein's sister-in-law and nephew. Anyone searching for Lepke would probably be looking for a dark, solitary gangster, not a family man.

Lepke lived in an apartment below the stairs: kitchenette, sitting room, bedroom. Over the next few months he would run the troop from the cellar, giving orders that changed lives across the country. The other boarder in the house was Eugene Salvese, a longshoreman from Italy. Though Salvese had come illegally to America, he was trying to set things straight. He had been several times to the American embassy, through lines that wound out the door. One evening he pushed back his blinds for a look at the street: storefronts, stoops, garbage cans. Across the way he saw a stocky man staring at the building. There was something suspicious about him. After a while he walked off; Salvese watched him go. A few days later Salvese was introduced to the stranger. "Eugene, I want you to meet someone," said Miss Porzia. "This is Abraham Reles. We have a new boarder, and Mr. Reles will give you that man's rent." Each week Salvese met the Kid at the Saratoga Avenue subway station, where he picked up Lepke's rent: fifty bucks. Salvese was paying ten.

One night, as Salvese was walking home from the docks, he met Reles in the street. "You're a good fellow," Reles told him. "Don't talk to anybody about the boarder in the basement. You work hard for a living. If you do as I say and don't talk to anybody and be a good fellow, maybe you won't have to work anymore."

"I have always worked for a living," said Salvese, turning away. "Why should it be different now?" After that, Reles told the landlady he did not want Salvese around when he came to see Lepke.

Each night, on his way home, Salvese picked up the papers for Lepke: the *Daily News,* the *Daily Mirror.* He had no idea of Lepke's fame and knew him only as a strange man who never went out, who lived for his newspapers. A snapshot of Lepke near the end: closed in a bunker, following his fate in the press, a blip on a radar screen. There were stories about the boss every day: some overzealous small-town cop spotting the name "Bukalter" on a mailbox and launching an investigation. Julius Bukalter turned out to be an eighty-three-year-old Lithuanian-born Jew, a retired teacher who once taught on Clinton Street on the Lower East Side. A letter from a man who spotted some crazy wandering the woods with a shotgun; could this be Lepke spying for Germany? "I'm pretty sure there are some airforce bases around here," wrote the concerned citizen. "Maybe this is the criminal out gathering information for the enemy."

In the spring of 1939 Salvese went to Cuba. His idea was to travel to Havana, turn around, and reenter America, this time legally. On the wall of the U.S. Immigration Office in Cuba, he saw a Wanted poster. The face on the poster was hard to make out, but he was almost sure it was the man in the basement. When no one was around, he took down the poster and folded it into his pocket. When Salvese got back to New York, Lepke had already moved on. Pulling aside his landlady, Salvese took out the poster. "Look at this," he told her. "This is a fine mess you've dragged me into, especially when I'm trying so hard to become an American citizen. I have lived in America fourteen years, and this might be the end of it."

Porzia told Salvese he needed a rest. She suggested he spend time in Saratoga. When he said he could not afford such a trip, she said money was no problem, that he should pack a bag and go the next morning to a corner on Saratoga Avenue. She knew some men who would drive him upstate and find him a cheap place to stay. When Salvese showed up, Reles was waiting. Taking Salvese's arm, Reles nodded to a car. "I went over to the car and I was very much afraid to get in," Salvese later said. "I thought I was going for a ride. But they hustled me into the back of the car and off we went, driving like the hammers of hell. All the time we drove, they spoke only to each other and seemed not even to notice me. They called each other Harry and Al."

Salvese was left at a rooming house on the edge of town. He spent a month up there, walking the woods, swimming—Lepke's way of paying a man for his trouble, buying his loyalty, his silence. When Salvese got back to Thirteenth Street, he was tan and relaxed, not a bad word to say of anyone.

Lepke was living with Dorothy Walker, the daughter of gangster Fatty Walker. After dinner Lepke would push back his chair and say something nice about Walker's cooking. He complained about the last person he stayed with, Miss Porzia, whose menu drove him to distraction. Sometimes it was spaghetti every night for a week. Reles was often with Lepke. When the gangsters talked business, Walker excused herself to the next room. She was not impressed with Reles. To his face she called him Shorty. Behind his back, who knows? The hideout was at 2720 Foster Avenue, a few blocks from Midwood High School, where my mom would eventually be a shy freshman in cat-eye glasses. Lepke slept in the back room of the brick house, a stoop and a porch out front, no different from a dozen other houses on that sad street. To the north the road climbed a rise before running off to the stores of Kings Highway. At Midwood the teachers must have discussed Lepke, how man is done in by crime, ruined by dark angels. And here, a short walk away, a newspaper spread across a kitchen table, was the wreck himself, looking no different than their fathers.

There was probably disagreement about Lepke in the high schools of Brooklyn. To teachers, who were often from middle-class Protestant homes, it was a simple case of a thug run amok. To students, who watched immigrant fathers struggle to find a place in America, Lepke was more complicated. While men like my grandfather had a clear sense of right and wrong, it was hard for sons not to admire gangsters. In Reles and Strauss they saw fearless Jews, men at war with an unfair world. As cops were combing streets for Lepke, Nazis were boycotting and tagging Jews in Germany, persecution that was maybe not well-known in the rest of America but was talked about in Brooklyn. Most Jews still had family in the old country, and the bad news came in letters that grew cloudier and cloudier, before the letters stopped coming altogether. In a time when the leaders of the West still hoped to strike a deal with the Fascists, gangsters were among the few who understood the enemy. When asked by Burton Turkus what he thought of the situation in Europe, Reles said, "It's a cinch."

"What do you mean, a cinch?" asked Turkus.

"They're just the same as the Combination," said the Kid. "We are out to get America by the pocketbook. When we have to, we kill people to do it. Hitler and Mussolini, they're trying to do the same thing, only they're trying to get the whole world. And they will kill people by the millions to get it."

The gangsters were a prototype of a new kind of Jew, the sporty, all-terrain model that would emerge from the ashes of World War II. Men like Lepke and Lansky were among the first Jews to know the truth about violence, that people pity the victims but yield to the victors. Long before the Holocaust, they knew about learning, how little it means when jackboots hit the landing. These men were not religious in the go-to-temple, keep-the-Sabbath way, but they were all for the Jews. The best of them knew there was no running away, that you either become more of yourself, running toward your identity, or become nothing at all, Jonah fleeing God. As the war came, they understood Nazis in a way most law-abiding adults could not. They knew what men are capable of, how far someone like Hitler would go, and they knew it could not be fought with reason or treaties or sanctions. The gangsters, who cared mostly about getting rich, knew some things were just not about money. They knew the only way to deal with Nazis was the way you would deal with them on the street. Not only would this win admiration from kids like my dad, it had a sound intellectual underpinning: it is hard for someone who has just had his lip split to believe he is a superman. "We knew how to handle them," Meyer Lansky told Uri Dan. "The Italians I knew offered help, but as a matter of pride, I wouldn't accept. I must say I enjoyed beating up Nazis. There were times when we treated some big anti-Semite in a very special way, but the main point was to teach them that Jews cannot be kicked around."

Pro-Nazi groups began organizing in America in the mid-thirties. Fueled by a rabid anti-Semitism, they had names like the German American Bund. "A pro-Nazi organization that spread Nazi-style anti-Semitic slogans," Lansky went on. "They strutted around and made threats, like throwing all Jews into concentration camps." By 1939 the American Nazi movement was strong enough to attract twenty-eight thousand people to a rally at Madison Square Garden. "I was always very sensitive to anti-Semitism, but during those years other people also became worried," Lansky said. "Important WASPs, as we would call them now, openly made anti-Semitic statements, and some magazines and papers backed them. This worried Jewish leaders, including the most respected of all, Rabbi Stephen Wise. He sent a message asking me to do something about this dangerous trend. Another Jewish leader who was worried was a respected New York judge, an important member of the Republican Party. We knew each other, and one day in 1935 he came to see me and said, 'Nazism is flourishing in the United States. The Bund members are not ashamed to have meetings in the most public places. We Jews should be more militant. Meyer, we want to take action against these Nazi sympathizers. We'll put money and legal assistance at your disposal, whatever you need. Can you organize the militant part for us?' "

When Bundists held a rally that spring in Yorkville, a German neighborhood on the Upper East Side, Lansky showed up with some friends. As they approached, it must have seemed they had stumbled into Berlin, sneers and swastikas, raised arms and thigh boots, Nazi banners snapping in the wind. "We found several hundred people dressed in brown shirts," Lansky remembered. "The stage was decorated with pictures of Hitler. The speakers started ranting. There were only about fifteen of us, but we went into action. We attacked them in the hall and threw some out the windows. There were fistfights all over the place.

Most of the Nazis panicked and ran. We chased them and beat them up, and some of them were out of action for months. Yes, it was violence. We wanted to teach them a lesson. We wanted to show them Jews would not always sit back and accept insults."

Out west, torpedoes like Mickey Cohen, a pugnacious flyweight of a gangster who made his name as Bugsy Siegel's bodyguard, were fighting similar battles. When Cohen was doing time in an Arizona jail, an outspoken Nazi sympathizer named Robert Noble was put in an adjacent cell. Cohen, who had been reading newspaper accounts of Noble's tirades, bribed guards to put him alone in a cell with Noble and his Nazi cohort. "All of a sudden the door opens at the other end and here comes Noble and this guy with him, these Nazis who hate General MacArthur," Cohen writes in his autobiography, *In My Own Words.* "They were real weasel bastards. I grabbed them both and started bouncing their heads together. With the two of them, you'd think they'd put up a fight, but they didn't do nothing. So I'm going over them pretty good. The wind-up is they're climbing up the bars and I'm trying to pull them down. They're screaming and hollering so much, everybody thinks there's a riot. After this got heard about, I'd get calls from places like the Writers' Guild to help with their problems with Nazi bastards. One time there was even a judge who called me about a Nazi Bund meeting. I told him all right, don't worry about it. So we went over there and grabbed everything in sight—all their bullshit signs—and smacked the shit out of them, broke them up the best we could. Nobody could pay me for this work. There ain't no amount of money to buy them kind of things."

The most legendary piece of Nazi fighting by a Jewish gangster happened around this time. Bugsy Siegel was having an affair with Dorothy DiFrasso, an Italian countess. In 1938 DiFrasso took Siegel home to the Villa Madama in Rome. The guest rooms were occupied by visiting German diplomats: Hermann Göring and Joseph Goebbels. When Siegel learned of this, he decided to kill the Nazis, charting their path through the day, comings and goings, when they could be taken. When he told the countess his plans, she frowned. "You can't do that," she said.

"Sure I can," said Siegel. "It's an easy setup."

According to actor George Raft, a friend of Siegel's who used to tell this story, Bugsy was dissuaded only when the countess explained what would happen to her and her husband—they would be killed.

No one knows just how closely this account stays to the facts, but it hardly seems to matter. Half a story or a sentence fragment is sometimes enough to bring solace, to give something as huge as the Holocaust a human dimension. Since the Holocaust often seems inevitable, those who ran it have the power of historical agents. The fact that Siegel was in position to kill two such agents makes the tragedy seem more manageable, something that might have been killed one Nazi at a time. You see, for people like me, who were born long after Germany was defeated, the worst part of the Holocaust was never the dead bodies; it was the way Jewish victims were portrayed. In history class at my junior high school in Illinois, we were forced to sit through films, spooled by some A/V geek, that showed images of the Holocaust: all those Jews waiting to be shot, looking ahead with already dead eyes, trees in the background, hands covering genitals. In none of those pictures was there even a faint suggestion of personality, an individual. There was only a silent, wide-eyed mass, the shame of being marched naked, being seen by women, by men. If, in just one of those photos, a condemned man had his arms stretched wide, a big circumcised prick swinging free, his eyes alive, then all the deaths would have been one degree easier to take. For forty minutes I would sit there, surrounded by non-Jewish classmates, my eyes burning, my neck starting to itch. At recess I would walk up to Clay Mellon, biggest kid in our school, the bully who ran everything, and say, "You stupid asshole." For people like me, what Siegel did, even if it was no more than a plan, made me dismiss the qualification my father tagged to the story: "Don't forget, Bugsy was an outlaw, a bad man." Fuck that. Bugsy was a kid at recess walking up to the bully, saying, "You stupid asshole."

For many gangsters, fighting Nazis was more than just an act of defiance; it was an expression of patriotism. For mobsters, taking on the enemy was a way to again feel part of the mainstream, a player in the national project. A few years later, when the Japanese attacked Pearl Harbor, even members of the military began to acknowledge this; it was something they could use. As intelligence officers grew increasingly fearful of enemy agents, sensing a spy in every shadow, whom did they turn to? Gangsters. In February 1942 the *Normandy,* a French cruise ship converted to carry American troops, caught fire while docked on the Hudson River. Experts suspected sabotage. German U-boats had already sunk 120 merchant ships off the American coast. Members of naval intelligence knew many dockworkers were immigrants from Italy, men like Eugene Salvese. Would these men help Mussolini? They could do so by telling foreign agents when military cargo was scheduled to depart or where troop ships like the *Normandy* were docked. *Loose lips sink ships.*

A few weeks after the fire, a naval intelligence officer contacted Socks Lanza, a thug who was said to control New York Harbor. When the officer explained what he wanted the gangsters to do—seal leaks, keep a lookout for suspicious doings on the docks—Lanza got in touch with Lansky. Meyer said only one man could fill the bill: Charlie Luciano. Though Lucky had already spent four years in prison, he still had ultimate authority on the docks. Moved to a better cell in a better prison, Luciano was soon sending word through Lansky to the waterfront capos. "I gave Cockeye [a mobbed-up dockworker] the orders," Lansky explained. "Go down to the piers and find out who is loyal and who is not loyal. You have to see that there are no strikes and that the job is done quickly when military stuff is loaded. And we have to make sure everybody keeps his mouth shut about troop movements. That means going into bars to make sure the crews and longshoremen don't start sounding off when they get drunk." Showing up at naval intelligence on Church Street in Manhattan, Lansky said, "I can promise you one thing. There will be no German submarines in the port of New York."

When the navy was planning the invasion of Sicily, Luciano had old friends draw detailed maps of their hometowns on the island. He also put officers in touch with the Sicilian Mafia, criminals who could steer troops through the roads, customs, and shortcuts of a foreign land. Just before the invasion, Luciano contacted navy officials: he wanted to accompany troops ashore. He would serve as a liaison, the perfect go-between. Maybe he saw himself returning home at the head of a vast army. Though his request was denied, the government did remember Luciano's contribution. In 1946, about a year after V Day, he was paroled. Tom Dewey signed the release. Along with freedom came an order of deportation: Luciano would be returned to Italy, where he would lose power, grow old, take a young wife, wear a smoking jacket, and, in 1964, die of a heart attack.

Luciano sailed from America on February 10, 1946. Pier Seven.

Bush Terminal. Brooklyn. A noisy, sad afternoon, photographers crowding out his last look at the city. Friends came to say good-bye. Frank Costello, Joe Adonis, Albert Anastasia, Meyer Lansky, Ben Siegel, Longy Zwillman, Owney Madden, Tommy Luchese, Joseph Bonanno, Carlo Gambino. The farewell swelled into a party, boasts, plans, promises to meet again, oysters, pasta, wine. When photographers moved in for a shot, they were blocked by a line of stern-faced stevedores, bailing hooks dangling from each hand. High in the sky, seagulls wheeled. When the foghorn blew and the ship departed, the birds flapped off across the harbor, over the tenements and clubhouses of lower Manhattan, the gray suits of Wall Street, the courtrooms and jails of Centre Street, the delis of the fast disappearing Jewish East Side, Ratner's and Katz's, and down into the early morning bustle of Little Italy.

Dead or Out of Town

LOUIS LEPKE HAD been two years in hiding, the back rooms and basements of Brooklyn. By 1940, when German tanks were rolling east, into the patchwork farms of the Ukraine, Lepke was losing his mind. His perceptions, distorted by months of confinement, ran red. From hidden rooms, everything on the street looked like a threat. He was not really that different from Joseph Stalin, a dictator surrounded by yes-saying sycophants, ruling from a throne in his mind. Lepke's paranoia was getting the best of him. Beginning in the late thirties, he directed a purge, killing off anyone he considered an enemy, anyone who might testify against him. In Brownsville the heady days of summer had run out into the long evening of autumn.

Lepke's orders were carried out by the troop, Brooklyn boys who wound up as little more than agents of another man's aggression. Bodies turned up in vacant lots and ditches and backseats: Leon Scharf (November 10, 1938); Isadore Friedman (January 29, 1939); Joseph Miller, a former Lepke business partner (March 30, 1939); Albert Plug Shulman, who was taken for a ride by Allie Tannenbaum and Knadles Nitzberg (April 28, 1939); Irving Penn, who, winning a kind of reverse lottery, was mistaken for someone else and filled with bullets (May 25, 1939); Hyman Yuran, who once ran a dress company with Lepke and was found in a lime pit near Loch Sheldrake (August 21, 1939); Max Rubin, who had told Joe Rosen to forget his candy store and get out of town, was shot in the head (survived); Moishe Diamond, an obese,

Polish-born teamster, was shot six times on the street by Happy Maione and Albert A.; Puggy Feinstein, who was killed by Strauss and Goldstein in the Reles living room. And so many others, at least thirteen men unseated from everyday life. In those days, reading the crime obits was like glancing at bar mitzvah announcements in the *Forward,* only instead of passing into adulthood these young men were passing out. "It is apparent that the Lepke mob is waging a war of extermination against its former and some of its present members," said Tom Dewey.

Lepke was trying to destroy government cases, steal witnesses from prosecutors, but his purge may have had the opposite effect. He may have created cases where there were none. All the killing created a jumpy, hostile environment, where assassins were locked in a race with cops: who gets the informant first? Men who might otherwise have not spoken to the cops now sought them out. What choice did they have? Once under Lepke's suspicion, they were as good as dead. It was the station house or the morgue. For some, their last days were a heart-thumping flight, a mad dash to beat the bullets to the cops. A few years later, when Lepke was tried and convicted, it was easy to view him with sympathy: the Man Gnawed to Death by Rats. But it was his fault—he created an atmosphere where a man must become a rat to survive. That's how it was with Greenie Greenberg, anyway.

Big Greenie grew up with Lepke and Gurrah on the East Side. He worked his way up in the rackets, breaking strikes, keeping order. In the twenties he spent summers at Loch Sheldrake, watching Allie Tannenbaum cut from the dining hall to the woods, where the boys taught him to fight. It was Greenie who got Tannenbaum his first job with Lepke, leading him from his upstate idyll to rough-and-tumble racket life. Greenie had been with Lepke through it all, planning, scheming, late night meetings in smoke-choked dives, shirt collars curled with sweat. So when the heat came on, Greenberg stood out like a target, something the cops might aim at. Lepke gave him the same old choice: Dead or out of town.

Greenberg went to Montreal. He was soon out of money. He sent word to the boss. Rather than simply ask for funds, he laced his request with a threat. "I hope you guys are not forgetting me," he wrote. "You better not." He was like Moses hitting the rock instead of asking it for water. "We all liked Big Greenie, but this was disloyalty," Doc Stacher later told Uri Dan. "Allie Tannenbaum was told to bump him off."

But when Allie got up to Canada, Greenie was gone. Tannenbaum chased Greenie to Detroit and lost him in Chicago. He went to wait in New York. For the next few months Greenberg was heading west, disappearing here, reappearing there. He followed dotted lines across the map, passing through towns in the dead of night, always a step ahead of the killers.

In the fall of 1939 Ben Siegel found Greenberg. Bugsy was thirty-six and living at 250 North Delfon Drive in West Los Angeles. He had come west a few years before from Scarsdale, New York, where he lived with his wife and daughters. He was sent by the Mob to put the L.A. underworld in the Syndicate. He was also invested in legitimate concerns, things to throw off the cops, like a hot dog machine company he owned with Longy Zwillman. "You put in ten cents and get a hot dog in cellophane, electrocuted, mustard," he told police. (Considering what would soon happen to many of Siegel's associates, I find his use of the word "electrocuted" oddly prescient.) Hardly a crime was committed in Los Angeles without Siegel knowing about it. So when Greenie ran out of country, washing up in Los Angeles, it did not take Bugsy long to find him; Greenie was living in a house at 1094 Vista Del Mar in Beverly Hills.

When news got back to Lepke, he put together a plan, something diffuse, a hit broken into a dozen pieces, a Cubist work in which the cops would never find the killer. Tannenbaum took a car from New York to New Jersey. At the airport in Newark he met Longy Zwillman, who gave him guns and $250. Allie took a train to Philadelphia, where he bought cartridges for the guns. He caught a plane at an airfield in Camden, New Jersey, and was met several hours later at Los Angeles Airport by Frankie Carbo, one of Siegel's men. Carbo left Allie at an apartment. A few hours later Siegel showed up. Everywhere Bugsy went, palm trees followed him through the door.

A few days before, Bugsy sent his driver, Whitey Krakow, to Hollywood and Vine, a corner where local wiseguys hung out just like back home. Krakow found Sholem Bernstein out there. He was in town visiting friends. Krakow pulled Sholem aside. "Ben Siegel wants you to clip a car." Sholem stammered. He was on vacation. He did not know the terrain and was in no mood to be a criminal. Krakow said it was an order from back east. "If you don't take my word for it, call up New York," he said. "Ask your friend Strauss."

A few days later Sholem dropped off an Oldsmobile. Bugsy said the car was all wrong; Sholem would have to clip another. Sholem listened, nodded, left the room, and headed east. When Siegel realized what had happened—that Sholem ditched—he became enraged. Quitting a job halfway, that was like abandoning someone midheist, what Mendy Weiss had pulled on Bug Workman. It was capital. *After Greenie is dead, we take care of Sholem.*

Ben Siegel worked out several days a week at the YMCA in Hollywood. Sit-ups, pull-ups, handball, massages. I like to imagine him there, figuring out the Greenie hit as some beefy guy pounds his back. A friend of Bugsy's would drive getaway. Tannenbaum, Carbo, and Bugsy himself would fill the contract. Bugsy was not expected to go along on the hit. He was one of the top members of the Syndicate, as big as Lepke or Lansky. He had only to sit back and give orders, which would keep him at a safe remove from the cops. Yet when the plans were laid, the weapons and getaway chosen, when Bugsy had only to wait for the call—*We got him*—he instead went along. Why? For the same reason other men go to the track. Because for Ben Siegel, killing was guaranteed fun.

In *Bugsy,* a film starring Warren Beatty, Greenberg is played by Elliott Gould as a doughy gangster who has hit bottom. There is a melancholy to this character, the desperation of those who wonder: Why me? The real Harry Greenberg could have had no illusions. He was complicit in every step of his demise. He had lived in crime, risen and fallen with its numbers. He was now having his own violence returned to him—fulfilling his destiny, the climax for all true gangsters. On November 23, 1939, the killers waited near his house. Greenie had no fight left in him. All those days on the road, knowing the realities of life had shrunk from years to hours, must have glazed his eyes and slowed his heart. He was shot dead in his own car. A driver took Allie up the coast to San Francisco, where he caught a plane to New York. "It was announced at a meeting that Ben Siegel had taken care of the matter personally," reads a police report. "The information, in effect, was that there was nothing to disposing of Greenie and not to listen to any stories."

A short time later, at a meeting in Jack Parisi's house—Parisi gunned for Albert A. and years earlier took Reles target shooting upstate—the gang discussed Sholem, how he ditched on Siegel. Anastasia was there, and so was Mendy Weiss, Louis Capone, Pep Strauss, Reles, and Siegel, who made a special trip. In my mind, the action resembles the court scene in *Planet of the Apes,* with orange orangutan faces peering at chimp barristers as Charlton Heston looks on in chains. "Siegel was so worked up he prosecuted personally," Burton Turkus writes in his book, *Murder, Inc.* "When he finished, there seemed to be no rebuttal against his deadly indictment. Walking out on a contract carried a death sentence."

Who will speak for the accused? Reles stood. In the way people like my father (businessmen, lawyers) dream of being gangsters, of meeting each setback, each humiliation, with a sneer and a shove, a threat of violence; gangsters like Reles dreamed of being businessmen, lawyers, whipping every enemy with words, and not caring a stitch about the getaway. It is a kind of transitive property, a formula that connects the lower and higher orders: George Raft dreaming he is a real gangster as Ben Siegel dreams he is a real movie star. Reles told the gangsters about Sholem, how he wanted to fill the contract but could not, how he was called on by a deeper loyalty. "When orating," writes Turkus, "the Kid was in a class by himself."

"The same day Ben gave him the contract, Sholem got word from New York that his mama is going to cash in," Reles told the gangsters. "Sholem is a good boy. His mama is dying; he figures he should be there. You all know how a mama is. It makes it easier to go if her boy is sitting by the bed, saying nice things. So Sholem does not even think about the contract. He didn't think of nothing. He lams out of L.A. and hustles home to be with his mama when she checks out. He drives day and night. All he wants is to hold her hand. He is a good boy. And that, gentlemen, that is why Sholem left town. Not on account of ducking the contract. But on the account his mama is kicking off."

"There was not a dry eye in the house," writes Turkus. "The judges did not even leave the bench to deliberate. The verdict was acquittal—unanimously."

In Brooklyn, the pressure was greater all the time. The faces on the street were fewer and fewer, a thinning mass, wood on a lathe. Being seen in the wrong window, the wrong door, meant the end of your adventures. And the cops were still combing the streets for Lepke, which put a freeze on all the old rackets. Sooner or later the detectives caught up with every thug who might have something to say. The cops would arrest a hood for some bullshit thing, and try to make a deal: Give up Lepke or we get you. Many of them made bail, then fled. *Dead or out of town.* Gangsters were being driven farther and farther from New York, clear across the map, where the blacktop turns to dust and everyone stars in his own personal western. Maybe no thugs went farther than Buggsy Goldstein and Blue Jaw Magoon.

Goldstein was a founding member of the troop. Short, dark, vicious. His walk was a side-to-side bulldog gait. Blue Jaw was a young troop member. Over the years he and Goldstein had become great friends. Probably they were friends for the same reason other people are friends. Killers are not just killers, you know. So when Lepke sent word—*Dead or out of town*—they went together, two men in a sedan, a car you see coming from a long way off, then—*whooosh*—is gone. It must have seemed like a dream, faces and colors, a desert over every rise, a party in every city, dry-mouthed and bleary in the morning. There are so many places you can go, vanishing into the flow of everyday life, where the cops can't find you, where Brooklyn won't look: they rolled into Canada, that outland of moose and poker and booze; they haunted the nightclubs of Chicago; they passed weeks in the safe houses of Kansas City, some well-paid politician holding the door; they ran all over the Midwest, roads running through fields and farms; and old heroic Texas, twangy music, hills rising likes notes, the road a trumpet blast disappearing over the rise. The boys were taking a victory lap, a last tour of the nation, like the Shah going hospital to hospital around the world. "Buggsy and I left Brooklyn and traversed the entire country in our travels, even entering Canada," Magoon later said. Their clothes must have become frayed and caked with dust.

Every few weeks they got off the highway and rolled through some southern or western or midwestern town where farmers and mechanics and factory hands in loose-fitting overalls or workclothes watched these dudes from the East make their way down dusty streets to the Western Union office, where Mendy Weiss sent the wire. A few hundred dollars. A few more weeks on the lam. And back on the road, rocking and roaring. They hit California like a couple of sight-seeing yokels, guys who return from Mexico in sombreros. "In California, we met Moe Suss, an actor in small and extra parts," Magoon said. "We also met Mack Grey, chauffeur of George Raft. Of gangland characters we knew Ben Siegel and Meyer Lansky, two of the chiefs of the major

Combination. Siegel was in California at the time of our sojourn. Buggsy [Goldstein] wanted to go see Siegel, but I declined. I said, 'What the hell do we want to let anyone know we are here for?' "

People found out anyway. After a few days on the coast, a letter arrived from Strauss. "He told us to get out of Hollywood," said Magoon. "Because everyone in Brownsville knew we were out there and Lepke did not care to have us apprehended." So the boys were back on the road, heading southeast, the lights of Juarez, a border town at night, and into Mexico, roads running like water down a drain. The lines of the North gave way to a tangle, colors running together, and at last they reached the other side, lammed it farther than anyone, the end of the underworld. There must have been a moment when they imagined staying, taking a Mexican wife, living in an adobe house, growing fat and satisfied and parched by sun, Brooklyn just a story told in town. *I hear the gringo was a killer in the North.* But soon they were back on the road, going the way they came, north, then east, going and going, and the road stretched ahead.

They watched the country roll back out the window, desert to plains to prairie to soft Hudson Valley hills, old stolid farms of the Northeast, rain on slate roofs. The road began to climb through the trees. From the top of a hill they would see the fields and silos of Newburgh, New York. A dirt road took them to a house. An elderly man sitting on the porch. This was Albert A.'s friend from the old days, the man who years before had taught Abe Reles to shoot. All the while, as the boys ran all over the continent, as Dutch Schultz was shot in a toilet in Newark, as Lucky Luciano was sent to prison, as Lepke, driven to basements, left a scatter of marks, this farm was up here waiting, impervious to time.

Magoon and Goldstein stayed several days in a guest cabin. Each night they played pinochle with the old man, purposely losing a dollar or two. "In this way we paid for our stay," said Magoon. One night Goldstein went to retrieve a money order in town. The attorney general's office had intercepted the wire, and the local cops were waiting. In jail, Goldstein slipped someone five dollars and a message for Magoon: Flee! The message was instead given to police. The cops reached the farm at midnight. When they asked Magoon his name, he said, "Harry Levinson." The police then showed him a mug shot of Goldstein. They studied Magoon's face. When he seemed to recognize the man in the picture, they brought him to jail. For many of the gangsters who got out of town, the road away from Brooklyn in the end led right back to the cramped cells they had been avoiding all their lives. Better than the lime pit in Loch Sheldrake.

Lepke could not stay forever in hiding. The heat on the street was greater all the time. In New York alone there were twenty-five detectives out looking for him. And ambition. Flat-out ambition is also part of the story. The federal and state governments were locked in a race not unlike the race that sent Russia and America into space. *Who will conquer the moon? Who will conquer Lepke?* As a leader of the Republican Party, Tom Dewey was working to unseat Franklin Roosevelt in the 1940 presidential election. If Dewey apprehended Lepke, it would show that his government could do something FDR's could not. Lepke was also thought to hold some of the Roosevelt administration's darkest secrets. Sidney Hillman, a member of FDR's kitchen cabinet who once headed the Amalgamated Clothing Workers Union, was said to have been in cahoots with Lepke, to have commissioned schlammings. If Dewey made the arrest, he might strike a deal with the gangster, a deal that would embarrass Roosevelt and put a Republican in the White House.

As autumn drew near, it seemed Lepke's best chance was to bargain, playing the feds against the state, striking a deal before the election, while his value was still high. Perhaps more anxious for a deal than even Dewey or J. Edgar Hoover were other gangsters: Lansky, Adonis, Costello. Hoover was threatening the bosses, saying he would arrest everyone unless someone gave him Lepke.

In the fall of 1939 Moey "Dimples" Wolensky came to see Lepke in hiding. Wolensky was a Jew from the old neighborhood, had long worked with Lepke and Lansky, looked like the number eight (round face, round body), was on the fringe of every conversation, in the corner of every room. He told Lepke he had gotten word from the G-men: If Lepke turned himself in, he would be tried for narcotics running only—a crime that would put him away for no more than ten years. A promise: No way would Hoover turn him over for trial to Dewey. Within a few days, Lepke must have set up and knocked down a dozen arguments. When he went for advice to Albert A., the gangster said the deal sounded screwy. He tried to get Lepke to see it from the point of view of the street, with the eyes of a free man. To Anastasia, only one thing was certain: As long as they can't get you, they can't hurt you. Once you surrender, the best deal in the world won't mean a thing. In the end, it probably came down to this simple truth: What was Lepke's life like now? All the hiding, all the running around, was it really that different from life in prison?

On August 5, 1940, Walter Winchell received a telephone call at the Stork Club. (Some say the call came elsewhere.) The Stork, at 3 East Fifty-third Street, was one of the hottest spots in town, a haunt of that immortal class of club-goer that seems to survive every rise and fall in the city. On brilliant nights they would arrive in limos and roadsters, leave keys with a valet, follow a broad back through the ropes and into the clink of glasses, voices, laughter, athletes, film stars, politicians, a collection of prewar night life, bold colors bleeding from made-up faces into the air. The place was put on the map years before by Winchell, when he went on the radio and called it "New York's New Yorkiest Place." He was there several nights a week, gathering stories for his column.

Winchell had softly handsome features, a picture never quite in focus. In the twenties he wrote for a number of papers before launching "On Broadway," a column for the *New York Daily Mirror.* The column, filled with things seen and heard, foibles of even the grandest celebrity, seemed to invent gossip, a culture that over the years has become American culture—what happens when the frontier spirit is locked in cities. By 1940, when Winchell got the phone call, his column was being syndicated in hundreds of papers around the country, and he could be heard each week on the radio.

When Winchell got to the phone, the voice on the other end was clipped, mysterious. "Don't ask me who I am," it said. "I have something important to tell you. Lepke wants to come in. If he could find someone he can trust, he will give himself up to that person. The talk around town is that Lepke will be shot while supposedly escaping." The voice told Winchell to contact his friend J. Edgar Hoover and get a guarantee that Lepke could come in unharmed.

Winchell could not identify the caller, but it was likely Albert Anastasia. Once Lepke decided he would (probably) turn himself in,

Anastasia, though he was against surrender, handled the arrangements. He was concerned with Lepke's safety. There were still $50,000 on his head. What would prevent some freelancing headhunter from taking a potshot? By surrendering to Winchell, Lepke hoped to get some assurance of safety. He was placing himself under the protective umbrella of celebrity. Nowadays, the prospect of killing both a media star and a criminal, maybe with a single bullet, would line the street with marksmen.

And there may have been another reason for choosing Winchell. What celebrity could better understand Lepke? The lives of the men, ambitions and dreams, seemed to reflect each other. Winchell too descended from Jewish stock, with roots in the Lower East Side. When discussing his own ethos, he could even sound like a gangster. "When someone does me dirt (after I've helped him or her) I return the compliment some day," Winchell wrote in his autobiography. "In the paper, on the air, with a bottle of ketchup on the skull. I don't make up nasty things to write about them. I wait until they get locked up for taking dope or pimping and then I make it public. Vindictive? You're gahdamb'd right! You botcha me, I botcha you!" In many ways, Winchell seems a precursor of the next generation, Jews who kept the ethos but shed the violence, who gave back twice again what they got.

On August 6, 1940, Winchell went on the radio and said, "Your reporter is reliably informed that Lepke, the fugitive, is on the verge of surrender, perhaps this week. If Lepke can find someone he can trust (I am told), he will come in. . . . I am authorized by the G-men that Lepke is assured of safe delivery. . . ."

Over the next several days, Winchell received many calls at the Stork—gangsters working out a deal. *Will Lepke be protected? What kind of sentence can he expect?* All the while, Winchell was rushing from the Stork to the Waldorf-Astoria, where Hoover had taken a room. Late one night, the mysterious voice asked Winchell if he had his car with the four lamps, which referred to the fog lights on Winchell's car. More than just choosing a vehicle they would recognize, the gangsters were probably giving Winchell a warning: We know you better than you know us. At three-thirty that morning, Winchell, following gangster directions, drove through the Holland Tunnel and out to the New

Jersey flats. He rolled around some vacant lot out there, headlights illuminating pavement. After fifteen minutes he got spooked and came back to Manhattan. He later decided the gangsters were making sure he would not be followed.

After a few more weeks and a few more errands, Hoover got fed up. He went to the Stork, where he found Winchell surrounded by admirers. Winchell must have seen him coming from across the room, a gunslinger in an old western. "I am fed up with you and your friends," said Hoover. "They can make a fool out of you, but they are not going to make a fool out of me and my men."

"They aren't my friends, John," said Winchell.

"They are your friends," said Hoover. "And don't call me John. I'm beginning to think you're the champ bullshitter in town. You can tell your friends that if Lepke isn't in within forty-eight hours, I will order my agents to shoot him on sight."

Winchell later said he was on the verge of tears. His credibility, his career, everything was on the line. He had wed his fate to the whim of hoodlums. Later, when the phone rang, Winchell related Hoover's threat—how he'd promised to shoot Lepke. "You people haven't been able to find him for two years," said the gangster. "How you gonna find him in forty-eight hours?"

A few nights before Lepke came in, Mendy Weiss called Albert Tannenbaum to a meeting. Lepke was still not sure he would surrender. If he did not come in, he knew there would be trouble. Some of the other bosses had sent a message. All this hiding was generating too much heat; cops were everywhere; no one could conduct business. They wanted Lepke to accept the deal. When Allie showed up, he was met by Weiss and Little Farvel Cohen. "I'm glad to see you," said Mendy. "We may have some trouble on our hands. Have you seen Workman?"

"No," said Allie. "He's not up in the mountains and he's not at home. But if I search, I can probably find him. Why? What's the trouble?"

"Lepke got a message," said Weiss. "Walk in or else."

Tannenbaum went to see Lepke, who was staying at a house on Third Street in Brooklyn. Allie asked if it was true: "Can the other bosses make you surrender?" Before Lepke answered, I imagine him sitting on the arm of a couch and sighing, like the father of a girl I once dated did before sharing a hard fact of life.

"When you've been around as much as me, when you've seen the things I've seen, you know what an ultimatum like that means, how serious it is, and what's on the other side of it," said Lepke. "These guys are strictly for themselves. They did it once before, and they wouldn't hesitate to do it again," he said, probably referring to the murder of Dutch Schultz. "To save you kids from a lot of trouble, the best thing would be to just walk in."

Mendy and Allie went to see Anastasia. They sat in a car outside his house, afraid to go in. Mendy was sure everyone was against Lepke now, and against his men, too. He knew Anastasia had a soundproof cellar and was afraid he would be shot down there. Mendy drove to a restaurant and called Albert, who came over to talk. Albert said he would go along with whatever decision Lepke made. The next morning the boys found the boss a new apartment, a place hidden from both cops and other gangsters.

In my mind, the members of the troop have, at this point, begun to wilt and fade. They are people who have been up all night, whose eyes play tricks, who startle easy. The day after they found Lepke a new hideout, they drove to an auction on Eighth Street in Greenwich Village. Eighth Street is now a shoe capital, with stores selling footwear from every era: platforms, wing-tips, pumps, spiked heels, flats, sandals, moon boots, moccasins. Manhattan absorbs styles, then, long after the moment is passed, continues to give them off, the way blacktop radiates heat even after sundown. The boys walked through the items set for sale, end tables, couches, ottomans, chairs, tables, looking for things that might serve a man well in hiding. They bought enough furniture to fill the hideout, made arrangements to pick up the stuff later, then walked off into the Village.

The next day Tannenbaum went to Loch Sheldrake. He was to wait there for word, a signal that would bring him blazing into the city. Lepke was scattering his pieces, hiding guns here and there. But in the end, Lepke must have known he stood no chance in a war. He was outmanned and outgunned. He would have to take on the cops and the other gangs. Gurrah was off in jail, and his own best days were behind him. The years in hiding had accomplished what his enemies never could: he was tamed, swollen at the cheeks and jowls, a man with not an ounce of energy left. A war would have been less a new beginning than a dramatic end, placing Lepke alongside those figures who fight instead of surrender—Texans at the Alamo, zealots on Masada, men whose last picture is an action shot. If Lepke had fought it out, how much more noble his end than the one that was waiting for him?

On the night of August 24, 1940, Winchell took a call at the Stork Club. A gangster told him to drive to Proctor's Theater in Yonkers. As Winchell pulled up to the building, a car stopped alongside. It was full of men. Someone got out, his face covered with a bandanna. He told Winchell to head back to town and wait in a drugstore at Eighth Avenue and Nineteenth Street. At 8:55 Winchell was drinking a Coke in back of the store when a stranger motioned him outside. The stranger told him to call Hoover and have him wait in his car on Fifth Avenue and Twenty-third Street between 10:00 and 10:20 P.M. After the call was made, the stranger followed Winchell into his car and told him to drive. Winchell was at first too nervous to get the key into the ignition. At 10:15 the stranger told Winchell to stop at Madison Avenue and Twenty-fourth Street. Winchell asked why he still had to be involved, why Lepke couldn't himself surrender to Hoover.

"Lepke won't do that," said the stranger. "He doesn't want to risk somebody shooting him for the fifty grand award before he gets to Hoover. If anybody hit you, it would raise a hell of a stink."

As the stranger left the car, he took a chain from around his neck, kissed a gold Star of David, and handed it to Winchell, saying, "Give this to Lepke."

At 9:00 P.M., Anastasia had come for Lepke at his hiding place. Lepke slid into the backseat of the car, and Anastasia went lurching off across Brooklyn. The boss was again disguised as a family man, with a woman and child at his side. His spaniel eyes were ringed and shadowed. His mustache hid a bent, uneven mouth. He wore a gray suit. They drove past the candy stores and newsstands of Brooklyn. Traffic, faces, streets going by. And soon they were crossing into Manhattan, where the lights of the financial district wink and shine. Lepke first crossed into the city years before, after his father died and his mother left him, off to the Rocky Mountains, leaving the boy to cross the bridge alone, steel blue arches and river scudding below. And here he was, all these years later, his true face hidden in the furrows of age, streaking toward surrender, a man of yesterdays taking a final drive through blocks he once ruled like a king. They drove by South Street, where pirates were once strung on the beach within view of excursion boats; by Cherry Street, where garment district looms still spun; by the courtrooms of Foley Square; by Chinatown; by the sinister East Side warrens of Monk Eastman and Arnold Rothstein. By 10:15 they had made it uptown. They pulled alongside a car idling softly, four lamps on dim, like a plane waiting out a storm on a runway.

Lepke slid alongside Winchell. At 10:17 they pulled in behind Hoover on Fifth Avenue. Hoover, who had a chauffeur, was in the backseat. Leaning in, Winchell said, "Mr. Hoover, this is Mr. Buchalter."

"Nice to meet you," said Lepke, getting in. "Let's go."

Albert Tannenbaum was still up in the woods. Sitting on a porch, feet propped on a rail, he would have seen the slope of a hill, a gray lake, a small curved shore on the far side. Maybe a sailboat tacked in the wind. What did Allie do? Probably he thought, waited, went on walks. The woods smell sickly sweet on August afternoons, everything overripe and bursting. He walked to town. When he came to a newsstand, the headline leapt out:—LEPKE SURRENDERS—like learning of your father's death in the obits. And here he was, waiting in the hills like some island-bound Japanese soldier fighting a war that ended years before.

Not long after he surrendered, Lepke realized he had been double-crossed. There never was a deal with the feds. There never was a promise to keep the boss from Dewey. The story Dimples told was a fiction, something you tell children before they go to the dentist. Lepke faced federal charges in December. Convicted on narcotics violations, he was sentenced to fourteen years in prison—a trial pushed to the back of the papers by more pressing concerns. Lepke had come in a week before Hitler invaded Poland.

Lepke's final days were a strange time for the troop. History is ending, and you continue on. Penny-ante heists, schlammings, crap games. And all the while the cops stayed after the boys, looking for any reason to run them in. For a decade the troop had been top dogs in Brownsville, a state within a state. A few months before Lepke surrendered, the police at last caught a break. Harry Rudolph, a small-time crook, a man in and out of jail, a thug doing time on Riker's Island, sent a letter to the DA's office in Brooklyn. He had a story to tell. Brought down in cuffs, Rudolph talked to Burton Turkus, a rising star in the office, about Red Alpert. In 1933 Alpert had been killed by thugs in Brownsville. Rudolph must have been excited as he spoke. Alpert had been Rudolph's best friend, and he still held a grudge, a neighborhood scorn, what Reles and Goldstein once held for the Shapiros. But why did Rudolph wait so long, coming forward seven years after the murder? Probably for the same reason dud bombs dropped and lost in World War II suddenly explode. Because time had allowed a change, some shift in chemistry that again made the contents deadly.

Red Alpert was one of a legion of low-level thugs who work the fringes, outlanders moving crime to crime. In 1933, while robbing a neighborhood store, he happened across a large haul. Uncut stones. Not having connections to move the jewels, he set up a meeting with Pep Strauss. Alpert was hoping Strauss would act as middleman, buying the stones, then passing them to a fence. When Pep showed up, he had the smug indifference of a rock star meeting a groupie. He said he would take the entire haul for seven hundred dollars. "You know what you can do with your seven hundred?" said Alpert. "You can go to hell." And that was it. A few sentences and Alpert's fate was fixed. How could Pep take that crap in his own territory?

A few weeks later, after two failed assassination attempts, Strauss told the story to Reles and Goldstein. *Jeez, Pep, the kid is only nineteen. You gonna kill him over a few dumb words?* So Reles and Goldstein went to see Alpert, hoping to get the dispute squared away. After looking at the stones, Reles said he would take the entire haul for seven hundred. Alpert shook his head, saying, "I told Pep to hell with him, and to hell with you guys, too." A few nights later, on November 25, 1933, Alpert was found dead. "I'll tell you who did it, too," Harry Rudolph told

Turkus. "Those Brownsville guys—Reles and Buggsy. They took Red when he came out of his house."

It was not a strong case. Rudolph was a criminal, a man trying to settle a score. In New York State the testimony of one criminal cannot alone put another criminal away. A story must be corroborated by a more trustworthy source. And still the cops pursued the Red Alpert murder case. It was part of a long-term battle they were fighting, arresting the boys again and again, hoping to harass or trick a member of the troop into a confession. A break in one case, they hoped, could solve a dozen others. So the next morning a few cops went to Brownsville, knocked on doors, stopped on corners, telling the local hoods to spread the word: Reles and Goldstein are wanted for the murder of Red Alpert. (Goldstein, after giving the police nothing on Lepke, was back on the street.) The police were also looking for Dukey Maffeatore, whom they had connected to the murder. When Reles and Goldstein got word—*The cops are looking for you*—they were probably not too concerned. Whenever anything bad happened in Brooklyn, detectives came looking for the boys. Between 1931 and 1940 Reles was picked up by the cops about once every seventy-eight days. Early the next morning the suspects went to the police station and surrendered.

Soon after the arrest, the cops went to work on Maffeatore. They put him alone in a cell. Sometimes they asked him questions or else told him about the other boys, how they were pinning everything on Dukey. They told him what he could expect of his final days: meal, walk, electric chair. It did not take long to break Dukey. He was just twenty-five years old, a comic book freak, a devotee of Li'l Abner and Superman. He came apart like wet paper, told the cops everything, how he got involved with the troop, stole kill cars, worked with Reles, Goldstein, Strauss. When Dukey said his partner was Pretty Levine, the cops picked him up, and he broke, too. The police soon had enough information to arrest most of the troop. Louis Capone, Happy Maione, Dasher Abbandando, Seymour Magoon, Phil Strauss, they were scattered in the jails of New York.

Reles was having a hard time in jail. He was physically worn down, and the monotony, the backbreaking sameness of incarceration, must have been hard on him. Prosecutors were moving him facility to facility, from Queens County Jail to Raymond Street Jail to the Tombs. Dank cells. Lost time. Variations on gray. In the Tombs he met up with Happy Maione, who was also an inmate. Maione was a tier above Reles. Before sleep, they would call to each other. Whenever Maione had the chance, he talked to Reles, standing before his cell until a guard chased him away. They also talked in the yard, beneath a faraway city sky, and in the jail chapel, whispering together as other inmates sang hymns. When a guard glanced over, they looked straight ahead and sang.

And then Maione was gone, off down the corridor, leaving Reles alone to think. And he had a lot to think about. Though he had been through many ups and downs, he was just thirty-four. He had a wife, a son, another child on the way. He had just opened a lunch counter, a place he hoped would carry his family toward the American dream. Now here he was, being run down by a crime he'd committed years before. What could Reles do? He saw himself as a clever man, someone who finds a way out of traps, who snickers at his guards, saying, "You can't build a jail to hold me." Yet when he sized up this predicament—life in prison or worse—his mind must have boggled. He was looking for loopholes, for scapegoats. So many gangs are broken this way—by a paranoid left alone in a cell.

In March 1940 the *Brooklyn Eagle* published a story about Pittsburgh Phil, how he was talking to the cops, giving up Reles to save himself. The paper was delivered to the Tombs, so Reles probably read or heard about the article. Though the story turned out to be false—it might have been planted to force the Kid's hand—it must have fueled Reles's paranoia: squeal or be squealed. He was pushed further down this road when his wife came to see him in the fall. Rose Reles told her husband she could not face life alone, two kids, no husband, and all those years. She begged him to help the cops, cut a deal, anything to get out of jail. "I knew Burton Turkus, the assistant district attorney on the case," Ralph Salerno told me. "Turkus was figuring a strategy, talking to him and her, trying to get a break. So he takes a gamble and lets Mrs. Reles talk with her husband. She cries, pleads, the whole bit. By the time she is done with him, he is jumping to make a deal."

Rose Reles went the next day to the DA's office in downtown Brooklyn. She was small featured, faintly attractive, suspicious, the kind of woman who sits on the edge of chairs, pauses before mirrors, whispers in hallways. Her hair was swept up into a turban, and she wore a beige coat with a wolf collar. She asked to see William O'Dwyer, the

Brooklyn DA. When Burton Turkus asked if he could be of help, she followed the instructions given her by Reles, saying she would talk only to the DA. Then she began to cry. "I want to save my husband from the electric chair," she said. "My baby is coming in June."

A few days later Turkus signed Reles out of the Tombs and brought him to the DA's office. Turkus recalled that encounter in his memoir, *Murder, Inc.* "I remember distinctly what I thought because I got the same thought every time I saw him afterward," writes the prosecutor. "It was that I could name one thousand and one more delightful companions for a stroll down a lonesome road on a dark night. There was something about Reles's physical bearing, a look in his eye, that actually made the hair on the back of your neck stand up."

That afternoon Reles sat in O'Dwyer's office, talking with the DA and his assistants, running through the merits of their investigation. In those days Reles wore a blue warm-up jacket zipped to the chin and smiled a fuck-you smile. He told O'Dwyer he had nothing on the boys, no facts, no witnesses. "You got no corroboration," he said again and again. "But I'm the guy who can tell you where to get it. I can make you the biggest man in the country." In exchange Reles said he wanted to "walk out clean." The men stayed in the office until four that morning, working out a deal. In the end, Reles was given immunity; he would go free when the last case was tried. "I am not a stool pigeon," he told Turkus. "Every one of those guys wanted to talk. Only I beat them to the bandwagon. They would be hanging me right now, if they had the chance."

Reles could not see himself as a rat. He hated rats. He instead must have seen himself as a resourceful man, someone who had found a way out. No different from the other boys, just smarter. "They would be hanging me right now, if they had the chance." When asked to explain his actions in court, Reles said, "I was expecting another child and had one already. I was disgusted with the way I was living. It was my life; I was fed up with my life."

"Your conscience told you to make this change?" asked a lawyer.

"That is too deep for me," said the Kid. "I just made a change."

Telling his story, Reles was like a man on a couch, working through the past. He spoke compulsively, giving Turkus names, dates, details of his other life, where to look, whom to ask, sharing a secret he had kept too long. Reles told the prosecutor not only what happened, but how to make the case. The Kid's testimony alone could not put a single thug away. He was a confessed killer, a man who would say anything to save his skin. So he told Turkus who could verify his stories—a man at a newsstand who saw the boys flee a scene, a gun dealer who sold them a murder weapon. When asked to recall the names of ten men he had killed, the Kid's voice was low, gruff. "Joey Silver, Rocco, Irving Shapiro, Jack Paley, Whitey Rudnick, somebody by the name of Mummy, Moe Greenblatt, Jake the Painter." He paused, then said, "How many is that, eight? Ruben Smith." He could not remember the last name.

When word about Reles got out, a panic ran through the underworld. Gangsters across the country began to think back, trying to remember if they ever had any professional dealings with the Kid, like a man quickly tracing his past when he hears an old lady friend is writing a tell-all memoir. Never before had someone so highly placed in the Mob turned rat. The Kid knew all the secrets. He talked about the killing of Dutch Schultz, Puggy Feinstein, Greenie Greenberg, Joe Rosen, Moishe Diamond, about the lime pit in Loch Sheldrake, about the history of the troop, from the war with the Shapiros to the invention of contract killing. Reles talked about eighty-five killings in Brooklyn alone. His confession filled seventy-five notebooks.

When it was all set down, the Kid's deposition read like a prose poem, the greatest hits of the Jewish underworld. When I look at those notes today, I am filled with shame—shame for Brooklyn, shame for the Jews. Not just for the crimes he committed, but also for the fact that, all these years later, he was singing to the cops. To most people, I suppose, the murders are where all the sin resides, all those bodies. But to me, turning rat only compounded what the Kid had done. It means his entire life, even the just battles, amounted to nothing. There never was a code, a boundary, a plan. When he cut his deal, he cast his vote for anarchy, where only the most fundamental laws of nature apply.

Reles's treachery now seems inevitable to me, an indispensable part of the story. He is the Judas of the Jewish underworld, the man whose treachery makes the legend possible. Without Reles, the Brownsville Boys would have grown fat and bloated, tired crooks in tired cells, or else petered out in Miami Beach, old men with bullshit old men stories. They will instead live forever, always young, angry, tough. What else can such men do but flame out, bitter and betrayed, a storm washing the sky clean, leaving nothing but blue vistas behind?

With the information given by Reles, the investigators were able to coax others into cooperating. This was sometimes done in ways that today seem extraordinary. Albert Tannenbaum was living near Grand Army Plaza in Park Slope when he was arrested for some ancient crime, tried, convicted, and sent to Clinton State Prison in Dannemora. Seven years hard labor. He was alone up there, far from the other boys, hours ticking past. In the fall of 1940 he had a visitor. William O'Dwyer, the DA, had come from Brooklyn. He told Allie what he knew and asked if he would cooperate. When Allie said he was no rat, O'Dwyer asked him to come along for a ride. The DA checked the gangster out of prison, and off they went.

They drove a hundred miles, roads singing over hilltops, farms grooved yellow in the distance. O'Dwyer, who would soon be elected mayor of New York, was a red-faced, old-fashioned machine-built city politician. He knew how to change a person's mind. It probably did not take Tannenbaum long to figure out where O'Dwyer was taking him—Loch Sheldrake, golden summer boyhood afternoons, Communists in the mess hall. They pulled off the road into a crowd of cops. Sholem Bernstein was in the middle of it all, telling the officers where to dig. The salt from the pit had eroded the bodies, but some of the features must have been discernible: jawbones, eye sockets. With a great heave, the cops pulled up the remains of Hyman Yuran, a corpse stinking on the autumn grass. The underbelly of Allie's life had been exhumed. A few days later, when he told O'Dwyer he would cooperate, his prison sentence was suspended.

Why was the government able to make cases where before they could make none? Well, mostly because of Abe Reles. When the Kid turned rat, it was game over. Past confessors had mostly been small-time operators, thugs like Harry Rudolph who knew only part of the story, who had just one of the fragments Lepke broke murders into. Reles had the whole picture, so when he started talking there was a chain reaction, one confession leading to another, until the air was full of voices. *Rats' feet on broken glass.* In just a few months, O'Dwyer and Turkus, who would actually try the cases, had turned several gangsters into informers: Dukey Maffeatore, Abe Reles, Sholem Bernstein, Albert Tannenbaum, Pretty Levine, Mickey Sycoff.

Over time, these men would serve the same basic function as

Josephus, the treacherous Jewish general who fought Roman armies in the time of Herod. When things got rough, Josephus surrendered his troops, moved to Rome, became a citizen (Josephus Flavius), and wrote *History of the Jewish War,* a book that preserves a story that would otherwise be lost. Like Josephus, the turncoat gangsters quit a losing team in a time of duress; like Josephus' book, their stories are the only thing that holds the past together, shedding light on a chaotic part of Jewish history. In the end, the rats destroyed their friends but preserved the legend.

When the nonratting members of the troop realized what was up, that they were being sold out by lifelong friends, they reacted in different ways. Some refused to believe it, blaming instead the cops and their bullshit stories. Others talked to their lawyers, looking for ways to poke holes in the stories the rats told. And then there was Strauss. Pep had always been the strictest member of the gang, a killer with a keen sense of old-time morality. When he heard Reles was talking, he told the cops he wanted to talk, too. But before he told his story, he needed time alone with the Kid. "Put me in with Reles, and more things will come back to me," he said. When the cops denied the request, the truth came out: "I just wanted to sink my tooth into his jugular vein," Pep said. "I didn't worry about the chair if I could just tear his throat out first." Maybe the most rational reaction was that of Mendy Weiss, who considered the situation, turned tail, and ran. He hid for a year, moving from Kansas City to Colorado, giving his name as James Bell, vice president of the Tungsten Mining and Development Company, Black Hawk, Colorado. The idea of Weiss, who was so New York (face, style, talk), selling himself as a western businessman was a joke even the cops could get. He was arrested in Kansas City on April 6, 1941.

By the time the trials began in spring 1942, the rats had been taken from the prisons and jails of New York and moved into a kind of fortress. How could the boys stay in lockup? For a rat, jail is more dangerous than the street, with a thousand inmates hoping to knife an informer. At home, even with a police guard, someone like Reles would have a life expectancy shorter than the Macedonian fruit fly, that fragile insect whose existence spans less than fourteen minutes. So the prosecutors moved the boys to the Half Moon, a hotel between East

Twenty-eighth and East Twenty-ninth streets on the Coney Island boardwalk. The place was known as the rat suite. For the boys, the stay in the Half Moon must have been a painful irony, a replay of long ago Florida getaways, only now locked up in the resort, closed off from the outside that makes the inside so pleasant.

A complex was built for the informers on the hotel's sixth floor, ten rooms that filled the east wing. Bedrooms. Sitting room. Living room. Kitchen. Suite 620. The front door was replaced with a bulletproof steel barrier: peephole, bar lock. The suite was guarded by a special police battalion, a unit headed by Captain Bals, a gray-haired, hawk-nosed New York cop. His unit consisted of eighteen officers, men assigned to guard the rats full-time: three shifts of six cops, each shift serving twenty-four hours, ten A.M. to ten A.M. When the boys went to sleep, a cop often sat in a chair in the corner. Sometimes a room was made up with three beds and a cop lay between two gangsters. "Machine guns and shotguns and what else they got," Sholem Bernstein said of the suite. "When I go to sleep, two detectives sit in the room all night."

For the rats in the suite, there was not much to do. They read the papers, talked. The prosecutors and the police guards did what they could to keep the informants sane. The cops stayed up talking with the boys and encouraged wives to visit. The guards bought Reles whiskey and sometimes even drank it with him. And the guards took the rats on outings, field trips to places like Heckscher Park in Nassau County, Long Island, where the boys played baseball and barbecued. I imagine the boys out there, smoke from the grill mounting into the night, stars in the east, Reles tearing around third and here comes the throw. But in the end there was really nothing to look forward to but the drama that would come in the courtroom, that would write the epilogue to so many Brooklyn lives.

The business of killing rides the wave of technology, grows with the nation, goes west with the country, on the trains and planes of America, blackjack to tommy gun, sedan to jet, always a step ahead of the cops, evolving away from the law like radioactive roaches, changing, melding, molding. The Murder Incorporated killers had grown out of the jazz age and the Depression, high and low. They had come up on speakeasies and shoot-outs, bosses and strikers. And now, with the coming of the Second World War, and the great unknown land beyond the war, their time was drawing to a close. Overtaken by the cops, they would soon give way to a new breed of killers, who would give way to a new breed of killers, who would give way to a new breed of killers, a chain stretching back to the pre–Civil War scrapes of the Dead Rabbits and the Plug Uglies and off into a future of cyberkillers and technothieves. For the Brownsville Boys, the story was winding down. Like so much of isolationist America, they would not survive the war. In Brooklyn the trains were all in; kill and crash cars parked in the garages; killers in the jails. This was the age of show trials. Well, here was another batch of killers ready for the dustbin of history.

On a morning he was to testify, Reles woke around six A.M., showered, shaved. Maybe he nicked himself. He put on a suit, knotted his tie. Maybe blood from the nick stained his color. He took an elevator down, cops sweeping him through the lobby into a car that whisked him to court. As the trials progressed and other gangsters came to see how damaging was the Kid's testimony, they began to lay plans, ways to take him out of the equation. It was a great riddle: the Abe Reles question. Marksmen were brought in from Detroit's Jewish underworld. The Purple Mob. They rented a room across from the Half Moon and set up a stakeout, dusty rooms clear through a rifle scope. When a rat wandered into the scope, a marksman would take him out. Pffft! Gone. But the guards were careful to keep the informers in the east wing only, rooms that looked out on nothing but sea. O'Dwyer learned of the marksmen and ran them off. When Turkus got word of a more sophisticated plot—a manufactured traffic jam would slow the car taking Reles to court; a sharpshooter would then kill the rat and his guards—he ordered an armored vehicle to shuttle the Kid back and forth.

Charlie Workman was the first of the boys to stand trial. Murder of Dutch Schultz. Brooklyn prosecutors let the rats testify for the state of New Jersey. Workman wore a dark suit to court. His eyes were black as buttons. He was already a different man, a captured criminal, vanquished. He was hung up by his own words, how he told everyone about the killing, vowing to get even with Mendy Weiss. Tannenbaum took the stand, telling what he could remember. Reles talked about a New Year's Eve party where Workman griped about the hit. Workman's parents sat in the gallery. His brother was there, too, a kid impressed by his older sibling.

Workman was found guilty and sentenced to life at hard labor. As he was led from court, he called over his brother. The conversation, overheard by a cop, hints at the future, an attitude that would help clear the landscape of Jewish gangsters. "Whatever you do, live honestly," said Workman. "If you make twenty cents a day, make it do you. If you can't make an honest living, make the government support you. Keep away from the gangs and don't be a wiseguy. Take care of Mama and Papa and watch Itchy. He needs watching."

Workman was sent to Trenton State Prison. A few months later, when the Japanese attacked Pearl Harbor, he sent a letter to the feds, volunteering for a suicide mission. His offer was declined. Workman was paroled in 1964. He got a job in the garment center, his old stomping grounds, only now lugging a sample case instead of a gun. He was twenty-three years in prison.

After the Workman case, the convictions began to stream in, one, two, three, just like that. It was as if something had gone wrong, as though someone who was supposed to be born never was, like that movie *It's a Wonderful Life* if the guy Jimmy Stewart played decided to stay unborn, and now the boys were living in some kind of historical oxbow, a place that is not supposed to exist. In 1941 Harry Strauss and Buggsy Goldstein went on trial before Judge John J. Fitzgerald for the murder of Puggy Feinstein, the ex-prizefighter killed with rope and ice pick in Reles's living room. The gangsters wore their best clothes to court, dark suits, cuff links, mouths turned down, cold serious eyes sometimes laughing, playing the crowd, mistaking star-struck pedestrian sighs for true love. Everyone likes to watch a man die. Strauss glared at Reles as he testified. The Kid twisted a red bandanna in his hands. A defense lawyer, trying to cast the Kid's stories in doubt, painted him as another con man trying to save his skin. "When you talked to the district attorney of Kings County, you were interested in escaping the electric chair, weren't you?" asked the lawyer.

"Yes, sir," said Reles.

When the attorney asked Reles why anyone should believe he was telling the truth, he said, "Because Judge O'Dwyer told me if he found out that I told so much as a lie, he would send me to the electric chair the same as the rest of them, and that is why I am telling the truth."

After watching Reles on the stand, the judge had his own opinion. "For the record I will say this man never had a conscience when he killed men. He killed men as a business. He had no sympathies. He was killing other men for money. He is a living tiger."

Each day in court, Reles was facing off against his oldest friends, those he had turned to when he was nobody, nothing. He was lashing at the forces that built him. For most people, such struggles take place in nightmares. But Reles was fighting his demons in the open, a stenographer taking it all down. Goldstein and Strauss sat side by side at the defense table. Goldstein had a million wiseguy teeth and a real underworld smile. His eyes were big, bloodshot, unbelieving. He leaned forward to get each word the Kid said, sat back, shook his head, looked at Pep, who just stared ahead, trying to bore a hole through Reles. Strauss had let his hair grow and now had it swept into a pompadour. Each day his eyes were smaller and colder, a star collapsing on itself. He was a human cold front, a personification of anger, an exclamation point out walking around.

As the weeks passed and it seemed clear the men would be convicted, each criminal reacted in his own way. Buggsy was growing, developing, evolving into the perfect movie gangster. When his old road companion, Blue Jaw Magoon, took the stand, Buggsy jumped to his feet. "For God's sake, Seymour, that's some story you're telling," he shouted. "You're burning me."

Strauss was turning inward, a man not connected to the world. He stopped shaving and showering. At one point, while at the Raymond Street Jail, he was forcibly shaved. The barber was told to use clippers only; no one trusted Pep around a razor. Mostly he sat mumbling in his cell. When guards came each morning to take him to trial, he refused to leave, holding the bars, screaming. When an attorney asked questions—"Did you kill him?"—he answered with non sequiturs—"Over easy, please. Plenty of toast." There is a picture of Pep taken at this time, wearing a V-necked sweater, his hair long, his beard wild. When it ran in the newspapers, this picture was said to show a crazy man, someone who had lost his mind, but really he looks like professors I had in college. Insanity is like the high jump—they keep raising the bar.

At the time, Pep thought long hair alone could get him off the hook, dismissed as a nut, not fit to stand trial. He was a precursor, maybe even a model for, Vincent "the Chin" Gigante, the recently convicted head of the Genovese crime family, who for years wandered through Greenwich Village, muttering, in robe and slippers, a man telling the world, "How can I run an organized crime family? I'm a lunatic." But Pep? His routine fooled nobody, especially not his friends. When Goldstein saw him in court, he said, "Geez, Pep, you make me sick to look at you."

A few weeks after Goldstein and Strauss were convicted, they were back in court for sentencing. As the judge read their death warrant, Strauss looked on through hooded eyes. When the judge asked if the boys had any comment to make, Goldstein said, "Before I die, there is only one thing I would like to do. I would like to pee up your leg, Judge."

The men were taken to Grand Central Station, where they would catch a train to Sing Sing. In those days this was one thing the condemned could look forward to, a last glimpse of Manhattan, the vaunted, echo-filled hall, ceiling and walls jumping away, sunlight breaking through faraway windows; briefcase businessmen; the scream of newsstand headlines; office girls in hats; the card shuffle of the departure board: Trenton, Camden, Philadelphia, Wilmington—a lonely windswept platform waiting for a traveler. As the men moved across the floor, they were surrounded by reporters. Cops cleared a path. Strauss moved through it like an exotic fish, a man who's played crazy so long, he half believes it himself. Goldstein was maybe more relaxed, gratefully taking it in, one last boisterous mob to see him to the door. Before he ducked into the terminal, he turned and said, "Just tell that rat Reles I'll be waiting for him. Maybe it'll be in hell. I don't know. But I'll be waiting. And I bet I got a pitchfork."

I have a picture of Strauss on the train a few hours later. He is wearing a rumpled gray suit over a T-shirt. He has not showered or shaved, and his greasy hair is pushed back. He looks like a singer out on tour or a killer out on an errand. He looks like Clint Eastwood in a spaghetti western, like Kurt Cobain in his first videos, like my father in pictures taken while he was in the army, like Yitzhak Rabin before 1948, like a kid I knew at camp and liked so much that I started to walk like him and borrowed his expressions: "decent," "wicked," "fuckin' all right!" He looks like everyone I ever admired. Calm, cool, sane. He is looking into the distance, feet up, smiling. He is cuffed to Goldstein but hardly seems to notice, as though Buggsy is just an accessory, something that looks good with this particular outfit.

Goldstein and Strauss were executed on the night of June 12, 1941, just a few months after they were sentenced. After a last meal, they were led down the final mile, a tunnel of eyes. And now their lives were reduced to this last room, the place where all the trains, planes, cars, buses, highways, and hallways were leading. In pictures of the death chamber, the shadows are dark and heavy as liquid. I have seen electric chairs in movies and newsreels. On a tour of Angola State Penitentiary in Baton Rouge, Louisiana, I even sat in an impotent old electric chair. What did I learn? That an electric chair is not a comfortable chair. It is really one of the least comfortable chairs I have ever sat in. Why should this be? After all, it is the last chair you will ever know, shouldn't it at least be okay? In my opinion, the electric chair should be a La-Z-Boy or a recliner of some sort. When creating a death chair, here is the one word designers should keep in mind: comfort.

Strauss was electrocuted a few minutes after midnight. He washed and shaved. He had decided to go out sane. When he died, it was without a word, though I imagine him talking to himself: Okay, we got through everything else. We will get through this, too. Goldstein died a few minutes later, climbing into a still warm chair. For Buggsy and Pep, there was little chance for redemption. Execution came so soon after sentencing. How could they feel anything but hatred? Even at the end, their minds must have been occupied by anger, images of Reles warm in his hotel suite. A few days before Goldstein died, he told reporters, "Too bad I can't hold Reles's hand when I sit in the chair."

Dasher Abbandando and Happy Maione went on trial early in 1941. They were charged with the murder of Whitey Rudnick. In courtroom pictures Abbandando looks sheepish, someone who does not believe in his own crimes. His lawyer was selling him as the all-American boy. Abbandando had once been a terrific baseball player, a professional prospect. "Ball players don't kill people," his lawyer told the jury. "In all my experience, I cannot think of a single baseball player who ever killed anybody."

At his side, Maione was a shadowy presence. He was built like a human cannonball and wore beautiful suits and elegant ties. They called him Happy, an outdated, ill-fitting nickname. The mood of the trial was set by his anger, his fiery temper and antics. One afternoon, as he passed Reles in the hall outside the courtroom, he lunged at the Kid, yelling, "You stool pigeon son of a bitch. I'm gonna kill you. I'm gonna tear your throat out."

When Reles mentioned Maione's house on the stand, Happy, leaping to his feet, flung a glass at Reles. "You son of a bitch, leave my home out," he yelled as the glass shattered against the wall. "You never was in my home."

The jury brought back a guilty verdict, and the judge sent the men to die in Sing Sing. Appeals pushed the execution back to February 19, 1942, by which time Happy and Dasher at least had the satisfaction of seeing one of their enemies die.

By the time Abbandando and Maione were convicted, the rats had been locked in the Half Moon hotel for over a year. They were in those rooms hours, days, months at a time. The variety of their lives, the excitement of the underworld, hit, getaway, chase, had been reduced to three gears: eat, sleep, testify. The outside world was just something through a window or a story a cop tracked in from the street. The boys read newspapers, played cards, or argued. If my mom was staying in the suite, she would call the boys "the Bickersons" and tell them to knock it off. More than even prosecutors or cops, they had come to hate each other. Why? Because they were rats. Reles felt about Magoon the same as Goldstein had: "That's some story you're telling, Seymour, you're burning me up!" And Magoon felt about Reles the same as Maione had: "You stool pigeon son of a bitch. I'll tear your throat out!" Everyone hates a rat.

So did they hate themselves? I don't think so. Everyone has reasons, justifications, for even the most treacherous things they do. Reles tells himself it is not his fault, that he is about to be ratted out himself, that his responsibilities as a father outrank his responsibilities as a gangster. And how can Tannenbaum find himself to blame when he was never meant for this life, when the boys tricked him down from the mountains, when taking the back door out is only the right thing? But such justifications have room for only one, and the others remain rats without reason. So what are you left with? Aimless gangsters who must pass the day with rats, in small cramped quarters, where you are forever being pulled by another's gravity, where every cough, sigh, comment, cuts like glass. By the fall of 1941 the suite had become a maze, where each rat must find his own why and how to live, his own method to cut away the monotony.

How did Reles deal with life in the Half Moon? He became aggressive, obnoxious, impossible. He was like a class clown, a kid who fights schoolday tedium with pranks and wise-ass remarks. He stopped showering, did not change his clothes, smelled. He put on weight, his face filling like a balloon. He talked while he ate, making his point with a fork, spitting, in everyone's business. At night he got drunk and abusive. He once insulted Sholem Bernstein's wife. The next day Bernstein tried to knife Reles. You see, the rats were like fighting fish shut in a tank. They had all this energy and nothing to do. You know what they were like? Subjects in an MIT stress study. Reles, who was in failing health, would cough blood into a glass and leave the glass brimming with red phlegm on a windowsill. He was sick and spent many nights in a secret room in a nearby hospital. "I didn't even like the idea of being in the same room with Reles," said Tannenbaum. "He used to spit in his hand and cough in your face, and every time he would bring up a mouthful of blood, he would bring it around and show everybody. Then he would spit into a glass and wait until it got full until he got rid of it. I was under the impression he had consumption."

Reles loved to play pranks, especially on the cops who were guarding him. No matter how far he went, he knew the cops would not retaliate. Reles, a star witness, could not be touched. Maybe it was unfair, but it was also fun. It was the Kid's way of passing time, and also of showing the other boys he could still outsmart the law. The pranks were mostly like something from the thirties, boxcar afternoons, hobos rolling west. Reles would sometimes duck under a table to give a cop a hotfoot, slipping a lit match into his shoe. As the officer went howling around the room, Reles collapsed in laughter. If a cop was fool enough to fall asleep near a radiator, Reles would tie his shoelaces to the pipes. When he was in the mood for something simple, he would wad wet toilet paper into a ball and fling it in a cop's face. "What's that?" he might ask during a meal. When a detective turned to look, Reles would spoon pepper into his food. In addition to being a killer and a rat, Reles was a jerk. He used to tell his guards they couldn't hold him, that he could leave whenever he felt like it. "You guys are tin badge cops," he would say. "I can get outta this sardine can any time I want."

Reles shut down and shut up only at night. He would listen to the radio for hours, voices fading in and out of dreams. On September 15 he was in bed early. His wife had come by before with a bottle of Rémy Martin brandy. "When I saw him, I was shocked," Rose Reles later said. "He looked horrible. He didn't have any hair. His head had been shaved in the hospital. I couldn't say anything. I just looked at him. He didn't even ask for the family."

Reles took his wife to the bedroom. The other boys were playing cards in the living room. The whispering laughter of a couple getting drunk turned into shouting. Rose was sick of this life. She could see her husband only a few times a week, and even then with cops all around. Her kids did not have a father. The shouting was replaced by tears. "I never asked him, but he knew I wanted a divorce," said Rose. "I told him it would be for the children. He told me to forget about it, to never mention it again. But that night I came with the intention of asking him. I knew he would never sign any legal papers, so I asked him if he would just sign a regular piece of paper, something saying I would never have to come to him for another signature. He looked at me. He must have thought I was crazy. He didn't say anything after that."

At eleven P.M. the boys in the next room heard the bedroom door open, saw Rose straighten her dress, wipe her eyes, and walk out. The Kid was sick, stir crazy, and now his wife, the one he was doing all this for, who got him to rat in the first place, was trying to break clean. When she walked out the steel door, he went into his room and shut the light.

Now and then a detective stuck his head in, and always there was Reles on his back, eyes closed, radio warbling. The radio was clear all night. It caught the sounds of the country, twangy jug playing Appalachia hillbillies, vaudeville Jews with lame take-my-wife gags, newsmen with nowhere voices, crooners, politicians, voices from Chicago, Colorado, Boston, make-believe cities with their own make-believe gangsters, baseball games, situation comedies. The religious programs were funnier than the comedies, with cracker evangelists talking about sin. In the early morning, the dial was a junkyard of choruses and maritime bands.

The police later made a list of the shows and personalities Reles might have listened to that night: *Uncle Don* on WOR; *WPA in Action* on WNYC; *Movie Gossip* on WMCA; sports with Clem McCarthy on WHN; army and civil defense with General George C. Marshall on

WEAF; *Li'l Abner,* WJZ; *Here's Morgan,* WOR; *Amos 'n' Andy,* WABC; boxing on WOR; *The George Burns and Gracie Allen Show,* WEAF; the Whitman Orchestra on WEAF; sports with Ed Dolley, WNEW; *Are You a Missing Heir?* on WABC; *Keep 'em Flying,* WMCA; news in Yiddish, WEVD; *Jewish Philosophers,* WEVD; *Can You Top This?* on WOR; *Battle of the Sexes,* WEAF; *The Avengers,* WHN; Bob Hope on WEAF; Red Skelton on WEAF; *Youth's Stake in the Fight for Freedom,* WJZ; President Roosevelt's Armistice Day Address, WOR; *All-Night Jamboree,* WEVD.

Also on that night (WABC) was an address by Sidney Hillman, FDR's adviser and the former head of the Amalgamated Clothing Workers Union, who once worked with Lepke. If Reles heard Hillman talking of the workingman, optimism, the future, he must have felt the distance between success and failure, lucky and unlucky. The Kid had lived twenty years in the line of fire, betting it all, and where had it got him? A crappy little rat-infested Coney Island hotel suite, Sidney Hillman on the radio. At 7:10 A.M., when a cop stuck his head in the door, Reles was asleep.

On the morning of November 12, 1941, William Nicholson, head of the Brooklyn Draft Board, was sitting at his desk in Coney Island. The United States was just a few months away from war, and his mind must have been filled with the news from Europe. Looking up, Nicholson could see out his window, across Twenty-ninth Street to the Half Moon. The hotel was set back at the second floor, leaving the first-floor roof exposed. Nicholson saw something on the roof, a splash of color. He called the hotel manager and told him there was something on the roof.

Detective Viktor went to investigate. He stepped through a second-floor window and onto the roof. It was around thirty-five degrees that morning, with a thirty-mile-an-hour wind coming off the ocean. The body was maybe twenty feet from the wall, face to the pebbly roof. It was approximately eight A.M. The detective turned over the body. Abe Reles. Looking into the sun, Viktor could see the sixth floor, where a window was open. Reles had fallen five stories, forty-two feet from his room to the roof of the hotel kitchen. He landed first in a sitting position, breaking his spine at the fourth and fifth vertebrae. The fall also ruptured his liver and spleen, and his abdomen hemorrhaged, filling his insides with blood. It must have been a spectacular stunt, a cartoon cat of a fall. The Kid's face was studded with pebbles. He was fully clothed. A checkered cap was stuffed in his back pocket. According to Edward Hefferan of the Brooklyn DA's Office, one of the first people on the scene, "Reles was fully dressed including his shoes, and his costume was not such as he might wear around the room but more as he wore in court. His shoes were new." Crime scene photos show Reles on his back, one arm pointing up, the other pointing down, a kind of necrophile's disco dance. His shirt is open, his skin white and pasty. His rubbery face is full of cuts. Doctors said he may have lived for as many as thirty minutes after the fall. At his side are sheets cut into strips and knotted together. When asked if Reles had scissors, Detective Boyle said, "Yes, he used them to trim the hair in his nostrils."

The hotel was soon awash in prosecutors and cops. Burton Turkus was there, and so was Captain Bals. They went to the suite to investigate. The Kid's room was shadowy and cool, still geared for sleep. Reles slept in a single bed on a plain wood frame. The blankets still showed the shape of his body. Newspapers and empty bottles were scattered across the floor. The walls were high and white, and the plaster cracked and peeled by a leaky radiator. A wire was tied to the radiator, and the window was open. Looking out, the cops would see the low roofs of coastal Brooklyn, billboards, streets running to the sea. Looking down, they would see Reles, face small and unshakable, being lifted onto a stretcher. Seen from a dozen angles, through a dozen lenses, it still amounted to the same dead body.

Tannenbaum shared the room across the hall with Meyer Sycoff. "I had my alarm clock set for eight-thirty," Allie later said. "I knew I had to go to court. I wanted to get up early, shave, and get dressed. About eight that morning, I heard a lot of doors banging. I opened up my door and walked out and saw the detectives excited. I asked, 'What is the matter?' And they said, 'Abe went out the window.' "

News of the death flashed through the underworld. *The New York Times* ran a front-page story. "Behind him in the room, lights still burned," it reads. "Behind him the little radio that had played all night still blared and babbled. The informant looking southward could see surf break against jetties. He could hear the dolorous clanging of the buoy as it rocked in the tide. He could see far down the deserted boardwalk. It was shrouded in morning mist."

The death of Abe Reles was the last great scandal of prewar

America. The story, which made front pages around the nation, was like something drawn up by underworld bosses. When Reles went out the window, he took with him cases against at least two major mobsters: Bugsy Siegel, Albert Anastasia. (Though Lepke had yet to stand trial for murder, Reles had already appeared before the grand jury, testimony that could be used in a criminal trial.) When the degree of the setback became clear, people wondered: How did this happen? How did a star witness, a man locked in a steel-doored fortress, a man under the protection of sixteen cops, at least one of whom is supposed to watch him as he sleeps, go out the window? The officers on duty that morning said they last looked in on Reles at 7:10 A.M. He was asleep. The head of the draft board spotted the body at 7:45. So whatever happened, happened in that half hour. When asked to explain their actions, what they had seen or heard in those thirty minutes, the police guards shrugged. They had been taking a leak or had gone for a smoke or else had drifted off to sleep. They did not know what happened.

Over the next few months the New York Police Department conducted a massive investigation. Detectives studied boxes of physical evidence and interviewed witnesses. "He had a smile on his face," Tannenbaum said of the last time he saw the Kid. "But it was just his mouth that was smiling." Reles's body was examined, cut apart, examined again. In the end, however, even the most solid findings of the investigation would seem suspect. After all, the report relied mostly on the police guards and their boss, Captain Bals, men who probably had the most to hide.

So it fell to the public to ponder. It was a great game in New York, a public murder mystery, a riddle running through heads in the subway, solved at lunch counters, argued over dinner. The death of Reles was the Rubik's Cube of the time, a puzzle on which everyone hopes to prove his wit. To this day, when I explain the death to friends who don't believe in Jewish gangsters, their eyes go glassy. They raise a finger. They are thinking. They ask me to read back testimony. *Now, you say Reles had only two dollars and thirty-five cents in his pockets when he died?* In the months following the death, as people awaited and then digested the official police report, a kind of consensus emerged, explanations floated by unnamed detectives, excited journalists, busybody amateur sleuths. Everyone had a solution.

Some thought Reles died trying to escape, that he hoped to swing from the suite on a sheet like Batman. The sheets were cut into strips, tied into a rope, roped to a wire, wired to a radiator. Though this rope was only long enough to carry Reles down one floor, he could have gone through a fifth-floor window, down the stairs, out a door. But he seemed otherwise unprepared for escape. He had only a few dollars, and Reles would not try to flee broke. Besides, the sheets were not strong enough to carry him. An FBI lab later said they could hold no more than 110 pounds. Reles, who weighed 170, made his name by knowing such details, by plotting perfect getaways. And the knots holding together the sheets were loose, amateurish. One good tug would pull them apart. If the boys learned anything on all those hits, it was how to tie a knot. And what if he had made it to the street? Reles would have a target on his back in Brooklyn. Escape? Escape to where?

Others said Reles must have committed suicide. What did he have to live for? By betraying his friends, he cast himself into a void, a place without meaning or rules. And what if he did finally earn his freedom? What if he sat through all the trials, sent all his friends to jail? Then what? What kind of a world would he be returning to? The place he left, the anything goes life of underworld Brooklyn, was gone, destroyed by his very treachery. That was the irony of the decision made by so many of the informants. By ratting, they prevented themselves from returning to the very life they were saving. Freedom for such men was life on the run, a new name in some shit-kicker city. Dead or out of town. Now, on top of everything else, Reles finds out his wife is leaving, taking with her the children and the only thing that might justify his behavior: My responsibilities as a father outweigh my responsibilities as a gangster. And so the reasoning goes: With nothing left to live for, Reles, at thirty-seven, already in failing health, followed Pep and Buggsy and Happy and Dasher the way he had sent them.

But how do you explain the sheet that followed Reles out the window? Why did he take a hat? Why would a man want to make his suicide look like an escape attempt? And how did he get so far from the wall? Around twenty feet, as if he'd been shot from a cannon. Even if he got a running start, the Kid could not clear twenty feet. Besides, no one thought suicide was in the Kid's nature. He was not morose, introspective, or self-pitying. He lived on the surface of life, waiting for the change that makes everything look different. Suicide is just not in the makeup of most gangsters. Any time you hear a gangster killed himself, you can turn the channel, knowing somewhere a killer is being congratulated for a job well done. When the suicide theory was brought to police headquarters, Captain Bals dismissed it. "[Reles] was more concerned about his physical well-being than anyone I know," he said. "He was more in fear of harm from the outside, he never indicated that he would do harm to himself. My observation was this: I considered him cowardly that he would never hurt himself."

Some figured Reles must have been killed by those with access—the other men who frequented the suite. He was hated by the cops and by his fellow rats. His every entrance was marked by a tightening in the gut, his every exit by a sigh of relief. Who knows? Maybe Tannenbaum, sick of glasses filled with blood, snuck in from across the hall and pitched Reles out the window. Maybe Sholem Bernstein, thinking of how Reles had insulted his wife, helped with the heavy lifting. And what about the cops? Men with wads of wet toilet paper still stuck to their faces, their soles still smarting from a hotfoot, their dinner still ruined by pepper? Why wouldn't one of these men toss the rat out the window? "The detectives were not sorry to see Reles dead," *The New York Times* reported. "They made no bones about this. He had been arrogant, surly, unclean in his habits. An internal condition, accompanied by frequent hemorrhage, which he took no trouble to conceal, heightened their distaste for the man." When faced with such theories, Captain Bals defended his men, saying they would not jeopardize a case because they were grossed out. "The detectives were apprised of how important these witnesses were," he said. "They were also made conscious of the fact that, by keeping people in confinement of this type, it required a lot of humoring, and that they were here to guard them and keep them in the best of spirits at all times."

More sophisticated sleuths stayed close to motive: Who would most profit from the death? That is the killer. But it sometimes seemed half the city would profit from Reles's end. There was talk of politicians, high-ranking Mobbed-up power brokers whom Reles might out. And what about the heads of the police department, bribe takers whose careers Reles might ruin? "Some people—politicians and minor officials—had a practical reason for their hatred of Reles," Burton Turkus later wrote. "In this connection it must be recalled that John Harlan Amen, then conducting a special investigation of corruption, had requested District Attorney William O'Dwyer to 'loan' Reles to him for questioning on the subject of protection and official corruption."

Of course, those with the most to gain were probably mobsters, men like Albert Anastasia and Bugsy Siegel, who must have seen the death of the Kid as a second chance. "As long as Abe Reles was alive we had a perfectly good case against Albert Anastasia," William O'Dwyer said on the radio. "But the day Abe Reles went through the window, that particular case, for want of corroboration, was no longer a clear case."

When they finished their investigation, the police department had come up with an entirely different explanation, something worthy of Mark Twain. According to the police, Reles died by misadventure. His plan? To swing on sheets down to the fifth floor, jimmy open a lock, climb through a window, come up the stairs, knock on the door of the suite. Hilarity ensues. The night before, the hotel front desk received a call from the suite, asking if the room below, 523, was occupied. It was not. Was this Reles making sure he had an empty room to bust into? Investigators also examined the fifth-floor window lock, looking for any evidence it might offer up. The tarnished brass lock is now in a box at the New York Archives in lower Manhattan, the office that houses the records of the state's case against Murder Inc. Looking at the lock, holding it in your hand, sliding the mechanism back and forth, you can see how a slim device might keep a person from finding a way back into the world.

For weeks Reles had been calling his guards tin badge cops, saying he could leave any time he wanted. Well, here was a chance to prove it. Not only did the misadventure theory fit with Reles's history of practical jokes, it let everyone off the hook. Who was to blame? No one but the Kid's bad sense of humor. When the report was made public, the officers on duty that morning were demoted, but none were fired. Rose Reles, the last to talk to Reles, seemed to support the theory. One night years before, when Abe was staying at Louis Capone's house, he played a similar prank. He was drunk upstairs, head spinning, walls flying away. He pulled a sheet off a bed, tied it down, went out a second-story window, feet finding ground. He stumbled home laughing. When questioned about her husband's death, Rose remembered that night. "I think I am the only one who solved this mystery," she said. "When you asked, 'How come you weren't surprised or shocked?' I couldn't have been because I suddenly remembered that night he had come down the bedsheet. He was in a stupor. He was amongst friends. He didn't want to escape. When he came in, he just stared. He didn't know why he did it." The cops said the Kid had gone out the window with hopes of repeating the stunt. The fact that he was no longer the same man, that he was sick, overweight, depressed, that he would now be working six stories off the ground, did not seem to bother investigators.

When the report was made public, New Yorkers must have had a good laugh. All those interviews, all those tests, and this is what they come up with? Death by practical joke? Oh, don't get me wrong. I think it's a great way for a life to end. Death by practical joke is my all-time favorite way for someone (not me) to die. It is funny until someone loses an eye, and even more funny after. The people of Brooklyn must have felt lucky—they had lived to see yet another great example of Mob humor.

Even as America fought the Second World War, Reles continued to intrigue New Yorkers. There was always some fresh piece of news, some fact, some theory. He continued turning up in newspapers, beaming out from old photographs, refusing to stay dead. A true crime brochure put out after the war shows a too close photo of Reles above the words "His Death Haunts Underworld Kingpins." Inside, the Half Moon is pictured at many angles, the sixth-floor window a speck in the sky. In 1951 Kings County Court launched a new investigation into the death. Though eighty-six witnesses were interviewed, the report shed little light. "Abe Reles met his death while trying to escape, by means of a knotted sheet which was attached to the radiator in his room," it reads. "He fell to his death while suspended from or supporting himself on this sheet, when the wire parted as a result of his weight on it. We find that Reles did not meet with foul play and that he did not die by suicide. It would be sheer speculation to attempt to discern his motive for wanting to escape."

Men familiar with the case came forward to dispute the findings. "On the basis of available data, I believe Reles was murdered," wrote Burton Turkus in 1951. "Here is why I believe that Kid Twist Reles was murdered: A far greater number of persons wanted to see him dead than wished for his continued well-being. He was hated by every hood in Murder Inc., because he had helped the law. The very witnesses who were under guard in the hotel with him—mobsters all—despised him."

For years after, the police department continued to receive letters from people convinced they had stumbled upon some new angle:

Dear Mr. Silver:

Did it ever occur to you Mr. O'Dwyer said, "Abe Reles was afraid to even cross the street for a cup of coffee without the aid of a cop." Why then would he even attempt to commit suicide if he was afraid?

Confused

3/20/51

Dear Mr. Halley;

While in Florida, a man by the name of Max Bogan met a retired detective who said that he was one of the detectives who cut the sheet which Reles was descending on. By getting in touch with Bogan you might be able to get more information on the Reles murder.

SINCERELY (Prefer to remain anonymous)

Dear Mr. McDonald:

Would it not be possible to bring in the six policemen who were responsible for the murder of Reles and make them sing? This I know would stop these rumors going around and discover who ordered the boys to pitch him out.

In the coming years, as first-generation Jewish gangsters wilted in exile or jail, as their past slowly overcame their present, a more believable version of Reles's death began to emerge. "It was Frank Costello who came up with the plan," Doc Stacher told Uri Dan in Israel. "You mustn't forget that Frank's role all those years had been to bribe the police and other officials. Like the rest of us, Costello reasoned that if Reles could be silenced permanently, the case against Bugsy and maybe those against some of the others would be finished. . . . So he got to work and found out which room Reles was in at the Half Moon—not so hard because cops had a round-the-clock guard on it. But then Frank really showed his muscle. He knew so many top-ranking cops that he got the names of the detectives who were guarding Reles. We never asked exactly how Costello did it, but one night he came back with a smile and said, 'It cost us a hundred grand, but Kid Twist Reles is about to join his Maker.' "

Meyer Lansky had his own version of the story. "The way I heard it was that Bals stood there in the room and supervised the whole thing," he told Uri Dan. "Reles was sleepin' and one of the cops gave him a tap with the billy and knocked him out. Then they picked him up and heaved him out."

Even now, over fifty years after Reles went out the window, people still puzzle over the death. They receive the mystery on a low frequency, a station at the edge of the dial, a station that also brings news of lost pirate treasure and UFO sightings. You cannot go to Twenty-eighth Street and the boardwalk in Brooklyn without feeling Reles in the air. His death haunts Coney Island, setting it adrift, neither past nor present, a desolate strip of old immigrant America. The Half Moon is gone now, replaced by a massive two-building complex, a Jewish geriatric center, which seems fitting, as if the property itself has aged right along with Jewish America, from a wild, seafaring youth to a tottering walker-using dotage. People still stand in front of the property, though, pointing out where the suite once was, tracing with a finger the trajectory Reles followed from the window to the roof below. "Right there," they say. "It happened right there." And somehow they know what happened was more than the death of a single ratting mobster. What happened on this desolate flyblow strip, under the gulls and beyond the horns, the husk of amusements marking the distance, was the end of something, a way of life, a stage of history, a style that came from the Jewish slums of Brooklyn, where the corner boys learned to hold nothing back, to fight without shame or fear. The death of Reles was the great symbolic killing of the Jewish underworld. It was a sacrifice, an offering full of ritual and symbolism. It was a death to pay for all the other deaths, blood to wash the other blood clean. But did it mark the end of the tough Jew in America? No. Of course not. Tough boardroom Jews today crowd the lobbies of Wall Street, Hollywood, Silicon Valley, the Loop. But the death of Reles did mark the end of the beginning, the passage of the pioneer generation, a necessary finale, like the first stage of a rocket blowing away, letting the capsule glide into space.

Lepke went on trial in Brooklyn three days after Reles fell. The DA's office had had a hard time putting the case together. After Lepke was convicted on federal narcotics charges, federal prosecutors were in no rush to turn him over to New York for trial. Though the Brooklyn DA had put together a strong case, the Department of Justice wanted Lepke to serve his federal sentence before releasing him to New York. "They had the worst time trying Lepke for murder because he'd been convicted on federal narcotics charges, and Franklin Roosevelt and his Department of Justice didn't want to turn him over," Ralph Salerno told me. Maybe FDR was reluctant to give Dewey access to the gangster, who, to save his own skin, might expose the corruption of a high-ranking federal official like Sidney Hillman. Dewey was planning to run against Roosevelt in the 1944 presidential election, and a federal scandal would help his cause. "If Lepke told the truth, he would say that when he was in garments, breaking heads for unions and everything else, one of the leaders he killed for was Sidney Hillman of the Amalgamated Clothing Workers," Salerno went on. "Then Dewey could say, 'The man I'm running against hired a man who hired Lepke to kill people.' "

The federal officials hemmed and hawed, raising objections, anything to keep Lepke out of New York. But when Reles began talking, elevating the DA's case against Lepke from racketeering to murder, the feds had to turn over the mobster. Sheltering a murder suspect would be the biggest scandal of all. While in a jail awaiting trial, Lepke received a note from his old partner Gurrah Shapiro, who was serving his sentence in a penitentiary in Atlanta. The note was a one-line reference to the long-ago meeting where only Gurrah pushed for the killing of Dewey: "I told you so."

The trial began on September 15, 1941. Lepke was said to have ordered at least seventy murders. He was now on trial for one of those killings, the death of Joe Rosen, the Brooklyn man killed in his candy store. On trial with Lepke were two of the men who carried out the order: Mendy Weiss and Louis Capone. The testimony of Abe Reles, spelling out the mechanics of the Combination, was read to the jury. When it was Allie Tannenbaum's turn to talk, he must have felt his stomach turn over. Tannenbaum was facing off against his old boss, the man who found him up at Loch Sheldrake, taught him to be tough, and gave him a life in the city. Allie probably killed his real father when he first went off with the gangsters, and now he was killing a second father. Double patricide. He told the jury about the day back in 1939, when he overheard the boss talking to Max Rubin, saying he was sick of Joe Rosen. "That bastard, he's going around shooting his mouth off about seeing Dewey," yelled Lepke. "He and nobody else is going any place and do any talking. I'll take care of him."

Then Max Rubin took the stand. He was handsome, white haired, patrician. He had tried to save Rosen, first telling Lepke the trucker was no threat, then telling Rosen to stay out of town. A few years later, when Lepke was purging the underworld, Rubin was shot in the head. He recovered and was now paying Lepke back. When Lepke's lawyer tired to discredit Rubin, implying he was himself a crook settling a score, Rubin grew red with anger. "I am fifty-two years old," he said. "Until I met that man Lepke, I never did anything wrong. And only to do him a favor, I got into trouble. I was never a murderer. You're filthy swine to call me such names. I'm not involved in this thing. I came here voluntarily."

When he finished talking, Rubin glared at Lepke, who had shaved his mustache and cut his hair and again looked like a man of the street, cool, calculating gangster eyes searching for the answer, adding the faces in the courtroom, soft heads in the jury box, fun seekers in the gallery, Rubin on the stand, and coming up with no answer. The jury convicted the defendants after six hours of deliberation. "Louis Buchalter, alias Lepke, for the murder of Joseph Rosen, whereof he is convicted, is hereby sentenced to punishment of death," said Judge Tailor. "Within ten days from this date, subject to any legal impediments, the sheriff of Kings County shall deliver the said Louis Buchalter to the warden of Sing Sing prison, where he shall be kept in solitary confinement until the week beginning Sunday, January 4, 1942, and upon some day within the week so appointed, the warden of Sing Sing prison shall do the execution upon him."

These were the final words on Murder Incorporated. Brooklyn had been swept clean of a league of killers, some gunned down in alleys, some lit up in the electric chair, some awaiting the death penalty, one out the window. Over the next few weeks, the rats still living in the Half Moon would quietly drift off, like college seniors after the last exam. They vanished into the fabric of American life, down roads that disappear at the horizon. Sholem, Meyer, Blue Jaw. I don't know what became of them. I do know that Allie Tannenbaum turned up in

Florida in the fifties and later in Atlanta, where he lived near his brother and worked as a lampshade salesman. When I think of Allie's life, how he slipped into the underworld and then slipped away, I feel something like admiration for him. I admire Allie because he seemed to be in it for the adventure; because at the end he could not get along with Abe Reles, who repulsed him; because he never wrote his memoirs or served as a technical adviser on a movie; because, when he left, he was gone; because his nickname referred to his personality and not his prowess as a killer; because he changed with the country; because he was the kind of exciting young man who becomes just another ho-hum old man; because when speaking to a detective in 1996, I referred to him as "Albert," and the detective corrected me, saying, "Allie"; because even in the worst picture he ever took, where he is shielding his face and frowning, his eyes are still smiling. I do not know if Allie lived long enough to see Israeli soldiers storm Entebbe. Probably he died before that. But Jews like him, who thrived on the same streets, in the same slums, who learned the same lessons and fought the same wars, did live to see the emergence of a strong Israel, and they must have seen it as something to rejoice over, proof that not everything the gangsters believed in was wrong.

Soon after the trial, Lepke, along with Capone and Weiss, took his last train trip. Looking out the window on the way to Sing Sing, I wonder if Lepke thought: That is the last oak tree I will ever see; there goes the last hill; look, it's my last car with three people, my last road with two lanes. Lepke could still appreciate the old things: revenge, street justice. Even though it did not affect his case, he must have been happy when Reles went out the window. Also when Albert A. took care of Dimples Wolensky, paying back the traitor. Maybe God uses gangsters to visit justice on other gangsters. But Lepke was now more spectator than participant. He had been locked up for three years and spent the year before that in hiding. His gangster metabolism had slowed, and he was a strange sight in jail, a man whose demeanor does not fit his legend. He is the only boss in Mob history to receive the death penalty. Robert Lowell, the poet, who spent time in jail, saw Lepke in his final days and recorded his impressions in the poem, "Memories of West Street and Lepke":

Given a year,
I walked on the roof of the West Street Jail, a short
enclosure like my school soccer court,
and saw the Hudson River once a day
through sooty clothesline entanglements
and bleaching khaki tenements.
Strolling, I yammered metaphysics with Abramowitz,
a jaundice-yellow (it's really tan)
and fly-weight pacifist,
so vegetarian
he wore rope shoes and preferred fallen fruit.
He tried to convert Bioff and Brown,
the Hollywood pimps, to his diet.
Hairy, muscular, suburban,
wearing chocolate, double-breasted suits,
they blew their tops and beat him black and blue.

I was so out of things, I'd never heard
of Jehovah's Witnesses.
"Are you a C.O.?" I asked a fellow jailbird.
"No," he answered, "I'm a J.W."
He taught me the "hospital tuck,"
and pointed out the t-shirted back
of *Murder Incorporated*'s Czar Lepke,
there piling towels on a rack,
or dawdling off to his little segregated cell full
of things forbidden to the common man:
a portable radio, a dresser, two toy American
flags tied together with a ribbon of Easter Palm.
Flabby, bald, lobotomized,
he drifted in sheepish calm,
where no agonizing reappraisal
jarred his concentration on the electric chair—
hanging like an oasis in his air
of lost connections. . . .

Fate seemed determined to push Lepke off stage, to render his closing moments invisible. His appeals would normally have made front-page news, but his conviction came on the eve of Pearl Harbor. So what happened over the next several months, the jockeying and deal proposing, was pushed to the wings by the European drama. Again and again the execution was delayed by appeals. Before a date could even be scheduled, the federal government had to pardon Lepke, excusing a debt he would not be alive to pay. The feds for a time stalled, perhaps concerned what Lepke would say when the federal government no longer had a hold on him. This battle was waged in the papers, in back, near the sports, until FDR at last signed the release. Then, as the weeks rolled by, Dewey went to work on Lepke, holding death over his head, a stick to beat out a confession. Living through these final days, Lepke must have remembered what Albert A. said while urging him not to surrender. *As long as they can't get you, they can't hurt you. Once you surrender, the best deal in the world won't mean a thing.*

On March 2, 1944, Lepke, Weiss, and Capone had their heads shaved, were dressed in white socks, black shirts, white slippers, and black pants. A slit was cut in each left trouser leg for an electrode. The men were led to a grim holding tank. The boys could talk in this cell but could not see each other. They called it the dance hall. A death row guard asked Lepke what he would have for his last meals. For lunch Lepke said he would have steak, salad, fries, pie. For dinner: roast chicken, salad, shoestring potatoes. Capone and Weiss said they would have what the boss was having—these men would stick with Lepke to the end, leading him into the unknown, like Pharaoh's servants.

After the meal, when that part was over and only the chair remained, a phone rang. In the movies it is a red phone, and the ringer echoes along stone corridors. A reprieve. Dewey had given the boys forty-eight more hours of life. "At least we get more good eats." said Mendy.

A lot was written about Lepke in these last days. It was an ideal scenario for crime reporters: the Mob boss who goes out in nameless gray convict garb, no better than all the illiterate psychopaths who sat in the same chair; intrigue heavy like fog; time running out; the bleak factory grounds of Sing Sing, pale smokestacks reflected in the muddy Hudson; reprieves in the wind and everyone wondering, Will he talk? If Lepke did talk, he would be no better than the rats who put him there, no better than Reles and Tannenbaum. If Lepke did talk, he would be giving up the one thing the government could not take away: how he saw himself. He was a true gangster, the real thing, the child of Arnold Rothstein, the hoodlum who feels the bullet in his chest and still waves off the cops, saying, "I'll take care of it my own way."

After the execution was stayed, Lepke had a visitor. Tom Dewey sent the Manhattan DA, Frank Hogan, to cut a deal. Hogan wanted to know about the old days: Was the boss ever on Sidney Hillman's payroll? Rumor had Lepke collecting three hundred dollars a week from the union chief. Did Hillman ever discuss schlammings or killings with Lepke? Rumor also had the men meeting at the Clinton Hotel in Manhattan. Lepke was desperate, frenzied, clinging to life, but he was no rat. "We reeled off one name after another and just drew blanks," Hogan later said. "Lepke knew what he was doing every minute, even though he was two days away from the electric chair."

"You ask, 'How can he do it? He knows he's going to die in the chair. How can he not make a deal?' " said Ralph Salerno. "Well, Lepke had a wife, a child, a brother. And even if he opened up, Dewey could not let him out of jail entirely. And then he would have to be isolated, or else he would be killed as a rat. So he would sit alone in a cell for the rest of his life. The Mob wouldn't kill his wife, his son, his brother. But they wouldn't take care of them, either. But if he kept his mouth shut, his wife, son, and brother would be taken care of." Salerno smiled and said, "Lepke was what you call a macho gangster. "

The next morning the newspapers were full of rumors: "Lepke offered material to the Governor that would make him an unbeatable Presidential candidate," reported the *New York Daily Mirror.* That afternoon, perhaps concerned by such stories, by the last image he would leave in the world, Lepke got word to the press: Be at the Depot Square Hotel in Ossining a half mile from Sing Sing prison. Around thirty reporters were there to meet Lepke's wife at the hotel bar. She wore a lamb collar and dark glasses. "My husband just dictated this statement in his death cell," she said, holding up a yellow legal pad. " 'I am anxious to have it clearly understood that I did not offer to give information in exchange for any promise of the commutation of my death sentence,' " she read. " 'I did not ask for that! The one and only thing I asked for is to have a commission appointed to examine the facts. If that examination does not show that I am not guilty, I am willing to go to the chair.' "

Lepke, Capone, Weiss—what were they doing with these last forty-eight hours? They were supposed to be dead, so now they were in the bonus. Did everything around them, floor tiles, veins in their hands, the little details that together make up the big detail of life, look sharp and clear? Did they notice the shadows their limbs cast on the wall? The way sound echoes? Or were their revelations interior? I don't believe these men were necessarily unsentimental or unfeeling. Lepke and Weiss were raised as Jews, with the bar mitzvah at thirteen, the High Holy Days after, and they said they believed in God. This belief was not something they talked about. It was probably something they held in reserve, like a gallon of gas in the trunk. When they needed it, there it would be. Like most of us, they probably set the big questions aside, believing they would solve them later, when there was time. And who knows? Maybe there was time, and maybe they did solve them.

Sing Sing. Night. March 4, 1944. The months of delays had conditioned the boys to stops and starts, the politics of the chair. Even on the last day, they must have waited for the call, the reprieve that gives them one hour more. Who can believe in his own death? As the gangsters waited in the dance hall, their last meal done, the guards whispered together, deciding who would go first, a task as rarefied as setting a batting order. Capone would lead off. He had a bad heart, and what if he died before they could kill him? When the warden asked Capone for a last statement, he said nothing. Switch. Charge. Next. Mendy Weiss was strapped to the chair. "I am here on a framed-up case, and Governor Dewey knows it," he said. "I want to thank Judge Lehman. He knows me because I am a Jew. Give my love to my family and everything." *Zap!* And then Lepke, marching across the room and sitting down, the last seat on a crowded bus. When the warden asked for a statement, he instead took a final look around, maybe remembering every face, people he might have a chance to meet again. When the executioner pulled the switch, his head snapped back. His body rang like a bell. His thoughts flew off like birds. The last voice he heard was that of Rabbi Jacob Katz, singing Kaddish—the Jewish prayer for the dead.

The Warriors

THE JEWISH GANGSTER did not survive the Second World War. The most daring among them had been locked up or executed or purged. In the coming years, the few who did survive, the ragged ends, drifted off or fell away, like Little Farvel Cohen, who was killed in the fifties in upstate New York, some drug thing, a "who cares?" death that flickers in the papers like outtakes shown over closing credits. And when this generation was gone, when the thugs born in Brownsville in the first years of the century were forgotten, who would take their place? No one. This was the last car, the caboose, and the train was going away. In the coming years, as Europe ran out of Jews to send across the ocean, as the ghettos dried up, as the universities and medical schools and law firms filled with Jews, as the Jewish people prospered in America, the gangsters would fade even from memory. "Allie Tannenbaum's generation was the last generation of Jewish gangsters," said Ralph Salerno. "The ghettos broke up and the Jews left, so who was there left to recruit?"

When old-generation gangsters like Meyer Lansky cast about for young, lawless Jews to flesh out their schemes, they came back with nothing. Zero. And this, I like to believe, is how they would have wanted it—a community strong enough to forget the street. For Jewish gangsters, crime was a ladder they pulled up behind them, a one-way "this generation only" shortcut to power. "Lansky realized that it was no longer going to be easy to recruit tough Jewish kids," Salerno went on. "They were all going to college. Moshe Dayan had this same problem in Israel. He said he had trouble finding people to drive taxicabs and work in factories. They all wanted to go to school. They didn't want manual jobs. Lansky realized this early, that there were not going to be any more tough Jewish kids who would take guns in their hands and have the guts to shoot them."

By the end of the Second World War, an entire gangster generation had been wiped out. Louis Lepke, Abe Reles, Charlie Workman, Pep Strauss, Buggsy Goldstein, Mendy Weiss, Greenie Greenberg—all killed within the previous decade. The curse of Jewish criminality, a plague once discussed in seminars and at temples, had drifted off in the course of the war. You wake up, and it's gone. But the war had also changed those Jews who survived. When the extent of the Holocaust came clear, when refugees began turning up with stories and tattoos, Jews who had never really considered the virtue of violence, considered it now. The old cerebral way, the rising above and muddling through of so many prewar scholarly Jews, Jews who filled those seminars on the evils of Jewish crime, now seemed like a failure. Brilliant, well-mannered Jews had been led by thousands to their deaths. Now, when people looked to the war for meaning, they came back with lessons the gangsters had accepted years before, what Meyer Lansky learned from the soldier who scolded his neighbors in Grodno, Poland: "Jews! Why do you sit around like stupid sheep and allow them to come kill you? You must stand up and fight."

The Holocaust had bred a new kind of Jew, a hybrid of uptown and downtown, brains and swagger, for whom confrontation or violence may not be the first option but is certainly not the last, a style that would manifest itself in Israel, the Jewish state that overcame more populous Arab enemies with sheer determination. In *Wanderings,* his history of the Jews, Chaim Potok acknowledges this change in character. "Most of the gentle Jews are dead," he writes. "The gas chambers and ovens have brought a new kind of Jew into the world. Even the Hasidim are no longer gentle. . . . From Auschwitz to Entebbe in a single generation." The gangsters were dead, but what made them strong, their driving, fight-to-the-end philosophy, lived on. Though Pep Strauss did not survive the war, his ethic, part of it, anyway, not only survived—it prevailed.

For my father and his friends, there could be no better teacher of the new lessons than dead gangsters. These were men who had, in a way, given their lives for their beliefs. When they could have ratted, they chose not to. And the fact that they were gangsters, that they operated beyond the law, past what is acceptable, gave them a kind of legitimacy, the instant credibility of the outsider. For most people, though, a dead gangster will always be preferable to a living gangster. A dead gangster is just easier to get along with. While a living gangster might be a bully, a jerk, a mean, greedy, psychotic, foul-mouthed bastard, a dead gangster is whatever you want him to be.

All across Brooklyn, kids were imitating gangsters, aping a way of life that had just vanished. In dead gangsters they saw something they needed, an essential vitamin. In the end, it would fall to this generation to carry the legacy forward, to extract lessons and memories from the painful history of the Jewish gangster. In a movie, I imagine editors cutting straight from Lepke in the electric chair, head snapping back, to the corner of Eighty-sixth Street and Bay Parkway in Bensonhurst, beneath the west end el, where my father and his friends hung out the way the wiseguys once hung out in Brownsville, only without the mayhem and killing.

My father still remembers every detail of the corner, approaches, getaways, a cityscape frozen in his mind, a model he carries wherever he goes. When asked to describe the corner and the surrounding streets, he closes his eyes and waits for the picture to flicker on. "Okay," he says, smiling. "I see it now. . . ."

Looking south down Bay Parkway, you see the narrow red brick buildings of the Italian section, pushcarts, pizza joints. That's the way you walk to school, stepping into the street to let the ladies pass. But school is over, so you head the other direction, past Richland Clothing, where no one you know can afford to shop, past Vim Sporting Goods, where a loudspeaker pipes Frank Sinatra tunes into the street. If you take a right on Twenty-first Avenue and ditch the junior high punks who are always tagging along—maybe you lose them in F. W. Woolworth's; you can lose anything in Woolworth's; a friend of yours lost his virginity in Woolworth's—you can go into Sam Maltz's candy store. You hate Sam Maltz. He is always peering at you through the glass candy case, his waxy candy head floating above the ring-dings. "No money? Get out!" So one day you go in with a pocketful of nickels. "Hey, Sam, you can't kick me out. I got money." And you walk to the jukebox and play Frankie Laine's "Wild Goose" twenty-seven times. Sam Maltz pushes the machine out the door after you, cursing. Still laughing, you head to Feder's Feedbox, a drowsy diner full of walk-up workingmen. Your friend Bernie has just read an article about food, some nutritionist saying since all food mixes in your stomach, it doesn't matter what you eat together. "It's mind over matter," he keeps saying. "I like pickles, I like ice cream, so I can eat pickles with ice cream." So you cover Bernie's ten dollars with a ten of your own and call over the waitress. "My friend will have ice cream with baked beans, scrambled eggs, pickles, chocolate syrup, and a glass of milk." As Bernie vomits into some poor stranger's lap, you take your twenty dollars, walk out the door, take a right, and now you are back on the corner, a warm summer night. Now and then a train goes rattling down the tracks overhead, sending down a shower of white sparks.

My father and his friends were sometimes on the corner late into the night, telling stories, laughing, helping each other through the rough terrain that runs from adolescence to adulthood. They must have sensed they were part of a tradition, the art of hanging out, an art perfected by Lepke and Luciano at the Hotel Arkansas in Little Rock. Each night after dinner the Bensonhurst boys walked to the corner from houses and apartment buildings around the neighborhood. The first to turn up got a seat on the bench; late arrivals leaned on the stop sign or else against the store windows.

Sid Young, then Sid Yalowitz, walked over from Seventy-fourth Street, where he lived in an apartment with his parents. Sid then was Sid now, just shrunk down, an imagination waiting for a body to grow. He was small, with a round face and a broad smile. He was playing basketball all the time, stories and sentences set to a dribble. *Hear what happened?* Dribble. Dribble. *I'm comin' down the street and run into the cutest girl.* Dribble. Dribble. *And then.* Fade back. *I ask her to go out.* Shoot. *And she says.* Swish. *Yes.* Sid would dribble from bedroom to kitchen, kitchen to living room, and then, when his mother told him to take it outside, he would dribble on every stair on his way out.

There was a grocery on the ground floor of Sid's building. The store was owned by an immigrant named Jagoda, a merchant who saved his best dreams for his son, Asher. Sid first met Asher on the street in front of the building, and they became friends. Together they played basketball, went to school, the corner, the world. From the beginning, Sid knew Asher was special. He was a born aristocrat, the handsome sailor of Melville. His features together made the kind of darkly mysterious face actors like Rudolph Valentino and Tyrone Power had prepared the women of America for. In high school Asher attracted the attention of adults, who put him in magazine ads. At seventeen he began posing for the covers of romance novels. You would be walking by the drugstore window and there, looking out from some glossy cover, would be Asher Jagoda, shirt undone, girl in his arms, under words like "Exotic" and "Adventure." Everyone knew Asher was bound for some other place, far from Bensonhurst, where words like "Exotic" and "Adventure" came from.

By the time Sid and Asher turned on to Bay Parkway, the corner was full of faces. Sam Deluca, a thick-wristed football player who later, as a member of the New York Jets, would snap the ball to Joe Namath; Sandy Koufax, who would go on to pitch for the Dodgers; Peter Max, who would become a world-famous artist, filling walls with colorful outside-the-lines sketches. They were standing out there, heads together, talking fast, in a language only they could understand.

It was on the corner that the boys were first saddled with nicknames, a way to be seen outside the house. Some nicknames were simply chosen (Bucko, Noodles); some emerged over time (Ben the Worrier); and some just sort of presented themselves. Bernard Horowitz, when asked a question, said, "Who?" and when the question was repeated, said, "Ha?"—and was ever after known as Who-Ha. In school, Irving Kaplan, on a dare, drank an inkwell and was quickly dubbed Inky. In high school Inky could eat lit cigarettes; he is now a dentist. One kid, nobody knows why, was called Gutter Rat, even by his own mother. *Hey, Gutter Rat. Come in for lunch!*

Larry King, whose real name is Zeiger, was known as Zeke the Creek the Mouth Piece. Even then Larry was a broadcaster, announcing happenings on the corner. "Here comes Sam Deluca," he might say, into a rolled-up newspaper. Larry already had his trademark baritone—a voice designed to relate big, earth-shattering events. "Now Deluca is telling Zeiger to shut up," he would continue. "Now Deluca is approaching Zeiger. Now Deluca is lifting Zeiger off the ground. This is Larry Zeiger, signing off."

Larry was born in Brownsville, where his father, Eddie Zeiger, a hardworking immigrant (Pinsk, Russia), owned Eddie's Bar & Grill on Fulton Street, a favorite among cops on the beat. Eddie was short and broad shouldered with a wide-open face that seemed to say, "Me? I'm nothing. But getta look at my boy!" Every day after school, Larry walked under the Fulton Street el, the sun coming down in patches, and into the bar's dusty interior, where some old cop set him on the bar and asked him what was wrong. "Kid, don't you know I'm a cop?" he'd say. "I can fix anything."

One day, soon after his ninth birthday, as Larry made his way home from school, he could see, off in the distance, the dull throb of police lights. As he approached, he saw squad cars parked in front of his building. He heard screams. His mother. Before he made it through the door, a cop put him in a car and drove him to the Loew's Pitkin, a huge movie theater. And it was there, as John Wayne fought "Japs" in *Back to Bataan,* that the cop told Larry about the sad way things sometimes work out. "Your father died of a heart attack this morning," he said in the dark. "You're the man of the house now." And Larry sat there to the end—Wayne, machine gun in hand, fighting to the death as he's overrun by the enemy—in the very theater where, a few years before, Dukey Maffeatore and Pretty Levine spotted the long missing Gangy Cohen in a boxing movie crowd scene.

"Hey look up there," Dukey had said. "That's Gangy."

That fall Larry's mom moved her family to Bensonhurst. The Zeigers, now fatherless and on relief, took an attic flat on Eighty-third Street. "The city of New York bought my first pair of glasses," Larry wrote. "Wire-rimmed glasses that told the world you were poor and on Relief and couldn't afford a pair with frames." When school began, Larry had trouble settling down. To a boy who has lost his father, some things just don't matter. What did subjects like math and biology have to tell him? Larry never again got good marks. He was smart but reckless. Several times each week he was sent to the principal's office, and that's where he met my father. "Herbie Cohen was the first friend I made in Brooklyn," he has written. "If Brooklyn has produced its share of characters, Herbie may head the list. A better friend no man ever had."

When I was growing up, my father told me all his childhood nicknames had to do with his physical appearance, which he said was pretty incredible. "What did they call me?" he would ask. "Handsomo, Mr. Stunning. Mr. Charming, General Gorgeousimo Franco." One year, over Passover dinner, I asked my grandma Esther if my dad really had been called Handsomo by high school friends. My grandma is of the old-fashioned, Eastern European variety: low center of gravity, accent, puff of blue hair. Before answering, she chewed her food carefully, swallowed, then said, "Vell, I know that's vhat he asked them to call him." For kids in Bensonhurst, as it had been for the gangsters in Brownsville, taking a nickname was a kind of liberation, a way of taking hold of your destiny, renaming yourself, a kind of self-christening, a way to shrug off the past, creating a world distinct from that of parents, free of traditions and expectations. A guy named Bucko is not a guy you expect to keep the Sabbath.

Now and then someone would come to the corner with news of the gangsters. The boys spent hours talking about Lepke, wondering where he was hiding, why he was surrendering, how he would escape, and finally how he would die, bravely or like a coward. The plight of Lepke taught my father an early lesson: Escape is sometimes impossible for even the toughest men; sometimes the best you can do is lose with grace. "You fellows hear about Lep?" my dad said after the execution. "Didn't say a word. He's no rat."

My father was touched by the example of the gangsters. From them he learned to live by a code, despise a rat, cherish loyalty. For parents, the gangsters may have been a *schanda,* the shame of the Jews, but the kids on the corners knew the truth—that the gangsters had at least part of a secret they were looking for.

From the beginning, my father and his friends unconsciously patterned some part of their style on the gangsters. In the early fifties some of the kids on the corner decided to start a gang. The Warriors. They ordered jackets. The jackets were reversible, red on one side with a white W, white on the other side, the W in red. On the breast, below a member's name, were stitched the letters SAC: Social Athletic Club. One night Who-Ha stormed to the corner, pulled my father and Larry aside, and said, "Guys, I have a question." Who-Ha had a lazy, pseudoaristocratic way of talking. When he said "guys," it came out like "gauze." "Guys, why are we called Social Athletic Club?" he asked. "All we do is athletic. We don't have mixers or nothing. Where is the social?"

My father looked at Larry, then said, "Ya see, Who-Ha, the athletic is social, 'cause we talk when we play sports. The A is S, so it is SAC." Who-Ha smiled, sighed, and walked away.

The Warriors had a clubroom on Eighty-fifth Street between Bay Parkway and Twenty-first Avenue, the basement of a house owned by Mr. and Mrs. Horowitz, Who-Ha's parents. The basement had its own entrance, a creaky staircase that led down from the street. Sometimes a Warrior would pause at the top of the stairs, shift his head, cock his hips, framing himself in the doorway, then yell, "Hey, fellas." The Warriors paid forty bucks a month for the unfurnished room, money collected in dues. Over time, the walls of the club were lined with couches and chairs, furniture swiped from apartment houses in

Brooklyn. Walking into some lobby, my dad would ask for the super. "We're here for the couch," he would say matter-of-factly. "Got an order for reupholstering." As they carried out the couch, my dad would turn to the super and say, "Hey, pal, how 'bout getting the door?" Even now, walking through an apartment lobby on the way to see one of his kids or grandkids, my father will take a quick look around and say, "Easy score. In and out. But you'd want the whole set."

On the clubroom floor the boys sketched, in glow-in-the-dark paint, a huge Indian head. When they got girls back to the basement, the gutsiest among them might say, "Wanna see the Indian glow?" Who-Ha had a great-grandmother, an about-to-die old lady with terrible circulation. When her fingertips went blue, she was put on the floor and rolled. So even these romantic moments, as the stolen couches heaved and sighed, as the Indian glowed, were often set to the rumble of a geriatric being rolled across the floor.

"What's that?" a girl would ask, looking up.

"My heart," Larry would say, pulling her close.

The Warriors met often in the clubroom, aimless discussions that led nowhere or else to idiotic schemes, plots that could end only in embarrassment or ruin. These schemes were usually designed by my father, who always loved to test himself, getting into trouble mostly to see if he could get out. In even his earliest stories, those told by friends from grade school and junior high, Herbie is cast as the disruptive force, the troublemaker who is followed by otherwise sensible kids. In whatever situation he finds himself, my father seeks the gesture that will provoke, inflame, disrupt. If you turned up on a street in Bensonhurst in 1946, say, you might find him raising funds for the funeral of Gil Moppo, a kid that was alive and well in Arizona; or crashing a New Haven campaign rally, loading up on free doughnuts, then taking stage to stump for the candidate who he has never seen; or driving any number of forward-thinking public school teachers out of their minds. "Back in Brooklyn, Herbie was, as they say in Yiddish, a tombenik," writes Larry King in *Larry King by Larry King.* "And Larry Zeiger was always ready to go along for the ride."

In later years, when I was a kid, these schemes expanded in scope, from Brooklyn to New Orleans, where he tried to convince the Tulane English Department I was an A student; to a checkpoint leading from Hong King to China, where he told a soldier he wanted to go to China "just for a minute"; to Moscow, where he went through Soviet customs with a list of Jewish refusniks in his breast pocket. "Last place the Ruskies would ever look," he later explained. "Right in front of their eyes." There have been times I was thrilled by his recklessness, his compulsion to skate the edge, like when he skipped every line, convincing Egyptian custom agents we were a family of diplomats, and there were times I was embarrassed, like when he told my high school principal, who was trying to suspend me, "Look carefully, for the next thing you will see will be me going over your head."

In his memoir, *When You're from Brooklyn, Everywhere Else Is Tokyo,* Larry King writes about my father's need to sneak in, sneak out, circumvent. When Larry told my dad he would be at Madison Square Garden in New York, where the Democrats were holding their presidential convention, my father said he would meet Larry on the convention floor. "Herbie, you don't understand," said Larry. "I can't get you a pass. Everything is triple-checked here. Ed Muskie got thrown out yesterday because he didn't have a red badge. He's the secretary of state. There's a security guard at every entrance. I'll meet you outside the Garden for a bite."

"Herbie doesn't know the meaning of the word, 'Can't,' " Larry writes. " 'See you on the floor tomorrow,' he said.

"Herbie just walked into the Garden, found a likely looking entrance ramp to the floor, and marched full of confidence up to the stunned guard. He slapped him hard on the back and said, 'Great job,' and wham, he's on the convention floor. And the guard just stood there with a huge smile on his face. I looked up and it was Herbie."

Over the years, I have come to see my father's antics less as a good time than as a philosophy in action, proof of his belief that authority, whether it be Russian customs agents or security at Madison Square Garden, can always be outfoxed. It's his way of showing us that the world is still a manageable place, that all these rules—Do this, Don't do that—are just the construct of other men and can be defeated. As an adult, Herbie would make his living as a negotiator, strategist, and also as a speaker, a man sharing the findings of a lifelong investigation into authority. In his book, *You Can Negotiate Anything,* he says, "Everything is negotiable," which to me refers less to the price of a car than to that part of your fate that seems predestined. He believes in free will, in finding a way around those bigshots who tell you what you are not capable of. It's the wisdom of the street, negotiating your way to the promised land, never taking anyone's word for it—and all of it old gangster wisdom, learning summed up back in the twenties by Arnold Rothstein. "The majority of the human race are dubs and dumbbells," Rothstein told the *Brooklyn Eagle.* "They have rotten judgment and no brains, and when you have learned to do things and how to size people up and dope out methods for yourself, they jump to the conclusion that you are crooked."

I think my father learned his philosophy partly from boyhood experiences in Bensonhurst, partly from old movies, where the Brooklyn wiseacre always wins in the end, partly from the Jewish gangsters, who really saw authority as a rival gang, and partly from the Holocaust, which (he feels) began with the acceptance of another's power. No matter how small you feel, you can outsmart a Nazi; if you outsmart a Nazi, you undermine his power; without power, a Nazi is just another schmuck you take on in the street. My father's lessons have always been tangled in my mind with things I was told in religious school, the story of Abraham, the patriarch of the Jews, who came to distrust false gods the day he destroyed the idols in his father's factory. Recently, when I asked my father, "If I can kick Rebbe Menachem Mendel Schneerson's ass, does that mean he is not the Messiah?" he smiled and said, "Interesting question."

For my father, every run-in with authority is a test, an indication of how he will stand against genuine evil. When trying to explain why he is fighting some skirmish that to me seems irrelevant, he says, "This is 1941 and these bastards are killing Jews." When Herbie and Larry were fifteen, they were picked up by the police in Bensonhurst. They were on the corner, just back from their Friday night dates. As they talked about the girls, a squad car glided up. "Okay," said a cop. "You two, get in." As Larry protested, saying there must be some mistake, my father, knowing a good ride when he sees one, said, "Larry, when they got us, they got us." The cops were looking for two kids, vandals tearing up the neighborhood, and my father and Larry fit the description.

On the way to the station, Larry's eyes filled with water. "You got the wrong guys," he said.

"Knock it off, Larry," said Herbie. "I told you justice would catch up with us."

At the police station, the Warriors were put in separate rooms and questioned. In a movie, this scene is shown in split screen, Larry on one side, crying, my father on the other, confessing to this crime and any others still on the books. "I think he claimed responsibility for Pearl

Harbor," Larry later wrote. After a while the police figured these were not the kids, that there was some mistake, and what they had here was a wiseass and a crybaby. The cops called the boys' parents to come pick them up. When the Warriors were released, they were met by parents, aunts, uncles, friends, and my father's brainiac sister Renee. (Once, when I told my dad I felt dumb, he said: "You feel dumb? I had a sister who was three years older than me and seven years ahead of me in school. How do you think I felt?") When they came into the throng, my father turned and said, "Hey, Larry, they got the whole gang!"

As the Warriors grew older, the gangsters began to fade from their minds. The usefulness of their example began to flicker. My father and his friends would have chances of which the gangsters could only dream. College. Professions. Careers. In Bensonhurst in the forties, the promise of America was something real. For them, going to the street was not a way up, it was a way out. A failure. Already these kids were fixed on the future, a time when Jews would become gentiles, and some gentiles would even want to become Jews. In Jewish life, the day of the ice pick was over. What would the boys keep of the gangsters? A style, a toughness, a pose to strike in the world. Nothing more. They were growing up, forgetting, moving into the mainstream. With them they would take a Brooklyn style, which at some level is a gangster style.

My father and his friends still checked in with the gangsters, though, tracking them like half-forgotten friends. In 1950, when Senator Estes Kefauver from Tennessee launched an investigation into the underworld, an investigation that ran over two years and heard testimony from over six hundred witnesses, the Warriors watched the hearings on TV. Herbie and Larry stood before the set as gangster after gangster testified.

Hey, lookit. That's Mickey Cohen. He used to box. Terrific flyweight, Mickey Cohen.

No, it ain't! That's Meyer Lansky, guy used to go around with Bugsy Siegel. Siegel's sister lives in Brooklyn, ya know!

Sure. Who don't know that!

When he testified, Frank Costello, fearing media exposure, secured a court order barring networks from showing his face. So, for hours, for days, screens around the country showed nothing but the gangster's veiny hands. Costello, bothered by the tone of questioning, stormed out of the hearings. He was later found in contempt and spent eighteen months in prison. When Jake "Greasy Thumb" Guzik, a Jewish gangster from Chicago, was asked a question, he refused to answer, saying, "My answer might discriminate against me."

One afternoon, as my dad was standing on the corner, looking through the el tracks at the sky, he saw Larry running up Bay Parkway. Every few feet Larry paused to push his glasses up his nose. By the time he reached Eighty-fifth Street, he was out of breath. "Hear what happened?" he said quickly. "I just read it in the paper. They killed Albert Anastasia."

"Who killed Albert Anastasia?" asked my father.

Larry looked through the girders, then said, "I don't know."

Albert Anastasia was probably killed at the order of Vito Genovese, a coup aimed at control of the Luciano crime family. He was killed in the barbershop of the Park Sheraton, the same hotel where Arnold Rothstein was shot thirty years before, as if the producer ran out of sets. Anastasia was in chair number four at 10:15 A.M. He dozed as the barber worked. The chair was turned away from the door, so the gunmen, two men in suits, fedoras, and sunglasses, must have seen the jowly gangster in the mirror, his face wrapped in a steaming towel. When the barber saw the gunmen, he stepped aside.

They shot Anastasia through the chair five times in the back. When he fell to the floor, they shot him five more times in the chest. There is a picture of the body taken a few minutes later. Albert is on his back, face covered by one sheet, legs by another. His chest is thick as a tree trunk. With the killing, the Jewish Mob was pushed one death further into memory. Another body. Another spadeful of dirt. For Larry, having news of the murder was being connected to a world once frequented by Reles, Strauss, Goldstein. The chair Anastasia was shot in, chair four, was later sold at auction for seven grand. The gangster's estate in Fort Lee, New Jersey, was bought by Buddy Hackett. In the end, everything belongs to the comedians.

In the fifties, parts of Brooklyn started to vanish. Entire blocks would pack up and move off, to tract houses in New Jersey or Long Island, or else west, to wide-open one-season states. Jackie Gleason, who had set *The Honeymooners* in Bensonhurst, took his entire television crew to Miami. In 1957 even the Dodgers left Brooklyn, chasing fans to California. A few years later Ebbets Field was replaced by a housing project, a complex that did to the color brown what Hitler did to the name Adolf. And then people started vanishing from the corner. You would get down to Bay Parkway after dinner, and someone would be gone. A friend that used to be on the corner was not on the corner anymore. Maybe it was Sandy Koufax and he'd gone off to play with the Dodgers. Or maybe it was Inky and he'd gone off to Howard Dental School. And the next day someone else was gone. This time it was Who-Ha or Gutter Rat or Bucko or Sheppo or Moppo. And then someone else.

One day on the corner, as Larry, boasting of radio dreams, announced passing cars—*There goes a 1949 Ford Fairlane, ladies and gentlemen; a big hand, please!*—my father noticed Sid and Asher were gone. A few days before, Sid and Asher had lit out for California with vague plans of playing basketball, USC or maybe UCLA, teaching West Coast kids the Brooklyn style. Now and then a report would make it back to the corner. Sid and Asher are playing at some junior college; Sid and Asher are surrounded by women; Sid and Asher are drunk all the time; Sid and Asher are now Sid Young and Asher Dann; Asher Dann had a meeting with a big-shot movie executive; Asher Dann signed a contract with Universal Pictures; Sid Young has a job in real estate; Asher Dann is in a B movie called *September Storm* as a cabin boy who almost never wears a shirt; Asher Dann was voted the sexiest man in Hollywood. After that, Sid and Asher sort of faded from view, a signal getting weaker as it goes away.

Dead or out of town—as true for my father and his friends as it once was for anyone who might testify against Lepke. You have to leave town to claim your life, to birth yourself, to take possession of the world. If you do not leave town, sooner or later, ten minutes from now if not ten years hence, you wake to find you were never alive, that your town exists against a nothing background. You have to leave your town before you can claim it—this is something my father and his friends came to realize in the fifties, when it seemed the entire borough was packing up and moving off. Dead or out of town. Dead or out. Out or dead of town. Dead town out of. And of course, years later, when they did try to come back, when they stood on the corner and closed their eyes, they realized the old town was gone, had died while they were off living their lives. Yet inside them they kept some of that old town, a world that existed once, exists still, at night, when they are dreaming. Dead or out of town. Well, the ones who stayed died with the town—only they don't know it. The ones who left are different, too; they changed the way the town should have changed if all the other things had stayed the same. It reminds me of a series of paintings by the Italian artist Boccioni: *Those Who Stayed; Those Who Left; The Farewells.* On either side, faces are lost in a soup of color, the same yet different. But the middle is *The Farewells,* which are full of life, and the railroad clangs as a train whistles down the track. The departures are the main thing; the departures are your life.

In 1954 my father enlisted in the army. He had been living at home with his parents while taking classes at NYU. He had not done well in school. Each night, when he set his books before him, the street below his window filled with Warriors. "Hey, Herbie," they would shout up. "Come out!" My dad would look at his books, the window, books, window, then race down the stairs. He knew this could not go on, that he was letting his youth extend into a twilight. A war was being fought in Korea—a way out of town. When he signed his induction papers, he at first felt a kind of relief, as if he had at last given his life shape. His own father had served in the First World War, and his cousin Nathan had been part of the Allied invasion of Sicily, Anzio, and Normandy in the Second World War.

The night before he was to report, he sat alone in his room. His mind danced into the future, dying alone on a desolate beach in the South Pacific or else leading a group of GIs in a charge up a hill. He watched the sky out his window fill with stars and the white curtain flap in the breeze off Gravesend Bay. He listened to the Frank Sinatra record *In the Wee Small Hours* until each song was grooved in his brain, until he was lost in a blue funk. When the sky grew pale, he fell into a light sleep. A few hours later he hugged his parents good-bye, swallowed hard, reported for duty at Whitehall Street, and was immediately shipped to New Jersey. A few days after that his parents visited the base, loaded with matzoball sandwiches.

After training at Camp Chafee in Arkansas, my father was shipped to Europe, which was electric with cold war tension. He was stationed in Bad Kissingen, Germany, in a flat region known as the Fulda Gap, through which, in the event of a world war, the Soviets would probably drive their tanks. For a time he patrolled the border in an armored car, manning the shotgun in back. Later he became a clerk in courts and boards, coached army basketball teams, found loopholes in arcane regulations, went on trips to France, Spain, and North Africa, filled a photo album with postcards, and pretty much had the time of his life. These days, when any old-timer asks if he served, he smiles and, in a slightly southern accent, says, "Korean War veteran under Public Law 550. Yep. Saved us all from the Commies."

When my father joined the army, Larry was the last of the gang left in Bensonhurst. He did not go to the corner. No one hung out there anymore, just high school kids, babies. He took low-paying jobs (delivery boy, mail clerk, milkman), all the while dreaming of the radio. Being on the radio was something Larry had wanted since he was a boy. In 1960, on the advice of a radio executive, he went to Miami. "It's the coming city, a place full of kids on the way up and old guys on the way out," the man told Larry. "They have no union yet, so you can get a job quickly. Low pay. Long hours. But at least you'll be working in radio." Over the next few years Larry worked his way station to station. His first general manager said Zeiger was too Jewish and changed his name to King. He was soon a star in Miami. By the late sixties, in addition to a radio show, he was hosting a TV show, calling play-by-play for the Dolphins, and writing a newspaper column. The world had become his corner.

In these years, Larry, and other Warriors scattered across the country, were following the travails of another New York favorite. What Meyer Lansky went through in 1972 now seems like the story of the Jewish gangster in microcosm, what happens to a group of men when their place in the world vanishes. In 1970, Lansky, then living in Miami, heard he was about to be indicted for income tax evasion. Rather than stand trial, he fled to Israel. He was making use of Israel's law of return, which guarantees every Jew citizenship. As soon as he was settled in Tel Aviv, Lansky began waging court battles, fighting the Justice

Department's efforts to extradite him. The case went clear to the Israeli Supreme Court, which refused Lansky asylum. Someone later approached Golda Meir, the Israeli prime minister, on Lansky's behalf. When Meir heard the word "Mafia" she shook her head, saying, "No Mafia in Israel."

Lanksy flew from Tel Aviv on November 5, 1972. In Zurich, Switzerland, he was met by a friend with tickets to Rio and a connection to Buenos Aires. From there he would catch a flight to Paraguay, where he would pay off officials, take a new name, vanish. The FBI sent a bulletin to airports around the world, and the police caught up with Lansky in Argentina. After answering questions, he was allowed to board Braniff flight 949. When the plane landed in Paraguay, Lansky was met by police agents, who said he was not to leave the plane. He found the same stern keep-it-moving greeting when the plane stopped in Bolivia, Peru, and Panama. In those hours the seventy-five-year-old gangster seemed to live again the history of the Jews, arrivals and departures, exile, wandering. He looked out the window, his face a blank sheet of paper. He slipped a nitroglycerin pill under his tongue.

When the plane landed in Miami on November 7, 1972, he was met by a crush of newspaper photographers. *Flash. Flash. Flash.* He had been traveling for thirty-six hours. In the end, after all that, court cases, running away, coming and going, he winds up right back in Miami, where so many old Jews take their dreams to die. Over the coming years, Lansky faced two tax evasion trials. He was acquitted. He could be seen in his last days walking along Collins Avenue, an old man with his dog. He died of a heart attack in 1983. He was eighty-one years old. He had achieved the only victory that can ever really be had by a gangster: he died of old age.

When my father got back from the army, he finished college and went on to law school. He met my mother in the NYU cafeteria in 1956, and they were married less than two years later. My sister, Sharon, was born in 1960 and my brother, Steven, three years after that. My father then took a job as a claims adjuster with Allstate Insurance Company and began his slow march up the ranks, each promotion a new life in a new town. In the years before I was born, which my brother says were the best years of all, my family moved from Ocean Parkway in

Brooklyn, to Aurelia Court in Brooklyn, to Syosset, Long Island, to Berkley Heights, New Jersey, to Libertyville, Illinois, where I was born in 1968. As sure as Lansky's journey encapsulates one part of the Jewish story, the wanderings of my family encapsulates another: the trip from cramped city apartments to rolling suburban lawns; from East to West, or Midwest anyway. We were the only Jewish family in Libertyville. One fall my mother took my sister aside and said, "Good news. There will be another Jewish kid in school next year." When my sister asked who, my mom said, "Your brother Steven."

When I was four years old, we moved down the lake to Glencoe. There were plenty of other Jews in Glencoe, but they were different from my parents. They were old money, midwestern Jews. They handled silverware as deftly as surgical instruments and rarely raised a voice. Sometimes, when I found out some super-WASP-y family was actually Jewish, I would say, "You're shittin' me." In my house, the voices at mealtime made the glasses rattle. To see my dad on the street in town was to see a piece of Brooklyn out walking around. Life in Brooklyn seemed to speed him up, get him going, like pedals on a bike when the chain comes off. Once, when my brother got in a pile fight in a hockey game, my dad ran onto the ice and dove on the pile. He used to walk through the drive-in at the bank, waiting in line with the cars; he used to stand on the bleachers when I played hockey, a cigar in his mouth, shouting, "Move it!" When I brought a super blond friend home from school, he looked at the kid sideways and said, "Look, it's Rich's white friend." He often spoke in the far-seeing truisms of gangster movies. He spoke the way Don Corleone speaks in *The Godfather* when he says, "A man will come to you to set up a meeting with Barzini. You will be killed at this meeting. This man is the traitor." Once, soon after my grandmother got remarried to a man named Izzy, a man my dad did not like, we were driving on the highway and my dad said to me, "When I die, your mother will meet a man who will buy her gifts and flowers, who will do all the little things I was never good at, and who will ask your mother to marry. I tell you now so you know: This man is a schmuck."

You saw Brooklyn mostly in his basketball game. We played each night after dinner. I wore shorts and T-shirts. He wore button-down shirts and suit pants. Change jingled in his pockets. He smelled of steak. Setting down his cigar, he would say, "Make it, take it." And bang! He's around me. If the game was close, he would talk trash. "Punk like you never beats the old guy." If I went ahead, he would say, "You're adopted." If I began to pull away, he dropped his voice to say, "Your mother needs your help; I have her tied up in the basement." He employed an array of graceful old-time shots: set shot, one-hand push shot, fade away. His favorite was the hook. He could also hit the jumper. He was violent under the hole. Once, when I went over him for a lay-up, he drove me to the ground. "I don't care if I'm in a wheelchair," he said, helping me up. "I still beat you. I'm from Brooklyn. Where are you from? The hills." Though there are no hills in Illinois, my father always said my brother and I were from the hills, up where rich kids live behind gates. Weak in our refinement, we were lost in the mountains of Illinois. If my life were a book, I would call this chapter "Why Our Fathers Mock Us."

My generation of Jews *is* different from my father's. My friends and I are still one more generation removed from Europe, from the shtetl. In my case, I feel a lot of the tough, world-weary Brooklyn humor has been replaced with a nasal midwestern irony. When I was growing up, any mention of Jews as Jews would make me cringe. Other than my parents, I really knew of only one type of Jew: cerebral bourgeois kids-to-college suburbanites. *Do Jews get drunk? Do Jews trash hotel rooms? Do Jews defend themselves?* Questions I never thought to ask. Why? I had no way of knowing the past. After the bulk of the Jewish gangsters died off, after the ghettos were left to the blacks or Latinos, that part of Jewish history, a New York story, was mostly forgotten. It was the willful act of grandparents, I suppose, like letting a failed path grow over. For Jewish kids of my generation, Israel would have to take the place of gangsters. Here were tough Jews, Jews who fought back, were strong, met aggression with aggression. Jewish kids talked in squeaky voices about the Israeli army, the wars, the victories. But Israel was faraway, foreign. What could it mean in Glencoe? And unlike my dad, I did not have Jewish gangsters or even Jewish boxers. Who did I have? Michael Milken, Steve Guttenberg, Abner Mikva. On television and in movies, tough-looking Jews invariably played Italians. Henry Winkler as Fonzie in *Happy Days;* James Caan as Sonny Corleone in *The Godfather;* Edward G. Robinson as Rico in *Public Enemy.* In the Richard Price book *The Wanderers,* an Italian character, not believing a movie star is Jewish, says, "Bullshit, he's too good lookin' for a Hebe."

I first heard about the gangsters from Larry King, sitting in our kitchen in Illinois. Just the words—Jewish gangsters—seemed to bring the room to life. The air filled with bullets, curses, schemes. The hanging fern plant looked springier. The bird chirping in the next room sounded ominous, a foreshadowing. My own face in the mirror looked darker, tougher. Somewhere in there, in lines that had yet to appear, a gangster might be hiding. A Jewish gangster. People don't believe in Jewish gangsters because Jewish gangsters fall outside stereotype, thwart the expectations so many people have of Jews. The Jewish gangsters were among the first Jews to scrap the notion of Jewish exceptionalism, to set Jews adrift in a world of killers and thieves, to set them free. When Reles took a mark, he was not just ending a life; he was expressing the essential freedom of the Jew in America.

In Glencoe, if I were to tell one of my "white friends" about Jewish gangsters, they would have laughed in my face. And I guess that's why I clung so tightly to those words: Jewish gangsters. The very fact that Jewish kids were once running in gangs, fighting, shooting, changed everything. It meant anything was possible. People could no longer judge me on the stereotype because the stereotype was wrong. People would have to meet me, talk to me, look into my eyes, before they could think they knew what I was like. Once, when my dad was driving my brother and me through Bensonhurst, we saw a hard-looking man skulking down the street. My father rolled down the window and yelled, "Hey, Sheppo."

The man's face lit up. He ran over. "I don't believe it," he said, looking into the car. "Handsomo is back." And that's when I knew the world before I was born was a different place.

When my father left the East, he lost touch with most of his Brooklyn friends. It was part of being an adult, I suppose, of being a father, a husband. A person can lead only so many lives. In 1976, when Larry's mother died in Miami, my grandmother saw the announcement in the paper and went to the funeral. She spoke to Larry, showing him pictures of my dad and his family. Larry, who was well on his way to CNN and global fame, phoned my father. Though they had not spoken in a decade, it was as if no time had passed. They were soon talking the nights away. Larry then put more of the gang back together. In the eighties he heard Sid had breakfast each day at Nate 'n' Al's. When he was next in Los Angeles, Larry stopped by the diner. He saw Sid alone in a booth, reading the paper as he ate. Larry quietly slid in across from him. Sid is semiretired and has made enough money in real estate to enjoy his breakfast. When he set down the paper, he saw Larry, grinning. "What the fuck is this?" said Sid, dropping his fork. "The corner? Ain't that Larry Zeiger?" After a while, Asher turned up. Asher, who long ago quit acting, owns one of the biggest real estate companies in California. His face has grown old and wise, but the handsome kid is still in there. A few days later my father flew out and the old friends were together again.

In the last few years they have spent a lot of time together, carrying their excited chatter into elevators, down hallways. I have seen them drunk at black-tie galas, shouting down pious after-dinner speakers; I have seen them in stuffy uptown restaurants climbing on tables to dance; one afternoon I rounded a corner at the Four Seasons hotel in Washington only to find Asher chatting up a minibar attendant as Sid, in his underwear, swiped dozens of mini Absolut bottles. Once I found Sid in a hotel lobby, surrounded by three blond women, saying, "Tell me, ladies, when does the fun begin?" I was at a party where Sid and Asher made so much noise that Helen Gurley Brown stormed over and said, *"Gentlemen, please shut the fuck up."* And I have seen them in the early morning, talking together in tender voices, in shades of concern that can be learned only with time, upsets, put-downs, and all the things the years bring. Everywhere they go, they take the corner with them.

The old neighborhoods are mostly gone now. The names are still on the maps and some of the buildings stand, but the people are different. The accents on the street have changed, and so have the smells. In Brownsville the row houses where young men spent nights on the stoop have made way for projects that run clear to the horizon: the Van Dyck Houses, the Laughton Houses. The Loew's Pitkin is a clothing store. The corner once occupied by Midnight Rose's candy store has become the Brownsville Bargain Center, a desolate storefront looking out on all-night delis and cold-water flats. The house where Reles and Strauss fought over the spelling of the word "friend" is still there, a two-story brick building surrounded by barbed wire. The drapes in the window are tattered, like after a hurricane. The house around the corner where Strauss lived has been boarded up, and the planks are appropriately covered with gang graffiti: "The Bump Crew Here!" My grandparents' diner is gone, too, replaced by endless vistas of steel-shuttered warehouse. But the legends are alive. You can hear them banging on doors and running down alleys. And every time my father is together again with old friends, telling stories, talking of the old days, the Brooklyn of Reles and Strauss and Goldstein, the years fall away. So they keep talking, telling themselves again of long-ago nights, sharpies and sharks under the bridge.

EPILOGUE

Nate 'n' Al's

THE BREAKFAST CROWD has cleared out, and only the regulars remain at Nate 'n' Al's. There is the ring of silverware in the kitchen and the sound of laughter in back, where the boys are still talking about Brooklyn. Dishes are scattered across the table. Here and there a scrap of bagel or a strip of lox catches the sun. Grease pools at the edges of plates. The waitress, Kaye, has come twice to clear the table and has twice been waved away. "Get outta here," says Asher, holding up a hand. No one will admit the meal is over. Herbie is still picking, coming up with strange food combinations. For Herbie, any collection of plates is a buffet.

"What the hell," says Larry. "French toast and white fish?"

"It mixes in the stomach," says Herbie. "Mind over matter."

Asher undoes a button in his pants, and Larry is already talking about lunch. Sid asks for the check. "Okay," he says, standing. "Let's break outta this joint."

The men walk slowly toward the register, knuckles dragging on tabletops. Eyes follow them through the room. Each man grabs a toothpick. On the street they are men with toothpick mouths, patting their bellies. They have come to prize comfort and all day long walk around like Mafia dons, in bright-colored sweatsuits. At night they go to dinner in silky Hawaiian shirts decorated with fish or race cars or flowers. It's as if they passed right from the short pants of their youth, to the uniforms of their young adulthood, to three-thousand-dollar, made-for-me-special-in-Hong-Kong suits, straight out to John Gotti at the Ravenite Club—the comfort-all-the-time look you get only with a truly tacky sweatsuit. They look up Beverly Drive to Wilshire, cars streaming by, all those suckers off to work. Ahead of them lie at least ten more good years, meals, vacations, sprees. They are like the gangsters had the gangsters done like Lepke said and stayed out of town. The story of their lives is, after all, an expatriate story, men who have settled far from home, who talk of the past because the past tells them who they are. Just before everyone goes their separate ways, Sid smiles and says, "Same time tomorrow. Last one through the door, pays."

A Note on Sources

The material in this book comes from various sources. In addition to those books mentioned in the bibliography, much of my research was done at the New York Archives, where the glory days of the Jewish gangster can be followed in skeleton form. In the forties, in the wake of the trials that put so many of the criminals in prison, the Brooklyn District Attorney's Office gathered their evidence into boxes, which were then archived in a building on Chambers Street in Manhattan—boxes that contain not only transcripts and police reports but maps of getaway routes, ropes used to strangle informants, wiretaps, and bullets pried from bodies. At the archives, I held in my hand the bullets that ended Plug Shulman. I am indebted to Ken Cobb of the archives, who led me, box by box, through the history of Murder Inc., and also to the author, Robert Lacey, who first clued me in to the archives.

Much of my research came from interviews. Not many people who have firsthand memories of the old Jewish gangsters are alive today; not many of the living were willing to talk. The gangster is dead, but the fear lingers on. First among those who did speak is my grandfather Benjamin Eisenstadt, who has since passed away and who, during the Depression, worked in a diner frequented by the gangsters. My grandmother Betty Gelman-Eisenstadt, whose family owned the diner, was also of great help. Other people I spoke with include Dorrie Shapiro-Grizzard, granddaughter of the notorious gang leader Gurrah Shapiro; Arlene Brickman, who was called on *60 Minutes* the closest thing we have to a female wiseguy. I also interviewed several people on the law enforcement side, including Ralph Salerno, a retired New York detective who specializes in organized crime; Ben Jacobson, a retired police officer who now works as a private investigator; Robert Patterson, a federal judge who had a distinguished career as a prosecutor; Herbert Brownell, recently deceased, who, before serving as Attorney General under President Eisenhower, managed Thomas Dewey's presidential campaigns; John Cusack, a longtime agent for the Federal Bureau of Narcotics, now the head of drug enforcement in the Bahamas; J. Edward Lumbard, a federal judge and former U.S.

Attorney, who served in the U.S. Attorney's Office with Thomas Dewey; Judge Joseph Stone. I must also acknowledge the guidance of my sister, Sharon Cohen Levin, and my brother, Steven Cohen, both current assistant United States Attorneys in the Southern District of New York. Sharon is the Chief of the Asset Forfeiture Unit; Steven is the Chief of the Violent Gangs Unit. They were able to give me a sense of what it might feel like for a young prosecutor to face down notorious criminals.

Then there are the neighborhood stories, folklore that has come to me from my father's Bensonhurst friends, especially Larry King, Asher Dann, and Sid Young, who spent many afternoons with me at the Friars Club in Los Angeles, where Sid once made me order a tongue sandwich (tongue tastes like tongue—my tongue, your tongue; tongue with mustard tastes like my tongue with mustard) so he could eat it when I gave up. "Don't want that, Richie? Pass it over." More than any other sources, however, what inspired this book are the Jewish gangsters themselves—that vanished, half-forgotten breed, whose dramatic lives even now, so many years later, hang like smoke in the air.

Bibliography

Asbury, Herbert. *The Gangs of New York.* New York: Paragon House, 1927.

Amen, John Harlan. Report of Kings County Investigation, 1938–1942. New York, 1942.

Berger, Meyer. "Murder Inc." *Life* 9, September 30, 1940.

Cohen, Mickey. *Mickey Cohen: In My Own Words,* as told to Peter Nugent. Englewood Cliffs, New Jersey: Prentice Hall, 1975.

Dewey, Thomas E. *Twenty Against the Underworld.* New York: Doubleday, 1974.

Doctorow, E. L. *Billy Bathgate.* New York: Harper & Row, 1989.

Eisenberg, Dennis, Dan Uri, and Eli Landau. *Meyer Lansky: Mogul of the Mob.* New York: Paddington Press, 1979.

Feder, Sid and Joachim Joesten. *The Luciano Story.* New York: David McKay Company, 1954.

Finch, Edward R. Jr. "Hands in Your Pockets: A Survey of the Background and Work of the New York County Rackets Bureau," vols. 1 and 2. Senior Thesis, Princeton University, 1941.

Fried, Albert. *The Rise and Fall of the Jewish Gangster in America.* New York: Columbia University Press, 1980.

Gaebler, Neal. *Winchell: Gossip, Power and the Culture of Celebrity.* New York: Random House, 1994.

Howe, Irving. *World of Our Fathers.* New York: Random House, 1976.

Jackson, Kenneth. *The Encyclopedia of New York.* Yale University Press, 1995.

Katcher, Leo. *The Big Bankroll: The Life and Times of Arnold Rothstein.* New York: De Capo Press, 1958.

Kennedy, Robert F. *The Enemy Within.* New York: Popular Library, 1960.

King, Larry. *Larry King by Larry King.* New York: Simon & Schuster, 1982.

———. *When You're from Brooklyn, Everything Else Is Tokyo.* New York: Little, Brown, 1990.

Lacey, Robert. *Little Man: Meyer Lansky and The Gangster Life.* New York: Little, Brown, 1991.

McClellan, John L. *Crime Without Punishment.* New York: Duell, Sloan and Pierce, 1962.

McDonald, Miles F. Grand Jury Presentment, County Court, Kings County: The Investigation into the Circumstances Surrounding the Death of Abe Reles on November 12, 1941, at the Half Moon Hotel in Coney Island, Brooklyn, New York, 1951.

Mitgang, Herbert. *The Man Who Rode the Tiger: The Life and Times of Judge Samuel Seabury.* New York: L. B. Lippincott, 1963.

Nash, Jay Robert. *Blood Letters and Badmen: A Narrative Encyclopedia of American Criminals from the Pilgrims to the Present.* New York: M. Evans and Company, 1973.

———. *The World Encyclopedia of Organized Crime.* New York: Paragon House, 1989.

Pankhurst, Charles. "Our Fight with Tammany Hall." New York. 1895.

Petersen, Virgil W. *The Mob: 200 Years of Organized Crime.* Ottawa, Illinois: Green Hill Publishers, 1983.

"Probation Report." People of New York Against Louis Buchalter, et al. Court of General Sessions.

Roth, Andrew. *Infamous Manhattan.* New York: Citadel Press, 1996.

Sann, Paull. *Kill the Dutchman.* New York: DeCapo Press, 1971.

Schwartzman, Paul, and Rob Polner. *New York Notorious.* New York: Crown Publishers, 1992.

Sifakis, Carl. *The Mafia Encyclopedia.* New York: Facts on File, 1987.

Smith, Richard Norton. *Thomas E. Dewey and His Times.* New York: Simon & Schuster, 1984.

Turkus, Burton, and Sid Feder. *Murder, Inc.: The Story of the Syndicate.* New York: Farrar, Straus and Young, 1951.

Winchell, Walter. *Things That Happened to Me—and Me to Them.* New York: Prentice Hall, 1975.

Index

About the Author

Rich Cohen's writing career began at *The New Yorker* magazine, where, soon after he graduated from college, he wrote stories for "Talk of the Town." For the past several years he has been a contributing editor at *Rolling Stone,* where he has done everything from playing tennis with Andre Agassi in Australia to traveling the South with the Rolling Stones. His work has recently appeared in *The New Yorker,* the *New York Times,* and *Details.* He was born and raised in Illinois and now lives in New York City. This is his first book.